THE JESUS LENS

Bringing the Bible's Story into Focus

By Leroy Spinks

© 2018
Published in the United States by Nurturing Faith Inc., Macon GA,
www.nurturingfaith.net.

Library of Congress Cataloging-in-Publication Data is available.

ISBN 978-1-63528-049-4

Unless otherwise indicated, Scripture quotations are taken
from the New International Version (NIV)

All rights reserved. Printed in the United States of America

"In *The Jesus Lens*, Leroy Spinks devotes much of his work to analyzing one possibility for how the Old Testament came to be written, edited, and shaped into the document we know. Leaning heavily on the work of Richard Elliott Friedman, he traces the work of various writers who contributed to the development of the Hebrew Bible over hundreds of years and in different life situations.

"Spinks explains the varying images of God and depictions of acceptable morality in the Old Testament as progressive steps in divine revelation that culminate in the good news of Jesus, who should be understood as the key to interpreting the scriptures that come before. This book will be especially enlightening to readers who haven't previously been exposed to the contributions of critical scholarship to our understanding of the Hebrew Bible."

—*Dr. Tony W. Cartledge, Nurturing Faith Bible Studies writer and Professor of Old Testament at Campbell University Divinity School*

"Leroy Spinks draws on a lifetime of engagement with Scripture to show that the story in the Bible can't be separated from the story of the Bible. To those who are disillusioned by simplistic and insular biblical interpretation he offers an understanding of scripture that respects modern historical sensibilities while still treasuring the Bible's authority as God's message to us.

"Instead of forcing a dogmatic unity onto the biblical text, he listens to the different voices that emerge, valuing them all for their revelation of the nature and will of God. *The Jesus Lens* is full of insights that give meaning to the texts, introducing lay readers to the work of biblical scholars.

"Spinks' attention to the purposes and artistry of the human writers of scripture complement his confidence that God spoke through those human writers and continues to speak through the texts to readers today."

—*Dr. Dalen C. Jackson, Academic Dean and Professor of Biblical Studies, Baptist Seminary of Kentucky, Georgetown, Ky.*

"As a scientist trained to be skeptical even of events I observe, I am unable to read the Bible as a literal scientific or historical document, although I respect and sometimes envy those who do. I cannot reconcile what I understand of the natural world and evolutionary processes with a belief that the universe was created in seven 24-hour days or that Eve arose from Adam's rib.

"My skeptical nature is also triggered by inconsistencies. Why do there seem to be two versions of creation in Genesis? How can I reconcile the often-violent passages of the Bible with a loving God? In *The Jesus Lens*, Leroy Spinks explains how the Bible's message can be interpreted without abandoning an understanding of the natural world as we experience it daily.

"Spinks synthesizes the work of biblical scholars, historians, archaeologists, and others to tell the story of how the Bible was written. With this historical context, the reader is better equipped to interpret the message of the Bible. For example, by presenting evidence that the creation accounts in Genesis were written by two different authors, both motivated by a desire to explain humanity's relationship with God and with dismissing the Babylonian creation myths, Spinks explains how we can find a more fundamental message in Genesis, not science or literal history.

"Mysteries are part of both science and religion. Some mysteries can be understood through observation and experimentation, but the Christian faith ultimately relies on belief in an event that falls outside of the realm of science: the resurrection. No book can resolve all conflicts between faith and science, but *The Jesus Lens* is a valuable tool for those who, as Spinks explains, 'are conflicted about the Bible but are willing to keep reading and thinking.' As a scientist and practicing Christian with more questions than answers, *The Jesus Lens* helps me do just that."

—*Dr. Rick Kopp, Professor of Biology, Georgetown College, Georgetown, Ky.*

"Leroy Spinks' *Jesus Lens* is a wonderfully approachable, honest study of our sacred texts. Our biblical studies too often deal with discrete—even isolated—passages. Spinks' primary goal in this work is to reveal the continuity and connectivity that exist within our sacred ancient stories. In doing so, he reveals the power and beauty of the epic journey of God's faithful: a journey of space, time, and understanding. While reframing and reintroducing the famous stories, Spinks addresses his understanding of God's intentions and tackles questions left unanswered by the original authors.

"Spinks has provided historical commentaries about many of our commonly accepted understandings of religious themes and movements. However, the real excitement in reading the book is with his own interpretation from a lifetime of faith and service. With skill and ease he takes the pieces of our faith and molds them into an epic story that highlights God's great works and humans' evolution in knowing and understanding their God. Throughout the story the author never lets us forget that the Spirit has inspired and walked beside us from the beginning. There is a depth in each chapter that helps the modern reader and Bible student explore their faith and challenge their understandings in the quest for faithful discipleship with the true lens, Jesus.

"Rev. Spinks has given us a valuable retelling of an old and continuous story. The book will be a valuable addition to the library of novice biblical students, veteran Sunday School teachers, and those of us who preach on Sunday morning."

—*Dr. Thomas Quisenberry, Pastor, First Baptist Church, Chattanooga, Tenn.*

Contents

Foreword vii

Introduction xi
The Misunderstood Book

Part I 1
The Epic

Chapter 1 3
Birth of a People: The Rise of Ancient Israel in Canaan

Chapter 2 9
A House Divided: Israel Debates Its Monarchy, Priesthood, and God

Chapter 3 23
The River That Waters the Earth: The Garden of Eden in Historical Context

Chapter 4 33
The World's First Historian: Writing History from Documentary Sources

Chapter 5 39
Religious Warfare: Prophets of Yahweh vs. Baal

Chapter 6 49
The Temple Apologist: The Jerusalem Temple Tradition

Chapter 7 65
The Man Who Saw the Beginning: The Temple Theology of Creation and History

Chapter 8 75
Religious Warfare Rages On: The Prophets and the Decline of Judah

Chapter 9 83
The World's Second Historian: The Deuteronomist's Theology as History

Chapter 10 97
*At Last—the Torah: An Heir to the Temple Apologist Unites
the Founding Traditions*

Chapter 11 105
The Hebrew Philosophers: Seeing God's Wisdom in the Commonplace

Chapter 12 115
*Into the Wilderness Again: Completing the Hebrew Scriptures—
and Then Crisis*

Part II 127
Climax and Denouement

Chapter 13 129
The Climax of the Epic: The Good News of Jesus Christ

Chapter 14 143
The Radical from Galilee: Jesus of Nazareth as He Presented Himself

Chapter 15 151
Death of a Radical: Jesus' Preaching Leads to His Crucifixion

Chapter 16 159
Proclaiming the Impossible: Good News of Jesus' Resurrection

Chapter 17 169
Denouement: Unpacking the Story

Conclusion 175
So, What Has Happened to the Bible?

Glossary 181

Suggested Reading 183

Foreword

Humility is an important mark of Christian discipleship. One sign of such humility is admitting that we are imperfect and, therefore, interpret truth—even biblical truth—imperfectly through various lenses. The apostle Paul, in his famous "love chapter," confessed to this reality when stating that he "sees through glass, darkly" and therefore "knows in part" (1 Cor. 13:12). We too should confess our limited vision and cultural biases that impact even our best efforts in exploring biblical truth.

What we take out of the Bible is shaped to a great measure by what we bring in. Whether intentional or unintentional, recognized or unrecognized, we all have presuppositions and perceptions that shape our biblical interpretations. Christian humility calls for setting aside any arrogance that allows for thinking we can extract truth purely.

However, we are not left helpless and hopeless when it comes to the important task of seeking and finding the truth as revealed in these ancient and holy texts. Jesus himself affirmed that God's Spirit ("the Spirit of truth") will "guide you into all truth" (John 16:13).

Yet, it is Jesus who serves as the best lens through which we interpret biblical truth. Think of it in this way: You may choose between a candle and a searchlight to find your way out of a dark forest. It is a simple choice, isn't it?

Likewise, Jesus is by far the best filter—the most illuminating light—for interpreting the Bible. While God is revealed in various ways, Jesus is clearly—with no close second—the fullest revelation of God. Therefore, his life and teachings, death and resurrection, provide the best way to read, understand, and apply biblical truth.

The harsh reality is that many Christians talk about the Bible more than they read and study it. And it is simply stunning to observe throughout the history of Christianity and today propositions of biblical truth that do not align with Jesus.

Therefore, this book written by an experienced pastor and thoughtful student of the Bible is so very important. It reminds us of or redirects us to the best approach to bringing the entire biblical revelation to life: Jesus!

As the author writes, "*The Jesus Lens* shows that the validity and truth of the biblical revelation lie in the entire story as read through its climactic conclusion in Jesus of Nazareth."

May this timely book about the timeless biblical story that culminates in the good news of Jesus Christ be read carefully and gleaned for all the available insights. Most importantly, may it help us to read the Bible, again and again, with Jesus as the lens through which we understand and apply the divine truth found in each unfolding story.

John D. Pierce
Executive Editor, *Nurturing Faith Journal*
Publisher, Nurturing Faith Books

*I dedicate this book to my wife,
Annette Scoggins Spinks,
the love of my life,
the most truly spiritual person I know,
without whose encouragement and informed guidance
I would not have completed and published this work.*

INTRODUCTION
The Misunderstood Book

America exhibits societal traits that mystify and amuse the English and Europeans. Our national political narrative constantly echoes with debates over abortion, homosexual marriage, and capital punishment, each side quoting the Bible to sustain its views. Congressmen claiming the Bible as their authority have pronounced global climate change a fraud, the theory of evolution a "lie straight out of the pits of hell," and all abortions murder. At the same time, equally devout ministers and theologians have found no conflict between Scripture and climate change, evolution, or abortion.

Whether the subject is sex, evolution, alcohol, marijuana, political conservatism vs. liberalism, war and peace, the Democratic and Republican parties, Islam and "Christian America," Americans often use biblical arguments. Even the national budget, economic theory, and gun rights too often entice various contestants either to trot out a favorite biblical proof text or to lampoon the other's use of the Bible to prop up a sagging argument. Frequently several sides of any given issue are equally convinced their position is "biblical," supported by divine revelation, endorsed by none other than God.

Millions of believers have found in the pages of the Bible the keys to living in personal peace with God and inner security, guiding their lives by its moral and spiritual precepts. Accepting the entirety of the Bible by faith, they do not question anything about this historic book—its history, science, moral injunctions, or views of God. For these believers, the Bible is inspired by God and therefore inerrant[1] in every detail.

Millions of others, however, see in the Bible a pre-scientific mindset more compatible with primitive mythology than with modern cosmology and critical historiography. They view adherence to the Bible as demanding blind faith instead of rational thought.

Furthermore, they find many of the Bible's teachings—on slavery, the place of women, holy war and genocide, stoning and mutilation as judicial penalties, and sometimes even the character of God—ethically, morally, and spiritually objectionable. They cannot imagine how to square those teachings of Scripture with the Spirit of Jesus Christ. Finally, many of them have concluded that history has shown the Christ of faith to be largely mythology created several generations after Jesus and having little to do with Jesus of Nazareth as he actually was.

These competing mindsets have contributed to a nation in which radical contradictions and ideological conflict rage. Conservative evangelical churches have exploded into America's fastest growing and largest churches, with immense political clout that can even elect a president. At the same time, a host of believers reared in the church leave in young adulthood never to return. Simultaneously, our contemporaries exhibit a bewildering variety of competing types of "spirituality" and secularism—and the church constantly loses population share.

Possibly the fastest growing group in America are those I call "skeptical believers." They are still believers, although they do not necessarily refer to themselves that way. They believe in God, and they admire Jesus Christ; they just do not like Christians or the church. Most of all, they cannot swallow some of the ideas we have convinced them come from the Bible.

Although believers of a sort (they frequently call themselves "spiritual but not religious"), they are also skeptics. The latter descriptor means they insist on relevant evidence for any proposition they accept as true. They see the Bible as a book of myths, legends, parables, and metaphors, but not facts of history. Some of them even say the Bible is inspired; they just can't take it literally. They want to believe, but the conflict between their intellect and their desire for faith and spirituality leaves them paralyzed.

In *The Jesus Lens* I address all these people—believers struggling to correlate science and history with the Bible, those who have totally given up on the Bible, and those who are about to give up. I address those who are conflicted about the Bible but are willing to keep reading and thinking.

It may come as a surprise to some to learn that many of us who believe and love the Bible, follow Jesus Christ, and preach the Bible's message have wrestled with these same issues. We have struggled personally, devotionally, and professionally with these same intellectual, ethical, and spiritual difficulties. For many of us, faith has not been easy, certainly not automatic.

We refuse either to reject the biblical message or to harmonize and rationalize its difficulties. We also refuse to reject the well-grounded findings of a century and a half of scientific and historical research. Believing "all truth is God's truth," we value both the biblical message and the findings of scientists and historians. We have committed ourselves both to faith in God and a rational, scientific approach—even to the Bible. *The Jesus Lens* sets forth one such approach.

The Misunderstood Book

Interpreting the Bible

Many of us grew up hearing the Bible stories and fell in love with the narratives of encounters with God by Abraham, Isaac, Jacob, Joseph, and Moses. We loved the stories of Jesus of Nazareth as he revealed the God of love and grace. Along the way, however, we ran into disturbing facts about that simple Bible and the simple Christ—facts we could not ignore, facts that confused our childlike faith.

The Bible describes the God of love destroying with a flood the entirety of humanity except for eight fortunate souls. Those same scriptures describe Jacob's sons—Israel's patriarchs—massacring an entire city to avenge the seduction of their sister. A couple of biblical authors say the God of love commanded Israel to slaughter the Canaanites down to the last suckling infant, pregnant woman, and helpless old man. How could we square such narratives with the Spirit of Jesus Christ?

To understand such stories, we have to understand that the Bible must not only be read; it must be interpreted. So, how do we do that?

I am convinced that a significant portion of the difficulties many people have with the Bible is due to a lack of understanding of the historical process by which we received these inspired scriptures—and I do believe they are divinely inspired. We have not paid sufficient attention to the story of how the Bible came to be written.

I propose to tell that story in this book—at least, that story as I understand it. Of course, the story of how the Bible was written overlaps considerably with the Bible stories themselves and with the historical context of Scripture. Still, we need to keep straight in our minds which story we are telling here. Our concern in this book is with the story of the writing of the Bible.

A Different Viewpoint

The approaches to the Bible taken in this work do not constitute some wonderful new discoveries of this author. Most of them have been around for more than a century. Neither do I claim that the conclusions I draw in this work are universally accepted by all biblical scholars. As in all intellectual pursuits, the experts debate, argue, and even quarrel acrimoniously over many of these issues. This general approach, though, is widely accepted among biblical researchers who are also Christian believers.

The Jesus Lens does, however, represent a new approach to this subject in four respects:

1. It presents this understanding of the Bible as a story—an epic.
2. It tells the story of the writing of the Bible as a whole.
3. It tells this story in a popular style understandable by non-specialists.
4. It presents the findings of historical biblical scholars from a faith-filled, Jesus-centered perspective.

I know of no other work that combines these four characteristics.

By the nature of the case, no one can fully explicate all these themes in a single volume. For this reason, the reader should approach this book as a schematic rather than as an encyclopedia, a suggested approach rather than the final answer.

Furthermore, I do not claim that all biblical scholars adhere to all the opinions expressed in this book. All the views expressed here, though, do reflect sound scholarship held by numerous qualified, trained biblical scholars and historians. The suggested readings at the end of this work will help those desiring more detailed scholarly discussions of these matters.

The Grand Epic

In *The Jesus Lens* I present the story of the writing of the Bible as an epic as exciting as the *Iliad* or the *Odyssey*. The story of how the Bible arose is a saga as thrilling as those of any Viking skald. This epic began with a set of political and religious controversies. Those controversies led to an even greater problem: Who is God, and how can we come into relationship with him? The story moves through a complicated plot exploring that problem. This plot features traditionalists, historians, prophets, and wise men and women approaching the problem in a wide variety of ways and coming to sometimes contradictory conclusions.

Our epic eventually moves like a gigantic multi-episode televised drama to a crisis and a climax that solves the original problem in a single man—Jesus of Nazareth. This great epic concludes with a denouement that wraps up the loose ends. This denouement explains the meaning of the epic and its climactic resolution, states the moral and ethical implications of that meaning for our lives, and provides tantalizing glimpses of what is yet to come.

The Bible itself is not always laid out in exactly the sequence of events I present here. You see, the Bible was not written by one person but by dozens of authors writing sixty-six different books over a period of a thousand years. For this reason, the order of events as I present them will require the reader constantly to remember what story we are examining. I am not telling the

Bible stories we learned as children but rather the story of how the Bible came to be written—how we got our Bible. For this reason, the order of events in this book does not always follow the order of the events in the biblical narrative itself or the order of the books in the Bible. After all, we are recounting not the stories the Bible tells but the story of how the Bible we use came to be our Bible.

The Purpose of *The Jesus Lens*

In *The Jesus Lens* I show that the validity and truth of the biblical revelation lie in the entire story as read through its climactic conclusion in Jesus of Nazareth. In that story taken as a whole we see God revealing the divine nature, will, and redemption in spite of human intransigence and inability to understand the divine self-disclosure. That divine revelation, moreover, is a progressive revelation—progressively unveiling God and correcting our human misunderstandings about God and even correcting earlier misunderstandings in the earlier scriptures.

The Bible's inspiration flows from its authors' unique intimate communion with the Spirit of God as they wrote their various visions of the self-unveiling God. The Bible is the word of God in the words of men. Here we tell the story of those humans who put the revelation into words.

Its authority proceeds from its nature as the primary record of and witness to those human encounters with God and their understandings of it. The solution to the scientific, historical, ethical, and spiritual difficulties many find in the Bible lies in the story of its human words—how it came to be the book we possess today. While the Bible is a revelation of God, here we give attention to the humans who wrote it. Join me in exploring this monumental record of divine revelation.[2]

Notes

[1] The doctrine of biblical inerrancy holds that the original documents in the handwriting of the original authors (the autographs or *autographa*) are wholly without error (inerrant) in any respect—factually, historically, scientifically, ethically, or spiritually. *The Jesus Lens* does not subscribe to that theory, considering it contrary to the teachings, implications, and phenomena of the Bible.

[2] For readers desiring additional study of various topics included in *The Jesus Lens*, see "Suggested Reading" on pp. 183-184.

PART I

The Epic

In Part I we encounter the story of the writing of the Hebrew Scriptures, the Christian Old Testament. A series of conflicts in ancient Israel stimulated the writing of this library of books, an epic written over a period of approximately eight hundred years. From the late 900s to the mid-100s BCE traditionalists, historians, prophets and prophetesses, wise men and women worked to delineate Israel's faith in a variety of genres. As they labored across those eight centuries, their understanding of God's self-revelation grew, matured, and even changed. Through all the growth and development, though, we can discern an organic progression in the Israelite conception of God's nature and will for creation.

This great national library contains four large bodies of work written by God-intoxicated men—men drunk on their experience of the living God of Israel. The first large body of work—the ancient Hebrew founding traditions—appears in our Bibles as Genesis, Exodus, Leviticus, Numbers, and Deuteronomy. Jews call these books the Torah; Christians call them the Law or the Pentateuch. Most of us learned to love the stories of these books as Bible stories read to us by our mothers at bedtime.

The most ancient comprehensive history of Israel appears in the books of Joshua, Judges, Samuel, and Kings. Jews call these books the Former Prophets for reasons we will see as our story progresses. The author of these books utilized the work of a host of earlier chroniclers and historians to write a national history of Israel and Judah. He began with the arrival of Israel on the edge of Canaan and finished with the Babylonian Exile six hundred years later.

The Hebrew prophets—the Latter Prophets for Jews—differed greatly from the prophets of other nations. Instead of engaging in fortune-telling by reading sheep entrails and patterns of stars and planets, they proclaimed an ethic of justice, equity, and compassion in the name of Yahweh, God of Israel.

Hebrew philosophers stood in stark contrast to Greek philosophers. The Hebrew philosophical works, along with several other genres of literature, appear in that section of the Hebrew Scriptures Jews call the Writings. Instead of laying out elaborate logical systems of mathematics, cosmology, and metaphysics, wise men spoke through proverbial sayings, dramas, poems, essays, and short stories to describe the art of walking with God. Rather than spinning speculative theories, their philosophy consisted of truth experienced in relationships among people and between themselves and God.

This library of religious works records eighteen hundred years of religious experience written by inspired ancient Israelites and Judeans over a period of eight centuries. These works recorded divine revelation, but humans received that revelation as human experience. *The Jesus Lens* explores the human side of that experience of the self-revealing presence of God.

Now let us ease into that story by laying its background in the story of the rise of the Israelite people.

CHAPTER 1

Birth of a People

The Rise of Ancient Israel in Canaan

Thirty-five hundred years ago a highly creative people dwelled on the eastern coast of the Mediterranean Sea where we find Jordan, Lebanon, and Israel today. The land between the sea and the Jordan River was occupied by a variety of peoples known to the Hebrews as Canaanites. A few great cities—Hazor in the north and Lachish and Jerusalem in the south—dominated a host of smaller cities, towns, and villages dotting the region.

The Canaanites had a rich culture of art, architecture, literature, and agriculture. The Canaanites on the seacoast—the Phoenicians—developed a vast shipping empire that served the ancient Mediterranean world, a naval power we still remember today. They achieved fame as producers of purple cloth, from which the names Canaan and Phoenicia possibly derive. They invented the world's first alphabet shortly before our story begins, the prototype of all the alphabets in the world today.

For centuries during the second millennium BCE Egypt dominated the region, with Canaanite kings little more than puppets serving as vassals of the pharaohs. In the thirteenth century numerous conflicts disrupted the area. During those disturbances a people calling themselves both Hebrews and Israelites crossed the Jordan River into Canaan. These new immigrants distinguished themselves by worshiping a new God, residing in distinctive four-room houses, using a distinguishing pottery, avoiding pork, practicing circumcision, living according to a unique set of ethics and law code, and observing the Sabbath. Pharaoh Merneptah encountered this people called Israel about 1220 BCE and left a written record of the event, the earliest written evidence we possess of their presence in Canaan.[1]

By the twelfth century BCE, Egypt had lost its hold on Canaan and withdrawn into its own borders.[2] Egypt's retreat set loose a maelstrom of internecine and inter-ethnic chaos among its former satellite kingdoms. Hordes of other alien peoples joined the newly arrived people of Israel. Relatives of the Israelites, Arameans and Midianites, along with Amorites, Ammonites, Hittites, Hurrians, and Greek-speaking Sea People from the Aegean, flooded into the vacuum left by the retreating Egyptian armies. The hill country population exploded with hundreds of new settlements and towns having distinctive characteristics identifying them as Israelite villages. Canaan's population tripled in a single century to approximately 150,000 inhabitants—far greater growth than even an extraordinary birthrate alone could have produced.[3]

Through the 1100s and 1000s BCE, many Canaanites and various immigrant ethnic groups merged with these Hebrews into a single people and took on the God, religion, laws, customs, and name of Israel. Although they called themselves Israel, each ethnicity frequently continued to worship the gods of their ancestors. For the next several centuries the adherents of Yahweh contended vigorously—sometimes by persuasion, sometimes by violence—with the adherents of Dagon and Melech. Most of all, Yahwists struggled against devotees of the Canaanite Baals and Asherahs.

Shortly after settling in Canaan, the Israelites set up their central worship shrine called the Tent of Meeting (Tabernacle) at Shiloh.[4] By the eleventh century BCE, Shiloh had become the major Israelite religious center where the Levitical priests offered sacrifices, oversaw the Ark of the Covenant, and provided a spiritual base for their people.[5] Whatever gods many of the Israelites might actually worship, officially they gloried in having "no king but Yahweh." For the next two hundred years this new people calling themselves Israel had no king and lived an egalitarian, democratic, agrarian lifestyle. Their only leadership consisted of Levitical priests and occasional charismatic military leaders they called judges who arose to defend them from hostile armies.

In the early eleventh century the Levitical priest Eli served at the Shiloh temple that had replaced the Tabernacle.[6] The boy Samuel grew up there as his student and aide, offered sacrifices as a priest, served as prophet, and in time led Israel as its last judge. Although Israel had other shrine cities, Shiloh had no peer and proclaimed itself the only valid sanctuary in Israel.

The Israelites fought interminable wars with the Philistines. The latter people group constituted one segment of the Sea Peoples from the Greek isles who had invaded the coast of Canaan shortly after the Israelites arrived. During Samuel's youth, disaster hit Shiloh. The Israelite army carried the Ark of the Covenant into battle as a war Palladium.[7] The Philistines routed the Israelites, captured the Ark, and kept it at Ashdod for a time and then at Ekron. An outbreak of what appears to have been bubonic plague, however, convinced them the judgment of Yahweh had fallen on them for desecrating that holy chest. They quickly sent the Ark back to Israel, where it remained housed at Kiriath-Jearim for decades.

The Ark never found its way back to Shiloh. Archaeological digs indicate Shiloh was destroyed and partially burned ca. 1050 BCE and never fully recovered its former stature.[8] By adulthood, the priest, prophet, and last judge Samuel had moved to Ramah and did not even include Shiloh in his annual judicial circuit of Bethel, Gilgal, and Mizpah.

Six Controversies

Under the occasional leadership of the judges, the people of Israel experienced societal chaos. As the book of Judges put it, "In those days Israel had no king; everyone did as he saw fit" (Judg. 17:6, 21:25). As they approached 1000 BCE, the people of Israel decided they needed a king like the nations around them. Samuel, acting in the name of Yahweh, chose a tall charismatic farmer named Saul for the throne. This move represented the first highly controversial development in Israel, because of their conviction that they had "no king but Yahweh."

Saul reigned for twenty years and then died in battle against the Philistines. A lame son succeeded him. Soon, however, one of Saul's former generals whom he had exiled installed himself on Israel's throne, supplanting Saul's house. David's rise presented the nation with a second controversy: On what authority did David overthrow Saul's dynasty chosen by none other than God's own prophet Samuel?

David shrewdly united his politically divided northern and southern tribes through three strategic steps. First, he provided a neutral capital at Jerusalem, which had not previously belonged to either set of tribes. Second, he installed two chief priests: Abiathar, the great-great-grandson of Eli of Shiloh in the north; and Zadok from the south.[9] Third, to make his new capital both the religious and political center of the new nation, David brought the Ark from Kiriath-Jearim to Jerusalem and housed it in a new tent in the City of David.[10] It would remain in that tent until Solomon moved it into his new temple about 957 BCE.

Following Shiloh's loss of the Ark, the symbol of the divine presence, the Shiloh priests lost their preeminence as Israel's spiritual leaders. For a while under David they comforted themselves that Eli's descendant Abiathar had joint custody of the Ark in Jerusalem alongside Zadok.[11] That situation did not last long, though.

While the aged King David lay dying, his oldest surviving son, Adonijah, laid claim to the throne. Joab, David's military chief of staff, supported Adonijah alongside Abiathar, the northern chief priest. Quickly, however, the court prophet Nathan, supported by the southern chief priest Zadok, engineered the accession to the throne by Solomon, a younger son. Aided by David and David's wife and Solomon's mother Bathsheba, Solomon succeeded in wresting the throne from Adonijah. He promptly ordered both Adonijah and Joab executed and exiled Abiathar to his country estate at Anathoth.

With Abiathar's deposition as chief priest, the priesthood of Shiloh went into eclipse, never again to officiate at the altar of Yahweh. Zadok, on the other hand, through his support of Solomon gained for himself and his family the central role in directing the temple rites, forever displacing the descendants of the Shiloh priesthood.[12]

Solomon's rise to the throne presented Israel with a third conundrum: Did the royal dynasty have any legitimacy at all? David's younger son had supplanted his elder brother; David himself had earlier supplanted the dynasty of Saul; and Saul had been crowned king in violation of Israel's principle of "no king but Yahweh." The situation, however, was about to get even more confused.

When Solomon died, his son Rehoboam succeeded him. A man named Jeroboam immediately led an insurrection and assumed the throne over the northern tribes who claimed for themselves the name Israel. Rehoboam suddenly found himself ruling only the tribe of Judah plus Saul's tribe of Benjamin and possibly absorbing Simeon. Now the Israelites had an almost unbearable four-fold quandary. Even David's dynasty, whose legitimacy already stood in considerable doubt, had been rejected by most of the nation in favor of a usurper. Furthermore, the once unified nation of Israel had split into two nations—Israel in the north and Judah in the south. How could this highly religious people deal with such theological and political chaos?

In addition, the nation's priesthood also labored under a heavy load of doubt. For the previous two centuries Israel had been led by the Levitical priesthood with its home base at Shiloh. During David's reign these priests had been forced to share religious supremacy with Zadok, a man of dubious origins but presumably from somewhere in the south. Now with the rise of Solomon, the Shiloh-based Levitical priesthood had been set aside entirely in favor of Zadok, presenting the people with a fifth controversy.

Finally, in the northern nation of Israel, Jeroboam replaced the Levitical priesthood at Shiloh with pagan priests at shrines at Dan and Bethel, worshiping golden bulls designed to represent Yahweh. Jeroboam's actions created a sixth national scandal and religious confusion.

Birth of a People

How would the people of Judah fare before Yahweh if possible usurpers filled both their royal dynasties and their sacral priesthoods? How could Israel call themselves the people of Yahweh while their official state shrines offered sacrifices to pagan bull-gods? At this point two thinkers arose to address these problems in books providing somewhat divergent answers.

In Jerusalem, the capital of Judah, a layman of profound spirituality wrote a national epic. His narrative stretched from the Creation to Solomon's establishment on the throne of David. His saga validated the Davidic dynasty in Jerusalem and justified the Shiloh priesthood's loss of religious leadership, at the same time defending the ancient Yahwistic faith of Israel.

Simultaneously, in the shrine city of Shiloh in the northern nation now claiming the name Israel, a Levitical priest wrote a similar epic. His competing saga stretched from the patriarchs—Abraham, Isaac, Jacob, and Jacob's twelve sons—to Israel's exodus from Egypt and their wilderness experiences. This northern priest implicitly contradicted the southern layman at several points. He posited a different history of the divine name Yahweh and assigned different names to Moses' father-in-law and the mountain where Moses received the Law.

Sometime during the next two centuries a second Shiloh priest wrote a short codebook preserving traditional laws attributed to Moses. This work provided legal validation of the Shiloh Levitical priesthood in opposition to the Zadokite priesthood officiating in Jerusalem and also disqualified the pagan priests at the shrines at Dan and Bethel.

With these three literary ventures representing two somewhat different points of view, both Israelite and world history changed forever. These three authors launched the literary process that over the next thousand years produced the Bible we read today. Stimulated by one set of problems—those outlined above—they inaugurated an even greater project. They set out to answer the ultimate question: Who is God, and how can we enter into personal relationship with the divine? The process these authors set in motion with their three books would occupy the hearts and minds of the best thinkers and most devout spiritual minds in Israel for the next ten centuries.

Notes

[1] J.A. Wilson, "Mer-Ne-Ptah," in vol. 3, *Interpreter's Dictionary of the Bible* (New York: Abingdon, 1962), 355. Amihai Mazar, *Archaeology of the Land of the Bible: 10,000–586 BCE* (New York: Doubleday, 1990), 234, dates this event 10 years later than do most other archaeologists.

[2] Avraham Faust, "The Emergence of Iron Age Israel: On Origins and Habitus," in *Israel's Exodus in Transdisciplinary Perspective*, ed. Thomas E. Levy et al. (New York: Springer, 2015), 469.

[3] William Dever, *Who Were the Ancient Israelites and Where Did They Come From?* (Grand Rapids: Eerdmans, 2003), 96-100.

[4] Josh. 18:1, 8-10.

[5] Josh.19:51, 21:2-12; Judg. 18:31; 1 Sam. 1:3, 9, 24; 2:14; 3:21; 4:3-4, 12; 14:3.

[6] 1 Sam. 1:9.

[7] 1 Sam. 4:3-22.

[8] Israel Finkelstein, "Shiloh Yields Some, But Not All, of Its Secrets," BAR (January/February 1986): 22-41.

[9] 1 Sam. 4:19-21, 14:3, 22:20.

[10] 2 Samuel 6.

[11] 2 Sam. 15:24-29.

[12] 2 Sam. 8:17; 1 Kgs. 1:32, 38, 45; 2:26-27; 4:2.

CHAPTER 2

A House Divided

Israel Debates Its Monarchy, Priesthood, and God

None of the earliest Hebrews could read and write, as far as the record shows. Developing their memories phenomenally, they could recite long genealogical lists and family tales passed down orally from older folks. Throughout Israel's history various kinds of traditions developed. Messages by Israel's earliest prophets are represented in Miriam's Song[1] (possibly from the 1200s BCE), and Deborah's Song[2] (from about 1100 BCE). Their oral folk "literature" included the genre of the riddle as preserved in Samson's Riddle[3] (from about 1100 BCE) and that of the fable as represented by Jotham's Fable (from the eleventh century).[4]

More importantly, the people orally handed down memories of the patriarchs—Abraham, Isaac, Jacob, and his twelve sons, especially Joseph. The most important of all Israel's oral traditions had to do with the Exodus—the national memory of the Hebrews' escape from slavery in Egypt. Priests at the various shrine centers collected and memorized stories associated with their particular localities along with the traditional religious and civil laws of the people of Israel. The oral period of ancient Israel's traditions movement lasted until the time of David, about 1000 BCE. Then a momentous development began: writing in the Hebrew alphabet.

The Mesopotamians had invented writing around 3500 BCE and the Egyptians 250–500 years later. The Canaanites invented the world's first alphabet in the second millennium BCE, and early Israelites adopted it by the eleventh century. The Israelites then developed their own distinctive alphabetic script by the time of King David's reign in the tenth century BCE.[5]

Probably well before David's reign, anonymous Israelite authors began writing the oral traditions in coherent collections. The Bible says Moses wrote a book of the Covenant. We have no idea what script he would have used or what that book may have been other than a legal code. Many of the patriarchal and exodus traditional stories and laws would have been written down at shrines such as Shiloh, Gilgal, Bethel, and Shechem. Priests at Shiloh would have written narratives of the various judges, of Samuel, and of the Ark of the Covenant.

> **Who wrote the Pentateuch?**
>
> For 1,800 years Christians believed Moses wrote the first five books of the Old Testament. Possibly they drew that conclusion from the New Testament practice of citing verses from these books as being from Moses. Many contemporary scholars, however, conclude that this manner of citation only indicated that the author was quoting "the books of Moses," not that Moses wrote these five books as we have them. Careful analysis of Genesis through Deuteronomy suggests those books came from several different authors.
>
> The view presented in this book is a modification of the hypothesis first promulgated by Julius Wellhausen in the mid-1800s. Scholars who reject the Mosaic authorship of the Pentateuch hold to a number of different views, but most of them hold views similar to the one presented in this work.

Ultimately, Shiloh in the north and Jerusalem in the south became the two key sites where such traditions were collected, memorized, and eventually written down in compositions of great artistic and spiritual value. These works were not yet our books of the Bible, but many of them were eventually incorporated into our biblical books.

The Layman of Jerusalem

Shortly after the breakup of the United Kingdom of Israel into the northern nation of Israel and the southern nation of Judah, an anonymous Jerusalemite wrote a history of the Hebrew people from the southern point of view. Biblical scholars call this man "the Yahwist" and the book he wrote "J" (from the German spelling *Jahwist*).

We possess the Yahwist's monumental book as part of the narratives of Genesis, Exodus, Numbers, Joshua, Judges, 1–2 Samuel, and the first two chapters of 1 Kings. (The reader can see a reconstruction of J in R.E. Friedman's, *The Hidden Book in the Bible*.[6]) Friedman suggests the Yahwist wrote a two-volume work: Volume 1 contained the Hebrew traditions from the primeval period (beginning with Gen. 2:4) until Joshua's old age (Joshua 13). Volume 2 contained the J material from the period of the Judges (Judg. 8:30) to Solomon's accession (1 Kings 2).

Beginning with the Creation and concluding with the establishment of Solomon's reign, the Yahwist outlined Israel's origins and validated the monarchy. He also vindicated the Davidic dynasty as successors to Saul, justified Solomon's succession to David, and implied support of Judah against the breakaway kingdom of Israel to the north.

This encyclopedic thinker wrote volume 1 of his work from oral traditions, thus becoming the first major literary preserver of the founding traditions. In this chapter we examine only the traditional material from his first volume, reserving the subsequent J material for chapter 4: "The World's First Historian."

The Yahwist's primary motive in the first volume of his history, the founding traditions, was to pass along the stories of Yahweh's self-revelation to the people of Israel. The Yahwist had gained a great vision of the God of Israel from meditating on the traditions concerning the patriarchs—Abraham, Isaac, Jacob, and his twelve sons. That story reached its climax with Yahweh's deliverance of Israel from slavery in Egypt.

The Yahwist and his people were surrounded by a dozen pagan peoples, each with their own gods and myths. Many of these other people groups, along with many Canaanites, had become a part of his own people, Israel. He felt he must protect the religious purity of the nation from the gods, ideas, and practices of those other religions.

His second motive, closely related to the first, was to defend Yahweh as the God worshiped by all people—not just Hebrews—from the earliest times.[7] This claim and other distinctive characteristics of his narrative enable scholars to distinguish his J material from other materials in the Pentateuch.

Yahweh?

As various pagan gods were named Zeus, Mars, Jupiter, or Mercury, so the God of the Hebrews was named Yahweh. In deference to the command in Exodus 20:7 against taking the name of Yahweh in vain, the rabbis refused even to pronounce the word Yahweh. When reading the Scriptures aloud, they substituted for it either "the Lord" or "God."

In the Hebrew text the rabbis wrote the consonants YHWH with the vowels for *Adonai* (Lord), indicating the reader should speak the word for Lord rather than the divine name Yahweh. King James translators, not realizing the significance of the vowels of the received text, created in a few places the hybrid name Jehovah from the consonants of Yahweh and the vowels of *Adonai*. Most of the time they translated the name Yahweh as "the LORD" (in all capital letters).

Obviously, he did not know of the other traditional historian writing in the north at the time, but certainly he knew that other ideas circulated among his people. Consequently, he wrote to defend Yahwism as the original faith of the human race and of his ancestral patriarchs.

He appears to have been a layman, neither a priest nor a prophet, for he shows little interest in either profession. He hailed from Judah, for his interests centered on the southern of the two Hebrew nations. We deduce that he lived in Jerusalem, because he shows a decided interest in that city and its reigning Davidic dynasty. Besides, at the time he wrote, of the towns of Judah only Jerusalem possessed the archives and learning necessary for such an undertaking.

The Yahwist concluded his literary masterpiece with this climactic sentence: "The kingdom was now firmly established in Solomon's hands" (1 Kgs. 2:46b). He wrote, therefore, sometime after Solomon's accession to the throne of Israel in 971 BCE. Furthermore, since he focused predominantly on locations in the southern nation of Judah, he must have written after the northern tribes broke away from the Davidic monarchy—after 931 BCE. Considering all these factors, many historians date the Yahwist during the reign of Rehoboam of Judah (931–913 BCE).

A masterful storyteller, the Yahwist wrote long connected narratives; painted wonderful word pictures; and preserved many marvelous stories of Abraham, Isaac, Jacob, Joseph, and Moses. He always referred to God as *Yahweh* ("Lord," in all caps, in our English Bibles), reserving the word *Elohim* (Hebrew for "God") for quoting characters in his narratives.

The Yahwist pictured the God of the patriarchs in anthropomorphic terms—a human-like God who talked to the patriarchs, with whom they could reason and argue. Yahweh related to them personally rather than as an awesome, distant deity. Still, Yahweh was an authority to be obeyed. Yahweh was, moreover, a God of grace, counting faith as righteousness.[8] Contrary to the gods of the pagans, Yahweh was not revealed through myths or images, but through deeds and words—God's name, covenants, and promises.

He taught that Yahweh called Abraham and gave him a covenant promise that Yahweh would make of his descendants a great nation, give him fame and honor, and bless all the people of the earth through him.[9] Yahweh also promised to give Abraham's descendants the land of Canaan, later Palestine.[10] In that covenant Yahweh did not ask Abraham to promise anything; God made all the promises. These promises would become the basis for Yahweh's future actions on behalf of Abraham's descendants, as well as the basis for Israel's trust in Yahweh's benevolence.[11]

The Yahwist, though, did not present these promises to Abraham as mere nationalistic chauvinism. This devout man of broad spiritual vision believed all humanity had been commissioned by God to rule the earth on behalf of its creator. Since humanity as a whole, however, had failed in that task, God began again with Abraham and his descendants. The nation of Israel constituted representative humanity, called to become a blessing to the entire human race.

Then when Abraham and his wife Sarah were old and still childless, Yahweh appeared to him in a dream promising to make his descendants as numerous as the stars. The Yahwist recorded, "Abram believed the Lord [Yahweh], and he credited it to him as righteousness" (Gen. 15:6). From the beginning of the patriarchs' experience of Yahweh, their relationship with God was based primarily on faith—personal relationship—not law, ritual, or cultic practice.

The Yahwist's narratives also included significant events from the life of Moses, Israel's exodus from Egypt, and several key stories of Israel's wilderness experience following the Exodus. He called Moses' father-in-law Reuel,[12] in distinction from the Elohist who called him Jethro.[13] Both authors, however, identified Reuel/Jethro as a priest of Midian. Furthermore, the Yahwist referred to the mountain of revelation as Sinai,[14] whereas the Elohist called it Horeb.[15]

It does not seem likely that the Yahwist created his stories, since he shared many of them with the Elohist and also with the later Priest of Jerusalem. Such independent multiple attestation of several stories indicates they came from some common ancient source. Two possible sources are obvious: oral traditions and written accounts of the oral traditions passed along at the shrines and cultic centers of Israel and Judah.

The Yahwist, however, did not merely collect and organize traditions in a cut-and-paste pastiche. The J material gives much evidence of deep spiritual vision and careful artistic composition. The Yahwist knew the traditions intimately and knew when he began to write where his narrative was going. He selected stories that suited his purpose and wove them into a masterful narrative that combined literary artistry, spiritual elevation, and preservation of ancient tradition in a document that has survived almost three thousand years to our own day as part of our Bible.

A Priest of Shiloh

At the same time the Yahwist was composing his Hebrew history in Judah, another collector and interpreter of the Hebrew founding traditions worked on a similar project in the north, probably at Shiloh. Like the Yahwist of Jerusalem, the Elohist of Shiloh had come to a profound love of God through his meditation on the founding traditions of his people.[16] His first purpose was to set forth the pure faith of the patriarchs and the revelation of Yahweh that Moses had received against the mass of priests of other faiths surrounding him and at times threatening his very existence.

His second purpose was to refute the point of view of the Jerusalem priesthood that only descendants of Aaron were legitimate priests and that Levites were their menial assistants. Rather than taking on the Jerusalem priesthood directly, however, he attempted to undermine them by the stories he related.

The point that most distinguishes the work of the Elohist from that of the Yahwist concerns his view of the Hebrew covenant name for God: Yahweh. The Yahwist claimed that some members of the human race and especially the patriarchs had always known God as Yahweh. The Elohist insisted, to the contrary, that God's name was first revealed as Yahweh to Moses at the burning bush.[17] The biblical evidence indicates the Elohist's view on this subject was the universal priestly tradition in Israel.

Loss of the Ark of the Covenant and with it their premier place in the Israelite priesthood must have rankled the priests of Shiloh. The Tabernacle and the Ark of the Covenant had been their responsibility from the time of Joshua until the time of Samuel, the great prophet, priest, and judge who anointed the first two kings of Israel. Now the Zadokite priesthood in Jerusalem had replaced the Levitical priesthood and reduced its members to the ignominious position of mere country priests.

To rub sand into that wound, the prophet Ahijah of Shiloh had helped instigate the establishing of the northern nation by blessing Jeroboam to foment that insurrection.[18] Jeroboam, however, repaid Ahijah's assistance by establishing his capital at Shechem, snubbing Ahijah's hometown Shiloh. Even worse, Jeroboam established shrine cities and set up golden calves at Dan and Beth-el, saying, "Here are your gods, O Israel, who brought you up out of Egypt" (Exod. 32:4b). Incensed at the blatant idolatry and the snub of Shiloh, Ahijah pronounced God's judgment on Jeroboam and his kingdom for apostasy.[19]

Since adopting the Canaanite alphabet a century earlier, the Shiloh sanctuary had no doubt served as a repository for historical documents and written versions of Israel's oral traditions. Drawing on these narratives, this Shiloh priest probably wrote what originally was a complete traditional history of the patriarchal period and of Israel's exodus from Egypt. We now know that history as "E," because the author insisted that the patriarchs knew God only as Elohim (God) prior to the burning bush experience of Moses. In other words, he flatly disagreed with the Yahwist's idea that people had known God as Yahweh from the earliest times.

We do not now possess the entire E Document. The author who centuries later merged J and E into a single work cut significant portions of the works from which he drew and preserved more of J than of E. The E material does not show up in our present Pentateuch until Genesis 20. It appears that a later editor eliminated everything from the E Document before the story of Abraham's passing off Sarah as his sister to Abimelech. After Genesis 20, however, the Pentateuchal narrative frequently focuses heavily on the E materials and provides us with a fairly continuous story.

The Elohist showed himself a superb storyteller, preserving many of our favorite Bible stories—Jacob and Laban, Joseph, the Exodus, crossing the Red Sea, and Israel's stay at Horeb (which the Yahwist called Sinai). The Elohist also provided us with much of the legal material in Exodus, showing his priestly concern for ethical matters. This interest distinguished him from the lay Yahwist's lack of interest in legal and ritual concerns.[20]

While the E material is extensive in places in Genesis 20 through Deuteronomy, it is nonexistent in others, giving the appearance of extensive editing out of E material. Nothing of E appears in Leviticus, little in Numbers other than chapters 11–12 and 22–24 (the story of Balak and Balaam), and almost none in Deuteronomy (except for 31:14-15, 23). Nevertheless, the E material proves itself a written document by its consistent distinguishing traits and the continuity of so much of its narrative.

We can tell the Elohist lived in the northern nation of Israel after the division of the monarchy. For one thing, the E material elevates the prestige of Joshua, a northern hero from the tribe of Ephraim. The E Document also showed great interest in the northern shrine city of Shechem in Ephraim.[21] The stories of Shechem selected by each author hints at where he lived and his attitude toward this key cultic center—the first capital of Israel under Jeroboam. The southern Yahwist tells a sordid tale about Shechem,[22] a major cult center of Israel, and the revenge of the sons of Judah on that city. By contrast, the northern Elohist tells a positive story of Jacob's purchase of land at Shechem and building an altar there that he named El-the-God-of-Israel.[23]

The Elohist's narratives reveal a distinct interest in other locales in the northern nation—Bethel, Penuel, and Dothan—as opposed to those in Judah.[24] The Elohist also preserved many stories featuring Joseph,[25] the eponymous father of the two leading tribes of the northern nation, Ephraim and Manassah.

That the Elohist lived at Shiloh surfaces in his implied insults to the Jerusalem Zadokite priesthood. When the Elohist wrote his stories of the Exodus and the Wilderness, he chose, significantly, to include the story of Aaron's golden bull. While Moses was meeting with God on the mountain, Aaron made a golden calf and said to Israel, "These are your gods, O Israel, that brought you up out of Egypt" (Exod. 32:8 NIV), even though Aaron had made only one bull, not two. When Jeroboam of Israel later set up his two golden calves at Dan and Bethel, he used exactly the same words as Aaron in the wilderness. The Elohist clearly intended to imply a parallel between Aaron's and Jeroboam's apostasies, casting Dan, Bethel, and Jerusalem (where Aaron's descendant was the high priest) in a negative light. Furthermore, in contrast to Aaron who succumbed to idolatry, his ancestors, the Levites, had rallied to Moses' side and slaughtered three thousand Israelites who had joined Aaron in his apostasy.

Everything in the stories of Aaron's golden calf with its implied reference to Jeroboam's golden calves at Dan and Bethel points to Shiloh as the locale of the preservation of this story. The Elohist did not make up this story to embarrass the Zadokite priests in Jerusalem, but he did choose this story and so worded it to underscore his point. The Elohist also described Miriam and Aaron, putative ancestor of the Zadokites, as criticizing Moses for his Cushite (probably Nubian) wife, thus bringing down God's judgment on themselves.[26] In addition, the northern hero Joshua had not been involved in the episode with Aaron's golden calf, because he was on the mountain with Moses. Finally, Joshua himself had set up the Tent of Meeting at Shiloh.

The Elohist's overarching interest in cities, heroes, and issues related to the northern nation of Israel points to his writing after the division of the monarchy in 931 BCE. The fact that he could produce such a monumental work indicates he wrote before the Assyrians destroyed Shiloh in 722 BCE and took most of Israel's leaders into captivity.

Between 931 and 722 BCE, three periods stand out as possible dates for the Elohist with his preoccupation with the golden bulls of Jeroboam. Friedman's arguments, however, seem to indicate that the E Document came into being during the reign of Jeroboam I (931–910 BCE) in response to his setting up the golden bulls at Dan and Beth-el, using non-Levitical priests, and snubbing Shiloh.

To say E was written in the 900s BCE is not to say the Elohist created its stories and laws then. Multiple attestation of the parallel sequences of characters and events in E and J (plus P, as we will see shortly) indicates the traditional historians of Israel and Judah did not feel free to invent a national history. Rather, they drew from well-known traditions of their people to set forth their visions of the meaning of the origins of Israel in light of what was going on at the time and place they wrote. Their histories of the patriarchs and the Exodus were written records of and interpretations of the oral traditions as well as critiques of their own periods of history.

The Elohist's most famous story in Genesis is his narrative of Abraham's attempted sacrifice of Isaac, which God prevented. With this story, the priest showed God as full of grace, not desiring the sacrifice of children as practiced by the Canaanites.[27] In a single narrative he vaulted Israel more than a thousand years into the moral future of the human race. When the Elohist recorded this narrative almost a thousand years after Abraham, worldwide rejection of child sacrifice still lay many centuries in the future.

A Second Priest of Shiloh

Sometime during the two centuries following the breakup of the United Kingdom of Israel,[28] a second Shiloh priest wrote down a collection of traditional laws of Moses. Whereas the Elohist had undermined the Zadokite claims by implications from Israel's history, this second priest directly refuted the Zadokite contention from the Mosaic law code. This priest did not make up the laws he wrote, but he did select them with a purpose. All the laws this Levitical priest recorded no doubt belonged to the corpus of laws traditionally attributed to Moses, even though later case law had almost certainly become included in the code.

This priest selected laws that fulfilled several purposes. He recorded laws that enunciated basic ethical principles of Israel and stipulated the essential holy days and festivals of Israel. These points established the basic distinctives of the Hebrew faith.

He included laws validating the position of all Levites and only Levites as Israel's priests. This point flatly contradicted the claims by the Zadokite priesthood of Jerusalem that only they could legitimately serve at the altar and that all other Levites were merely their menial assistants.

The laws he preserved forbade the worship of any god other than Yahweh or the worship of any idol. These laws undermined the position of the non-Levitical priests of Jeroboam's state cult shrines at Dan and Bethel worshipping the golden bulls.

Careful analysis of the language, style, flow, and concerns of the book of Deuteronomy suggests that the original version of this book possibly consisted of chapters 12–26.[29] These chapters contain almost exclusively legislation given in second-person plural commands, presumably by Moses. Not all of the commands came from Moses, we may be sure, as other injunctions from later case law evidently were added to the original corpus of laws. Still, the whole of it belonged to the traditional Mosaic law.

The opening chapter of the book of the Law states that when the Hebrews arrived in Canaan, they should offer all their sacrifices and offerings at "the place that YHWH, your God, will choose from all your tribes to set His name there, tent it" (Deut. 12:5).[30] Multiple references in Deuteronomy 12–26 to God's tenting or tabernacling found fulfillment at Shiloh where the Tent of Meeting stood for a century or more.[31] Significantly, the most important piece of furniture in the Tabernacle—the Ark of the Covenant—shows up later at Shiloh.[32]

In the early days of the northern nation of Israel, Shiloh was the place most likely to have the people with the skill set necessary to produce such a work as the core of Deuteronomy. Abiathar,[33] descended from the Shiloh priests, served as one of David's two chief priests, giving evidence of the high level of prestige these priests held and suggesting a corresponding high level of education. Subtle additional turns of phrase in Deuteronomy 12–26 point to Shiloh as its place of origin.

We saw earlier that the Elohist most likely worked during the reign of Jeroboam I. If we accept Shiloh as the origin of E, similarities between the book of the Law (D) and the E Document strengthen the identification of Shiloh as D's place of origin. Both D and E refer to the place where God gave Moses the law at Horeb,[34] but J refers to it as Sinai.[35]

The Deuteronomist considered Moses a prophet and promised that after him God would raise up a prophet like Moses.[36] His law code warns against false prophets and provides tests for discerning them.[37] The Deuteronomist's and the Elohist's connection to Shiloh also shows up in their sharing a positive view of prophets, which would flow naturally from Samuel's having begun his ministry there. By contrast, J never speaks of anyone as a prophet.

Finally, the Elohist told the story of King Balak's hiring Balaam to place a curse on Israel. Then D refers to Balaam son of Beor in the only other Pentateuchal reference to him.[38] These similarities between E and D suggest a common tradition and an identical place of origin.

It has been claimed by some that since the book of the Law (Deuteronomy 12–26) was found in the Temple in 621 BCE, it was created at that time and placed in the Temple so it could be "discovered." In other words, the book of the Law (D) was a "pious fraud," probably perpetrated by the high priest Hilkiah. That theory would be credible if the book of the Law provided internal evidence to support it, but it does not.

Deuteronomy 12–26 bristles with passages not likely to have been written by a Jerusalem Zadokite priest or readily accepted by a king of Judah. When D speaks of armies, it does not refer to standing armies or professional armies but of musters from the people—citizen militias.[39] By Josiah's time, standing professional armies had served the kings of Judah for centuries. Militia musters of the locals wielding scythes and clubs lay in the ancient past.

Additionally, Moses told Israel that when they chose a king, he must not accumulate great wealth.[40] Furthermore, the king himself should write out a copy of the book of the Law and meditate on it his entire life so that he would not depart from it. King Josiah did accept the book of the Law, repent of his nation's failure to keep the laws of that book, and launch the nation into a vigorous campaign to correct its failures and abuses. No historian of ancient Israel, however, records anything of Josiah's shedding himself of any of his wealth or writing out his own copy of the book of the Law for his personal use.

A still more salient argument, however, comes from the attitude of Deuteronomy 12–26 toward the Levites and the priests. We will see in chapter 6, "The Temple Apologist," that the Jerusalem priests descended from Zadok held themselves above Levites, whom they considered mere aides to the priests doing the menial work of the Temple. The D document, by contrast, considers all Levites priests, regularly calls the Levites priests, and several times refers to "the whole tribe of Levi" as priests.[41] No Zadokite priest writing in seventh-century Jerusalem would have written such passages. The high priest's acceptance of this book, including passages so distasteful to his own vested interests, indicates he and his priests truly found the book—and it awed them into accepting it.

The date of the writing of D, however, does not equal the date of the origin of these laws. Surely the author of D worked from a corpus of laws received from the past, considered to have come from Moses himself. Later case law had clearly attached itself to the original body of laws, but this corpus of Hebraic law was ancient by the time the Deuteronomist wrote it sometime in the ninth to eighth centuries.

Two additional traits of the Deuteronomist's work require our attention. First, of the four authors of the Pentateuchal material, he bears down harder than the other three on the insistence that God commanded Israel to either enslave or to annihilate the Canaanites. The others generally said God only commanded them to drive out the Canaanites, contradicting the Shiloh priest. It seems his priestly sensitivities were greatly offended at the idolatrous and degraded orgiastic practices of the Canaanite worship of the Baals and the Asherim.

Secondly, he asserted that God would bless the people of Israel for faithfulness to Yahweh and curse them for unfaithfulness. This curse potentially extended to exile from the land. This point is known as "the Deuteronomistic theology" and would be taken up later by a highly significant historian.

Then in 722 BCE disaster struck the northern nation of Israel and the city of Shiloh when the Assyrians invaded, stimulating a new phase of the preservation of the ancient Hebrew traditions.

Notes

[1] Exod. 15:1b-18.
[2] Judg. 5:2-31.
[3] Judg. 14:14.
[4] Judg. 9:8-15.
[5] William G. Dever, *The Lives of Ordinary People in Ancient Israel: Where Archaeology and the Bible Intersect* (Grand Rapids: Eerdmans, 2012), 228-30.
[6] The remainder of this chapter follows largely the view argued by Richard Elliott Friedman in *Who Wrote the Bible?* (New York: HarperSanFrancisco, 1997), *The Hidden Book in the Bible* (New York: HarperSanFrancisco, 1998), and *The Bible with Sources Revealed* (New York: HarperOne, 2005). Friedman makes several crucial modifications to the 150-year-old Wellhausen Hypothesis in the light of more recent evidence. Possibly a majority of critics hold to somewhat different views from Friedman, but his arguments seem decisive to this writer.
[7] Gen. 4:26.
[8] Gen. 15:6.
[9] Gen. 12:2-3.
[10] Gen. 12:7.
[11] G.E. Mendenhall, "Covenant," in vol. 1, *Interpreter's Dictionary of the Bible*, ed. George A. Buttrick (New York: Abingdon, 1962): 717-18; G. Gordon Wenham, *Word Biblical Commentary: Genesis 1–15* (Waco, TX: Word, 1987), 326.
[12] Exod. 2:16-18, Num. 10:29.
[13] Exod. 3:1.

[14] Exod. 3:1, 18; 18:1-27.

[15] Exod. 19:11, 18, 23.

[16] Admittedly, many scholars now question or even deny the existence of the Elohist or an E document. We also have to recognize that we cannot find a full Elohistic narrative in Genesis–Numbers. A number of scholars, however, Joel S. Baden, *The Composition of the Pentateuch: Renewing the Documentary Hypothesis* (New Haven: Yale University, 2012), for example, still argue persuasively that the Elohist did exist and produced a written Elohistic (E) traditional history of the Hebrew people. Arguments supporting the position taken in this book can be found in Friedman's works, particularly *Who Wrote the Bible?* In *Sources Revealed* (HarperSanFrancisco, 2003), "Collection of Evidence," pp. 7-31, Friedman summarizes the evidence to support his view that all four documents—J, E, D, and P—existed as independent written documents. Baden's work offers a somewhat different defense of this view.

[17] Exod. 3:13-18.

[18] 1 Kgs. 11:29-39.

[19] 1 Kgs. 12:28, 14:1-16.

[20] To gain the full impact of viewing the various sources, I suggest reading Friedman's *The Bible with Sources Revealed* with its various source materials color-coded.

[21] Joshua 24.

[22] Genesis 34.

[23] Gen. 33:18-20.

[24] Gen. 28:11b-12, 17-18, 20-21; 32:25-33; 35; 37:12-18 (all E).

[25] Genesis 40–41 plus other verses (E).

[26] Numbers 12 (E).

[27] Otto Eissfeldt reported that Phoenician records from the Roman period (a couple of millennia after Abraham) speak of sacrificing a sheep instead of a dedicated child (Gerhard von Rad, *Genesis* [Philadelphia: Westminster, 1961], 238 fn). Much earlier the Phoenicians reported that the god Kronos sacrificed his only son to his father Uranus (John Skinner, *Genesis* [Edinburgh: T&T Clark, 1930], 332). Of course, the Phoenician story is myth, but it shows that the Phoenicians, who were seacoast Canaanites, had a memory of child sacrifice in their ancient past. As late as about 800 BCE (more than a thousand years after Abraham and near the time E was written), the king of Moab sacrificed his eldest son to win a war (2 Kgs. 3:27). Between 400 and 200 BCE the Phoenicians of Carthage buried 20,000 burnt children ages birth to two years. Archaeologists interpret these charred skeletons as evidence of infant sacrifice. Almost a thousand years after Abraham, the *Iliad* portrays Agamemnon sacrificing his daughter Iphigenia to ensure a Greek victory over the Trojans. Admittedly these stories were written down long after the presumed time of Abraham, but the ancients were still practicing child sacrifice long after the story of Abraham and Isaac revealed God's rejection of that horrendous practice.

[28] Baden, *Composition of the Pentateuch*, 128, argues this point persuasively.

[29] Ibid. Baden argues that Deut. 1:1–11:31 contains the original introduction to the laws of Deuteronomy 12–26. He further argues that this introduction shows dependence on the E material, further supporting Friedman's contention that both E and D came from the same location, Shiloh. Baden, however, believes the Elohist was a layman, but that idea is almost certainly fallacious.

[30] Translation by Friedman in *Sources Revealed*, 330. Perhaps a better translation than "tent" in this quote would be "tabernacle." See also 12:11, 14:23, 16:6, 26:2. Friedman's translation finds support in the work of G. Ernest Wright, "The Book of Deuteronomy," in vol. 2, *The Interpreter's Bible*, ed. George A. Buttrick (New York: Abingdon, 1953), 411-12.

Wright construes the Hebrew as meaning "to tent, to tabernacle" rather than simply "to dwell" (which is a different word in Hebrew).

[31] Josh. 18:1.

[32] 1 Sam. 4:3-22.

[33] 2 Sam. 20:25; 1 Kgs. 1:7, 2:26-27. Second Sam. 8:17 has almost certainly become corrupted and the names of Abiathar and Ahimelech reversed.

[34] Deut. 18:16 (D); Exod. 3:1, 17:6, 33:6 (E).

[35] Exod. 19:18, 20, 23; 34:2, 4 (J).

[36] Deut. 18:15-19 (D).

[37] Deut. 13:1-5, 18:20-22.

[38] Numbers 22–24 (E), Deut. 23:5 (D).

[39] Deut. 20:1-9, 24:5-6.

[40] Deut. 17:14-20.

[41] Deut. 17:9, 18; 18:1, 3, 6; 21:5; 26:11, 12, 13.

CHAPTER 3

The River That Waters the Earth

The Garden of Eden in Historical Context

Before the Yahwist ever set goose quill to parchment, he conceptualized the whole of his story. He would set forth for posterity the founding traditions of Israel followed by more recent history based on documented sources. Furthermore, he would set the stage for that grand epic with an introduction consisting of his theology of creation followed by his theology of history.

Of course, he would not have called these stories "theology." As his people always did, he was simply thinking about God through stories. Still, in our way of thinking, he was engaged in theology of creation and theology of history. These two narrative theologies would introduce the reader to the great themes he would subsequently develop in the stories of the patriarchs, the Exodus, and finally the founding of Israel as a nation.

Rather than speak in abstract terms like a Greek philosopher, though, in typical Hebrew style the author would present his theology as picturesque narrative God-talk.[1] The people around him—the Canaanites and other groups—told elaborate myths of the creation of the world. The Yahwist recognized that those crude myths could not possibly reflect the exalted spiritual reality he had experienced in Yahweh. As he meditated on the history of Israel and his experience of Yahweh, he conceived a point-by-point refutation of the pagan myths.

Although another creation narrative appears in the first chapter of our Bible today, the Yahwist wrote his story first (probably shortly after 931 BCE), so we will look at it first. We will take up chapter 1 of Genesis when we get to that place in history in chapter 7, "The Man Who Saw the Beginning."

The Yahwist's Creation Story

The Yahwist concerned himself solely with the issue with which his contemporaries were obsessed—the religious question: What is the meaning of our existence? His methodology, though, stood in direct contradiction to that of the peoples among whom he lived.

The priests of the Canaanite and the Babylonian religions sought answers by reading the entrails of animals, studying the movements of the heavenly bodies, and consulting mediums who talked to the dead and oracles who spoke enigmatic riddles that could mean almost anything. The Yahwist found his answers in rational, spiritual reflection on history in communion with God's Spirit. Through his profound contemplation of the history of his people received first in their oral traditions and later in nearly contemporaneous documents, God revealed something of himself to this perceptive Jerusalem layman.

Like all people of all ages, this Israelite theologian of necessity began where he found himself. Today, we cannot discuss the beginning of the cosmos without speaking of the Big Bang theory and billions of years of development. Similarly, the Yahwist could not speak of creation without dealing with the currently prevailing myths. Most ancient thinkers simply took over the ancient myths and elaborated on them without essentially changing them. The myths were holy and could not be changed without offending the gods.

This Hebrew thinker, by contrast, defied the prevailing wisdom and offered an alternative view of the origins and meaning of this world and humanity. He presented a high, exalted, sublime theology of creation and the nature of the world and humanity in personal relationship to a single invisible spiritual deity.

The Yahwist described God as planting a garden "eastward in Eden," with a river flowing through and out of the garden. He said the river "parted, and became into four heads" (2:10), meaning the single river split into four rivers. Rivers and tributaries work exactly the opposite way in the real world. Natural rivers flow *from* multiple headwaters, not *into* multiple streams. This oddity in the story provides our first indication that this narrative does not describe ordinary topography. Furthermore, although the four rivers of the Yahwist's story in Genesis 2 bear familiar names, they cannot be identified with any of the rivers on earth as he knew them.

Gordon J. Wenham suggests the odd description of these four rivers provides an indicator of the author's intentions.[2] He was signaling that we cannot locate these rivers anywhere on earth, even though he gave them the names of four great rivers watering the nations he knew. The River of Eden, the spiritual stream flowing from the Garden of God, waters the entire earth. "We are all out of Eden," the Yahwist proclaimed. We are all irrigated by God's Spirit, but we have been cut off from intimacy with the divine presence. Both our glory and our anguish flow from that now lost Eden.

This story represents a history of a sort, but humanity's spiritual pre-history, not the fact-based history researched by today's professional historians. The artifacts of Eden are all around us in our society—and within us in our psyches. We dig up those potsherds in that twilight zone between wakefulness and sleep when we face our own alienation from God—and from one another—and long for reconciliation.

Having formed the man's body from the earth, God breathed into his nostrils the "breath of life." (*Adham*, Adam, simply means "man" in the sense of humanity, but it sounds much like *adhamah*, the earth from whence he came.) And "man became a living soul" (Gen. 2:7). The Yahwist did not speak of the man's receiving a soul but rather becoming a soul. A human does not *have* a soul in the Yahwist's Hebrew theology; a human *is* a soul consisting of body and breath (in Hebrew *ruach* = wind > breath > spirit).

The Babylonian myths, the dominant mythology across the ancient Near East, said the gods created humanity from the blood of a god, but this Hebrew theologian rejected such crude nonsense.[3] Humanity did not begin as an offspring of the gods, or as a little god or as a piece of the gods. Our creator did, however, create us in a special way—for fellowship with God. We breathe the very breath of Yahweh, as it were, the Yahwist sang out.

Furthermore, Yahweh did not create the man to be a slave of the gods, as the prevailing myths of Babylonian origin had it, but to serve as God's representatives on earth, joining in the divine work of creativity. Yahweh God gave man a beautiful garden to live in, a garden watered by a great river and filled with beautiful trees, like a middle-eastern prince living on his lavish estate. Yahweh commissioned the man to take care of the wonderful garden he had given him for his home. This beautiful creation is not humanity's private possession, the Yahwist proclaimed, but God's; still, God made humanity as caretaker of that paradise.

Then Yahweh created from a rib of the man a woman to stand beside him. The Yahwist says Adam called her "Eve" (Hebrew, *hawah*, meaning life or living, from the verb *hayah*, to live) "because she was the mother of all living" (Gen. 3:20). In other words, The man named his wife Life, and Man and Life set up housekeeping in God's own garden. The account of the two trees—the Tree of the Knowledge of Good and Evil and the Tree of Life—proclaimed that Yahweh created humanity free, with the capacity for moral choice.

The Yahwist's creation story presented the ancient Hebrews with a fresh, thrilling anthropology. Yahweh God created humankind with the capacity to choose to act as God's viceroys on earth and to enjoy unimaginable bounty. We were created for fellowship with God and for one another in marriage. We were created, finally, for open fellowship with one another. "And they were both naked, the man and his wife, and were not ashamed" (Gen. 2:25).

With the story of Adam's naming the animals, this theologically minded layman recognized the significance of language. Language as we know it sets us apart from the animals; but the names of things come from the human mind, not from the gods as the myths had it.

Then the Yahwist described the temptation of the original human beings to depart from the purpose for which Yahweh created them. This temptation did not come, as he described it, from the devil or Satan but from a snake. This snake was a talking snake, to be sure, but otherwise a very natural reptile. Eve was tempted, not by some supernatural being, but by one of the creatures roaming the garden.

What was the temptation? "Ye shall be as gods," the King James Version translates it. "You shall be like God," contemporary translations put it. Both translations mean the same thing. The ultimate temptation facing the human race is to aspire to become our own gods.

The temptation to eat of the Tree of the Knowledge of Good and Evil does not mean the temptation was knowledge itself, nor that moral knowledge is evil, nor that sex is evil—three abysmally silly misinterpretations. Some interpreters believe the story said the basic human temptation is to know everything. "Good and evil" was a Hebraism meaning "everything." To our own day, that aspiration has not escaped us. This understanding possibly reflects what the Yahwist means, but another view of this story seems more likely.

Gordon Wenham points out that several passages in the Bible equate "knowledge of good and evil" with moral discernment and insist valid moral discernment comes only from knowledge of God's revealed will.[4] Such knowledge the Hebrews called "wisdom." To attempt to attain wisdom apart from God's revelation amounts to rebellion against God, to making ourselves our own deities.

This narrative presents profound theology in a beautifully picturesque story. The Yahwist proclaimed that we could have chosen true, full, rich life through fellowship with God. Instead we have chosen to become our own gods and consequently abandoned that relationship with our creator for which we were created. The Yahwist did not intend this story as an explanation for the origin of physical death. After all, Adam and Eve did not physically die the day they "ate of the fruit"; but they did die spiritually.

We should not imagine that someone with a camera could have captured Eve eating fruit in a digital recording. Still, it is history—of sorts. It presents a vision of what went wrong with the human race from the very beginning. The Yahwist began with a set of problems in Israel's royalty and priesthood; now the Yahwist identifies humanity's ultimate problem with which the rest of the biblical epic will deal. Humanity has lost fellowship with God. How can we get it back? How can we see God's face again? What is the way back to God's presence?

We lost the sense of God's presence, but we have not lost the attributes given us by our creator. We still breathe the spiritual breath of life given us from God. The river flowing out of Eden from God's presence still waters all the nations of the world, connecting us to our original home, irrigating our lives if we will receive it.

We were created to live in the Paradise of God's presence. How shall we live now that we are homeless wanderers? How shall we return to Eden? The Yahwist's tale of humanity begins with a longing for Eden—a longing and grieving for lost opportunity and lost fellowship with God. In this narrative the Yahwist foreshadowed themes that will occur again and again in the remainder of his work, signaling that he envisioned the entire tale before he first put quill to parchment.

The Yahwist's Theology of History

To complete his introduction to his story of the Hebrew patriarchs, the Yahwist followed his narrative theology of creation with a narrative theology of history. In these stories the Yahwist foreshadowed and set the theological stage for the history he was about to narrate and interpret. Drawing from the store of traditional stories of his people, he selected several stories from the primeval memories of the human race and presented them in such a way as to teach his vision of what God is about in this world. He brought to those stories revolutionary insights concerning the nature of the human race and its civilization and accomplishments.

Where did he get such insights? Yahweh's creation of Israel essentially from nothing taught him much about creation of the universe. God's redemption of Israel taught him about grace, and the nation's repeated backsliding from faithfulness to God taught him about sin. His people's experience with building a nation, cities, palace, temple, and defensive city walls taught him the limitations and corruption of human culture and cities. The Hebrew experience with warfare, violence, genocide, injustice, and child sacrifice taught him the deep depravity to which even civilized humans could descend.

Simultaneously, the Yahwist had experienced the grace-filled redemptive presence of God. He wrote, therefore, stories that subsequent generations would call inspired revelation breathed out by the very breath of God.[5] These primeval stories joined to his creation narratives set the theological background for the stories of the patriarchs and the Exodus. These descriptive narratives set the themes he would develop over many chapters to come.

Soon after The Earthy One and his wife Life left the garden Yahweh had designed for their enjoyment, the woman had two sons, Cain and Abel. Cain became a farmer and Abel a shepherd. Clearly the Yahwist was the recipient of traditions that told of the tremendously important advent of the twin skills of agriculture and domestication of sheep. Significantly, we now know these two historical developments arose around 10,000 BCE in the Middle East near where these stories originated. His ancestral traditions still possessed a rudimentary memory of those events. Cain soon murdered Abel and was banished from human society.[6]

Section one of the Yahwist's theological pre-history climaxes with a song Cain's son Lamech sang to his two wives celebrating his murder of a rival.[7] The first city, the Yahwist tells us, was built by a murderer who was the son of a murderer. Clearly, the Yahwist did not think much of cities with their corruption and violence. From the murderers Cain and Lamech develop all of civilization—Bedouin desert wanderers, domestication of sheep and cattle, music and its instruments, smelting and smithing of brass and iron, and cities.[8]

The Sumerian and Babylonian myths celebrated such human accomplishments as gifts of the gods or of super-human heroes—exhibits of the greatness of the ancients. Our Yahwist, however, presented all the accoutrements of civilization as entirely human accomplishments, developed out of a violent society, fathered by murderers in rebellion against God, and banished from God's presence. He saw civilization as standing under God's judgment for its violence and rebellion against the divine will, not commended for its super-human or even semi-divine accomplishments.

In the strange story of the Nephilim[9] the sons of God mate with daughters of men and sire a race of giants, or so the story has traditionally been read. The story in Hebrew, however, says nothing of giants, but speaks only of the Nephilim, literally, the Fallen Ones. The Nephilim "became mighty men which were of old, men of renown"—mighty heroes or warriors, possibly famous warriors fallen in battle. Traditionally the story has been seen as describing sexual intercourse between angelic males and human women. The angelic theory seems unlikely, because the Yahwist *never* mentioned angels except for the Angel of Yahweh, a personal manifestation of Yahweh (as in Genesis 19).

Whatever the Yahwist's own meaning of this odd story, its significance for us resides in what the Yahwist did with it. For him, the "men of renown," the heroes of yesteryear, were heroes fallen in battle—nothing more. They were not gods, demi-gods, nor even superhuman heroes as in the myths.

Having judged all civilization as hopelessly enmeshed in evil, the Yahwist then turned to God's judgment on all human accomplishments achieved apart from faithfulness to God. Throughout the Near East, the earliest historical event memorialized in extant records was the Great Flood, universally seen as having wiped out the previous generation with its cities and civilization, forcing survivors to rebuild civilization from scratch. Such a universally remembered event must have been based on some actual occurrence(s).

Archaeologists have uncovered several feet of flood silt covering ancient cities in Iraq from as far north as Nineveh and Kish to as far south as Shuruppak, Uruk, and Lagash near the Persian Gulf. These flood deposits, though, did not occur contemporaneously with one another. It appears that accounts of several local floods that destroyed various centers of civilization at different times eventually merged into a story of a single Great Flood wiping out all humanity. The Babylonians worked this story of the Great Flood into their mythology, but the Babylonian version differs significantly from the biblical account, notably in its theology of the flood.

The Babylonians said the gods decided to wipe out humanity because humans had multiplied so prolifically and had gotten so noisy the gods could not rest. The Yahwist, however, said the one God decided to destroy humanity in judgment for its evil.[10] During the flood, the Babylonians said, earthquakes and storms frightened the gods and they fled the scene in abject terror. The Yahwist, by contrast, portrayed God as fully sovereign over the situation.

During the flood, the myths said, humanity had been unable to provide food for the gods. Following the flood the hero of the Babylonian myth offered sacrifices, and the famished gods gathered around the oblation like flies. The Yahwist, on the other hand, portrayed Noah as offering a sacrifice, to which God graciously responded that he would never again bring such destruction on the earth.

The Babylonian myths concluded with the elevation of the hero of the flood to the status of a god or demi-god. The Yahwist portrayed Noah as a normal human being who began vita-culture (the raising of grapes for wine-making) and got drunk on his product. On top of that, his son Ham committed the terrible act of disrespecting his father by ridiculing his drunken nudity and reporting it to his brothers.

Throughout his flood narrative the Yahwist emphasized righteousness and justice as Yahweh's standards for humanity and the normal humanity of his non-heroic characters. The Yahwist saw these traditional stories in ethical monotheistic terms, stressing the mercy and grace of God, in stark contrast to the currently prevailing mythology of capricious gods.

In the Babylonian myths, following the Flood, Marduk, patron god of Babylon, commissioned the Council of the Gods to build Babylon. The gods labored for a year shoveling mud to make bricks to build Esagila, the great ziggurat, the step-pyramid for which ancient Babylon is still famous. The Esagila was crowned by a chapel to the gods where the deities gathered for a banquet climaxed with mugs of beer. The Babylonians saw Babylon as the Gate of the Gods and center of the earth.

The Yahwist made fun of that myth, remarking that the Babylonian ziggurat reaching to heaven was so puny that God had to come down to earth just to see it.[11] The Babylonians sought to unify themselves with this great temple, but it divided them instead. Rather than the Gate of the Gods, Babylon represented the gate to rebellion, confusion, and division.

Instead of signaling the apex of human accomplishment, Babylon signified the height of human arrogance. Instead of standing as the center of the earth as in Babylonian thought, Babylon represented the center of human strife and division. Instead of showing human wisdom, Babylon revealed human folly. Instead of receiving the word of Yahweh, these men became embroiled in the confusion of their own words. The confusion of multiple human languages became the perfect metaphor for describing human confusion and division.

Having begun with Adam and starting over again with Seth and then with Noah, God began anew once more with Abraham who had come out of Ur, then part of Babylonia. Whereas God judged the sin of the human race with destruction in the Flood, God began a new work of mercy and grace with Abraham. That vision of God's grace remains the central underlying truth of the Yahwist's subsequent narrative.

At this point the Yahwist has presented a new theology of history. The great accomplishments of civilization do not represent the successes of superhuman heroes, but rather the expressions of human rebellion against God. God not only judges our sin but also extends grace to transcend our sin. Yahweh is the God of beginning again, and again, and again. These will be the themes pervading the Yahwist's narrative of traditional history to come. With this twin foundation of a theology of creation and theology of history, the Yahwist is ready to launch into his stories of Abraham, Isaac, and Jacob, which in turn will introduce the Exodus (which we examined in chapter 2).

Notes

[1] I learned the expression "*picturesque narrative*" from Dr. J. Hardee Kennedy in his advanced Hebrew class at New Orleans Baptist Theological Seminary. The expression "God-talk" I learned from Anglican John MacQuarrie's book by the same name (New York: Harper and Row, 1967).

[2] Gordon J. Wenham, *Word Biblical Commentary: Genesis 1–15* (Grand Rapids: Zondervan, 1987), 66-67.

[3] Babylonian mythology was known all over the Near East, among Hittites, Hurrians, Canaanites, and Hebrews. A copy of a fragment of the Babylonian Gilgamesh Epic was found at Megiddo, in Israel. See T.H. Gaster, "Myth," in vol. 3, *The Interpreter's Dictionary of the Bible*, ed. George Buttrick (New York: Abingdon, 1962): 484; A.L. Oppenheim, "Assyria and Babylonia," in vol. 1, *The Interpreter's Dictionary of the Bible*, ed. George Buttrick et. al. (New York: Abingdon, 1962): 297-298, 303; Amihai Mazar, *Archaeology of the Land of the Bible* (New York: Doubleday, 1990), 168; Ziony Zevit, *Religions of Ancient Israel: A Synthesis of Parallactic Approaches* (London: Springer, 2001), 445 with fn. 11.

[4] Wenham, *Genesis 1–15*, 63-64.
[5] 2 Tim. 3:16.
[6] Gen. 4:1-18.
[7] Gen. 4:19-24.
[8] Gen. 4:2, 16-22.
[9] Gen. 6:1-4.
[10] Gen. 6:5.
[11] Gen. 11:1-9.

CHAPTER 4

The World's First Historian

Writing History from Documentary Sources

For the first two centuries after the people of Israel entered Canaan they had no ongoing government. Charismatic leaders called "judges" arose as needed to fend off invasions but then returned to their farms when the crisis passed. Then about 1020 BCE, a momentous change took place in Israelite culture. Under the influence and pressure of the Canaanites and surrounding nations, many of the people of Israel decided they had to have a king to lead them in defense against invasions. Under pressure from the people, the prophet Samuel took the controversial move of anointing a young farmer named Saul as the first king of Israel.

Saul stood head-and-shoulders taller than other Israelites and proved himself a ferocious warrior and ingenuous battle tactician. At the same time some emotional disability periodically incapacitated him—apparently depression accompanied by irrational suspicion that his subordinates were out to undermine him. In spite of his emotional problems, Saul became an effective king and unified the people of Israel into a nation of sorts. His own relatively large farm house probably served as his "palace." His "army" consisted of a militia of local farmers called up to fight off their enemies with whatever weapons or farm implements they possessed. Surrounding nations likely considered Saul nothing more than a contemptible local warlord; but for Israel he was their first king, and they were now a genuine nation contending with the great powers of the world.

When Jeroboam wrested the northern tribes from Rehoboam's control, the nation with no king but Yahweh now had two kings. The first king chosen by Yahweh had been succeeded, not by his son, but by one of his generals. That second king had been succeeded, not by his eldest surviving son, but by a younger son who, as some saw it, supplanted his elder brother. Then the northern tribes had broken away from the original nation to form another nation worshiping idolatrous golden bulls instead of Yahweh. In addition, the Levitical priesthood administering sacrifices before the Ark of the Covenant at Shiloh had been replaced and demoted by the Zadokite priesthood at the Temple in Jerusalem and the idolatrous priesthood of the golden bulls at Dan and Bethel.

What did this chaos in two national institutions say about the legitimacy of Israel's leadership and Yahweh's approval of them? How could this sequence of political events be squared with Israel's faith—and with the concept of proper social order? Without a king whose legitimacy the nation at large acknowledged, chaos would reign and the judgment of God might fall on them all! Without a legitimate priesthood to represent the people before God, would their sacrifices even be accepted?

In the midst of this political and religious maelstrom, shortly after 931 BCE, a devout layman in Judah wrote his theological assessment of the nation's history and the state of the nation. We have already met this man—the Yahwist—and the work he wrote—J. His history of Israel, however, covered far more than the nation's founding traditions included in the Pentateuch, which we have already examined. We now turn to the second volume of his work: his national history drawn from documentary sources. First, however, let's look at the historical sources on which he drew.

Ancient Israel's Earliest Historians

The conventional story holds that Herodotus (ca. 484–425 BCE) holds the title as the "father of history," since he supposedly made the first attempt to write a history based on documentary evidence rather than on myths, legends, and oral traditions. The Roman Cicero who gave the Greek that epithet clearly did not know of the ancient Judean who wrote his national history from documentary sources five hundred years before Herodotus.

Through the first few centuries of the life of the ancient Israelites, only oral traditions kept alive the stories of their ancient patriarchs, Israel's exodus from Egypt, and their early years in Canaan. By the time of Israel's first king, Saul, the Israelites had adopted the Canaanite language and alphabet. By the time of David, they had developed their own unique alphabet. Using this tool, learned men began to write narratives nearly contemporary with the events they described.

Those early documents were not our Scriptures; but the later authors of the Bible did incorporate a number of them into our Bible.[1] Samuel at Shiloh[2] and the Ark Narrative[3] were possibly written by the Levitical priests at Shiloh early in David's reign, or possibly even earlier, to preserve the history of their most notable native son, Samuel. The Rise of Kingship,[4] Saul's Battles,[5] and the History of David's Rise[6] were possibly written by someone in David's court to legitimate the monarchy and David's claim to the throne. The Throne Succession Narrative[7] was possibly begun in David's reign and completed in Solomon's to legitimate the Davidic-Solomonic dynasty.

The Prophet Narrative[8] was almost certainly written by the prophetic disciples of Elijah and Elisha to preserve the memory of their founders. Court annalists kept contemporary records of the court history of David and Solomon.[9] Someone had written a still more ancient work named the book of Jasher,[10] but we no longer have anything of this work except the stories borrowed from it and included in our Bible. Certainly, there must have existed many others.

Ancient Israel and Judah were hotbeds of historical research and chronicling. Probably nothing like this activity took place in any other civilization on earth at the time. These early historians of ancient Israel no doubt undertook this monumental enterprise because they were convinced that they had received a revelation of Yahweh through the history of their people—and in this insight, they achieved another monumental first in human history.

The First Major Hebrew Historian

The first Hebrew Historian to attempt a comprehensive history of his people, the Yahwist, probably wrote his great composition in two volumes.[11] The first volume (discussed in chapters 2 and 3) began with creation and primeval history through the patriarchs, the Exodus, down to Joshua's old age (the J material from Gen. 2:4 to Joshua 13). He based this first volume entirely on oral traditions or written accounts of oral traditions. That first volume, therefore, represented one of the strands of the Hebrew founding traditions.

The second volume covered Israel's history from the judges Abimelek through Samuel and the kings Saul and David down to the point that Solomon established himself securely on the throne of Israel (the J material from Judg. 8:30 to 1 Kgs. 2:46). The second volume thus began with oral tradition (Judg. 8:30 through his material in Judges) and then moved on to draw from written materials, some of which had been written near the time of the events they described (1–2 Samuel and 1 Kings 1–2). In other words, the second volume of J morphed from oral traditions at the beginning to documented history at the end.

The Yahwist completed his history of Israel sometime in the late tenth century BCE, probably during the reign of Rehoboam (931–913), completing the first comprehensive written history of any nation on earth. With this work—the J Document—the Yahwist established himself as the first major Hebrew Historian, and through his history accomplished several purposes:

- He communicated his vision of Yahweh—God of grace, love, faithfulness, and redemption.
- He showed how God relates to people personally, not as some deity totally removed from human contact.
- He validated the monarchy against those who insisted Israel had no king but Yahweh.
- He vindicated David's dynasty against those who believed David was a usurper who had no right to replace Saul's line.
- He justified Solomon's claim to the throne over his older brother Adonijah.
- He implied the illegitimacy of the insurrection of the northern tribes who had broken away from the United Kingdom of Israel to form their own nation, appropriating to themselves the name Israel.

The Yahwist adapted the already existing works cited earlier to accomplish these goals. In the process he preserved two versions of the Israelite settlement in Canaan. In his material in our book of Joshua, he presented the Israelite possession of Canaan as a blitzkrieg attack in which Joshua conquered all the kings and cities of Canaan in one fell swoop. In his material now appearing in our book of Judges, he described a longer, more involved occupation of Canaan by Israel. In this latter account he described the Israelite possession of Canaan as a long process of gradual conquest and occupation. His account of the period of the Judges concludes with these momentous words: "In those days Israel had no king; everyone did as he saw fit" (Judg. 21:25; cf. 17:6, 18:1, and 19:1).

These words set the stage for the rise of the monarchy to follow. Then he described the ministry of Israel's first great prophet, Samuel, the rise of the monarchy under Saul, the rise of David and his dynasty, and Solomon's accession to the throne of Israel. He concluded his history with the words, "The kingdom was now firmly established in Solomon's hands" (1 Kgs. 2:46).

The Yahwist's success is palpable. He preserved the stories of many of the judges, of Eli and Samuel, of Israel's first kings Saul and David, and finally of Solomon's rise to the throne. We can appreciate his success, for his work was later incorporated into a second and much larger national history that became a major part of our Bible today. Without his preservation of Israel's founding traditions and documented history of its earliest years, we would know almost nothing of this period of history.

Notes

[1] For a discussion of these early documents, see Ralph W. Klein, *Word Biblical Commentary: 1 Samuel* (Waco, TX: Word, 1983), xxviii-xxii, and Simon J. DeVries, *Word Biblical Commentary: 1 Kings* (Waco, TX: Word, 1985), xxxiii-lii.

[2] 1 Samuel 1–3.

[3] 1 Sam. 4:1b–7:2.

[4] 1 Sam. 9:1–11:15.

[5] 1 Samuel 13–15.

[6] 1 Sam. 16:14–2 Samuel 5.

[7] 2 Samuel 9–20, 1 Kings 1–2.

[8] 1 Kings 17–22.

[9] 1 Kgs. 11:41.

[10] Josh. 10:13, 2 Sam. 1:18.

[11] In this reconstruction of the work of the Yahwist, I follow the work of Richard Elliott Friedman in *The Hidden Book in the Bible* (New York: HarperOne, 1999).

CHAPTER 5

Religious Warfare
Prophets of Yahweh vs. Baal

We should not imagine that ancient Israel was a totally harmonious society united around its devotion to the one God of the Hebrews. When the Hebrews arrived in Canaan, they soon amalgamated to the local culture to a great extent. Today, archaeologists recognize Israelite settlements by the combination of their distinctive "four-room houses," lack of pig bones among their refuse, and the pottery they developed from Canaanite pottery.

Even so, the newly arrived Hebrews, like all other immigrant cultures in history, accepted much of the culture of their new home. They soon adopted the Canaanite language—Hebrew is simply southern Canaanite. Abraham and his kin had no doubt spoken Aramaean, for Abraham's brothers and nephews were known as Aramaeans. They also quickly adopted the Canaanite alphabet—the Hebrew alphabet is just a modified Canaanite alphabet.

Most significantly, however, they also quickly adopted the Canaanite gods—the Baals and their consorts, the Asherahs. They even provided Yahweh with a Canaanite female deity as a consort. Archaeologists have found small home shrines inscribed "to Yahweh and his Asherah."[1] In addition to archaeology, we know of Israelite Baalism from the Bible, for the prophets regularly inveighed against it.

Baalism represented a magical agricultural fertility religion. Through certain rituals, including cultic prostitution in their temples, the worshipers attempted to manipulate the gods into making their crops, livestock, and wives fertile. The Hebrew prophets of Yahweh found the Canaanite idolatry repulsive and declared it an abomination. (Whenever we find that word in the Bible, it usually refers to idolatry and its associated practices.)

The Nature of Hebrew Prophecy

The Hebrew prophets represented something totally different from what passed for prophecy in other nations. Pagan "prophets" examined the entrails of animals and the movements of the heavens to foretell the future. The mature Hebrew prophets communed with Yahweh and served as forthtellers of God's word to them. Rather than pious prognosticators and fortune-tellers, they burned brightly as flaming monotheistic ethicists passionately concerned with social justice in the courts, politics, and economy. In time their message would transform the world's ideas of ethics, justice, and righteousness.

These fearless preachers of righteousness did not defend "traditional morality" accepted by society at large. In addition to idolatry, the Hebrew prophets opposed the rich and powerful among the royalty and nobility who used their wealth, status, and power to victimize the poor and helpless. They preached the radical message that righteousness does not consist in ritualized worship and sacrifices but in legal, economic, and political justice and equity.

These bold ethicists did not gain honor, wealth, or political power from their status as preachers of God's word, for their contemporaries no more welcomed their message than the same message finds ready reception today. Both society and the political powers frequently persecuted, threatened, jailed, and even killed them for their preaching.[2]

Still, the preachers faced down kings, rebuked nobles, castigated the common people, and condemned even the priesthood for their venality and misuse of power. It is no wonder the Zadokite Priest who wrote the P Document did not give prophecy so much as a nod, for he himself had probably frequently felt the sting of their lashing words. Without a doubt, these prophets of God's righteousness and proclaimers of personal, social, legal, and economic ethics were the most courageous firebrand preachers of public righteousness this world has ever seen.

Early Hebrew Prophets

Two of the oldest prophecies still in existence came from women active during Israel's oral traditions period. Miriam, Moses' sister and probable author of Miriam's Song,[3] arose in the 1200s BCE as the earliest prophet in Israel's history after Moses. Deborah, the first prophet of the later prophetic movement and the only known woman judge in Israel, wrote Deborah's Song[4] in the 1100s BCE. These two prophecies rank among the oldest pieces of literature in the Hebrew canon, as well as among world literature.

Other women prophesied in ancient Israel. The prophetess Huldah prophesied during Jeremiah's lifetime.[5] King Josiah called on her to authenticate the book of the Law found in the Jerusalem Temple. Isaiah of Jerusalem called an unnamed woman, no doubt his wife, "the prophetess."[6]

Most of the prophets, though, and all of the writing prophets were men, as is to be expected in that male-dominated period. Few men in history have exercised such varied gifts and wide-ranging authority as Samuel. He served as priest at Shiloh, as the last of the judges, and as a prophet who ministered during the eleventh century BCE. He also initiated the monarchy by anointing Israel's first two kings: Saul and David.[7]

David's court prophet, Nathan, possessed the unusual capacity not to be corrupted by royal patronage. He retained the capacity to preach uncomfortable and unwelcome truth to power. Later, two other great prophets arose to preach the word and will of God to the nations: Elijah and Elisha, who ministered in the ninth century BCE.[8]

Along the way lesser prophets such as Jehu ben Hanani[9] and Micaiah ben Imlah[10] spoke for Yahweh. Most of these earliest Hebrew prophets did not write anything that has survived but proclaimed orally the revelations God gave them.

The early prophets, though, were far from perfect. From the eleventh through the ninth centuries prophets were called "seers" rather than the later designation "prophets,"[11] showing they exercised some of the functions of fore-tellers. For example, like a fortune-teller, for a price Samuel told Saul where he could find some lost asses.[12] The prophets were also prone to emotional excess. On one occasion Samuel's disciples were portrayed as lying outside naked all night in prophetic ecstasy.[13]

More significantly and shockingly, the earliest Hebrew prophets could exercise their vocation quite violently. Samuel famously hacked King Agag "in pieces before the Lord."[14] The famous episode in which Elijah confronted the prophets of Baal on Mount Carmel climaxed with the slaughter of 450 prophets of Baal.[15]

To be fair, though, had he not slaughtered the prophets of Baal, they would probably have done him a similar honor in this dark and violent period.

Elijah's greatest fame possibly comes from his "still, small voice" revelation after his slaughter of the 450 prophets of Baal.[16] The prophet left the cave where he received that revelation with a commission to anoint Hazael and Jehu to seize the thrones of Syria and Israel.[17] Unbelievable slaughter followed the palace coups of these two anointed usurpers.[18]

Elijah's experience in the cave has thrilled millions since; but ironically and almost forgotten, that scene bore such devastatingly blood-chilling fallout that the later writing prophet Hosea denounced and pronounced God's judgment on its results.[19] The prophets, after all, did have the capacity to critique one another's prophecies and ministries. Unlike some preachers today, they did not hold to the doctrine of prophetic infallibility or inerrancy.

Furthermore, the early prophets could act with political savvy. While David lay on his deathbed, court prophet Nathan conspired with the court priest Zadok and Queen Mother Bathsheba to ensure her son Solomon's succession to the crown of Israel.[20] Nathan no doubt had his reasons for supporting Solomon over his elder brother Adonijah, presumptive heir to the throne; and he was possibly correct in his judgment. Nevertheless, we cannot consider him purely a spiritual man of the cloth. He knew things also get done by those who do not stand and wait.

Finally, many of the earliest Hebrew prophets were professionals in the worst sense of the word. Chapter 22 of 1 Kings records a confrontation between professional prophets and Micaiah ben Imlah, a legitimate prophet of God. In that encounter Micaiah denounced the professional prophets as prophets for hire.

The earliest Hebrew prophetic movement represents a mixed bag, containing shining examples of courageous integrity and shameful examples of the worst kind of "prophecy." No movement, however, should be judged by its beginnings but by its ultimate fruit. The prophetic movement began in Israel in the 1100s BCE (the pre-monarchical period of the judges) with fortune-telling, emotional frenzy, religious violence, political manipulation, and mercenary opportunism. It matured, however, into the most stellar display of homiletic oratory and righteousness the world has ever seen.

We can see something of the growth of prophecy in the biblical record of the prophets Elijah and Elisha in the ninth century (1 and 2 Kings). Elijah "hewed [King] Agag in pieces before the Lord in Gilgal." His disciple and successor Elisha, however, exhibited a much more reserved and "civilized" temperament. Even with these two early prophets the movement was learning, growing, changing, and maturing.

Eighth-Century Hebrew Prophets

By 760 BCE, a century after Elijah, the Hebrew prophetic movement had transcended the mercenary practices, fortune-telling, emotionalism, and violence endemic to that earlier age. The best aspects of Deborah, Samuel, Elijah, and Elisha came to maturity in the eighth-century prophets. These men combined the traits of flaming passion for Yahweh alone, white hot zeal for social ethics, and ice cold cerebral calculations of the implications of their faith.

A century after the two firebrands Elijah and Elisha, two centuries after the Yahwist and Elohist wrote their J and E documents, Hebrew prophecy climbed to its zenith. During the eighth century BCE the Hebrew prophetic movement suddenly shone with the bright light of the greatest constellation of prophets the world has ever witnessed in one place at one time: Amos and Hosea in Israel and Micah and Isaiah in Judah. The firmament glowed from Dan to Beersheba under these supernovas of prophetic preaching of righteousness and call to ethics in politics, economics, and law. Their prophecies have provided the world spiritual light ever since.

Amos
Amos, the fig farmer from Tekoa turned prophet of God, had a short career—possibly of just a few days or weeks. One day about 760 BCE Amos walked boldly into the royal religious center of Bethel where the nation of Israel still worshipped Jeroboam's golden bulls. In a brilliant move he began by condemning the enemies of Israel for aggressive warfare, enslaving captive peoples, war crimes, and desecrating the dead. Then he condemned the nation of Judah, Israel's competitor nation to the south, for forsaking the revealed law of God.[21]

Having won the hearts of his audience by condemning their enemies, he moved quickly to the real point of his sermon. He condemned his immediate audience, Israel, for violating the will of God revealed in the law, especially for injustice to the poor and helpless. The rest of his prophecy continued in that strain, calling for justice in law, politics, and economics and warning of God's coming judgment on injustice. The wonder is that he survived to write down his prophecy or deliver it to some anonymous disciple to record.

Amos insisted that he was not "a prophet or a son of a prophet."[22] He was not commenting on his parentage, though, but insisting he did not belong to the guild of lying professional prophets who would tell the king anything he wanted to hear in return for the right amount of gold.

The high note of Amos' prophecy came when he roared that God did not want Israel's sacrifices, rituals, or liturgical music but instead desired justice and equity in law and economics:

> I hate, I despise your religious feasts; I cannot stand your assemblies. Even though you bring me burnt offerings and grain offerings, I will not accept them. Though you bring choice fellowship offerings, I will have no regard for them. Away with the noise of your songs! I will not listen to the music of your harps. But let justice roll on like a river, righteousness like a never-failing stream. (5:21-24)

Amos knew nothing of keeping politics out of his preaching. The king's chaplain of Bethel's golden bull rebuked him for his effrontery, but Amos answered as well as he received. Amos did not receive a plush retirement pension from the king but an invitation to leave town as soon as possible. We do not know the aftermath of Amos' preaching career, but he did not end up with a television "ministry," a Ferrari, and several million-dollar homes and condos in Palm Beach and Aspen. Likely, he returned to Tekoa to herd sheep and prune figs. At any rate, he simply disappeared from recorded history.

Hosea

Hosea, roughly contemporary with Amos, also preached to the northern nation of Israel—evidently the only writing prophet to come from Israel. (Although Amos preached to Israel, he came from Judah.) Hosea embodied a recurring trait of the prophets: he acted out his prophecy in his life.

Hosea had married a woman who turned out to be promiscuous. He apparently fathered Gomer's first child and named him Jezreel. That name served as a symbol of God's judgment on Israel for Jehu's violence in overthrowing Ahab at Jezreel in response to Elijah's prophecy.[23]

Gomer's second child was not Hosea's, so he named the poor girl Not-Loved. Her third child was not his either, and he named that unfortunate child Not-Mine. Hosea was not averse to using his children as sermon illustrations. Then he divorced the wanton Gomer.[24]

Out of that experience Hosea preached that Israel had acted unfaithfully to her marriage to Yahweh who would divorce Israel, breaking that long-established marital relationship with them. That message shocked his audience. The Israelites assumed their relationship with Yahweh as chosen and blessed by God to be inviolable. Hosea castigated the nation for idolatry, adultery, violence, dishonesty, false testimony in court, and theft. For its unfaithfulness, God would divorce Israel as Hosea had divorced Gomer:

> Hear the word of the LORD, you Israelites, because the Lord has a charge to bring against you who live in the land: There is no faithfulness, no love, no acknowledgment of God in the land. There is only cursing, lying and murder, stealing and adultery; they break all bounds, and bloodshed follows bloodshed. (4:1-2)

One day Hosea saw his former wife Gomer on sale as a slave. He bought her off the auction block, took her home, rehabilitated her, and restored her as his wife.[25] Again, Hosea preached out of his own pain. God, he proclaimed, loved Israel as Hosea loved Gomer. God would forgive Israel even for her terrible sins and rehabilitate and restore her. No other Hebrew prophet ever proclaimed God's grace with such pathos, power, persuasiveness, and empathy.

Within forty years of Hosea and Amos, the nation of Israel lay in smoldering ruins at the hands of the Assyrians. In 722 Assyria invaded Israel and burned its major cities to the ground. The warnings of the judgment of God from these two prophets were not void.

Micah

Micah, a contemporary of Amos and Hosea, arose in Judah to preach to Judeans. His message can be encapsulated in one verse from his pithy book: "He has showed you, O man, what is good. And what does the LORD require of you? To act justly and to love mercy and to walk humbly with your God" (6:8).

Even the gigantic Isaiah borrowed one of this great prophet's most powerful messages, now engraved on a statue in front of the United Nations building in New York: "They will beat their swords into plowshares and their spears into pruning hooks. Nation will not take up sword against nation, nor will they train for war anymore" (4:3, borrowed from Isa. 2:4).

Almost three thousand years later, Micah's vision touched the hearts of African slaves in America long before the UN borrowed his words. The African-American spiritual proclaimed "ain't a-gonna study war no more" in a folksy rendering of Micah's words. Micah's vision has not yet been fulfilled, but humanity still hopes.

Isaiah of Jerusalem

Isaiah of Jerusalem gave his name to the book of Isaiah. As it appears in our English Bibles, this book comes from the pens of three different men. The first of these, Isaiah of Jerusalem, wrote most of the first thirty-five chapters.

Like his three contemporary writing prophets, Isaiah spoke unpleasant truth to power. He confronted the rulers of Israel for injustice in the courts and economics and for engaging in alliances with pagan nations. He preached against the evils of other nations along with those of his own. Isaiah subscribed to the notion that everyone has something of God's moral law written on her heart and is culpable for violating the law of conscience.

Still, Isaiah held out constant promise of God's forgiveness upon repentance. Perhaps his most famous prophecy comes in the first chapter of the book bearing his name: "'Come now, let us reason together,' says the Lord.

"Though your sins are like scarlet, they shall be as white as snow; though they are red as crimson, they shall be like wool'" (1:18).

Legacy of the Eighth-Century Prophets

Amos, Hosea, Micah, and Isaiah played a major role in the development of Judaism into what has been called "ethical monotheism." Their ethical vision would eventually be that of the entire world, at least in theory, even if the world has conveniently forgotten the source of that vision.

The key trait of these four gigantic eighth-century prophets is their call to faithfulness to the one true and living God. These prophets called Israel to radical monotheism in the face of the crude polytheism and idolatry of their neighbors. Their message of God's "jealousy" has been popularly misunderstood as describing God as a petty, insecure, narcissistic, possessive lover. The Hebrew word for jealous, however, had the double meaning of jealous and zealous (the better translation). God's jealousy means God is zealous that we not become enslaved to the idolatry, polytheism, immorality, injustice, and violence of the those around us.

A second enduring trait of these monumental preachers and authors was their insistence that the service God demands goes beyond ritual and music. The worship God requires consists of righteousness in economics, in courts of law, and in courts of government and power.

Notes

[1] Amihai Mazar, *Archaeology of the Land of the Bible* (New York: Doubleday, 1990), 448.
[2] Elijah and Elisha, Amos, Jeremiah, Isaiah, respectively, according to tradition.
[3] Exod. 15:1b-18.
[4] Judg. 5:2-31.
[5] 2 Kings 22.
[6] Isa. 8:3.
[7] 1 Samuel 1–25.
[8] 1 Kings 17–2 Kings 13.
[9] 1 Kings 16.
[10] 1 Kings 22.
[11] 1 Sam. 9:9.
[12] 1 Samuel 9.
[13] 1 Sam. 19:18-24.
[14] 1 Sam. 15:33 (KJV).
[15] 1 Kgs. 18:40. The story does not tell us, however, why Elijah did nothing about the 400 prophets of Asherah currently practicing their trade.
[16] 1 Kgs. 19:12.
[17] 1 Kgs. 19:15-17.

[18] 2 Kings 9.
[19] Hos. 1:4.
[20] 1 Kings 1.
[21] Amos 1:1–2:5.
[22] Amos 7:14.
[23] Hos. 1:4.
[24] Hos. 2:2.
[25] Some interpreters deny that the slave woman in chapter 3 is the same as Gomer of chapter 1. That interpretation, however, makes nonsense of the entire story and renders Hosea's message irrational.

CHAPTER 6

The Temple Apologist[1]
The Jerusalem Temple Tradition

By the late 700s BCE, the priests of Shiloh possessed two complete books recording the ancient traditions of their people, in addition to many written records containing parts of those traditions. One of those books, E, was a complete narrative history from the patriarchs through the Exodus. The other, D, consisted of the law code of Moses.

Then disaster struck. In 722 the Assyrians burned most of Israel's major cities, destroyed their fortresses and temples, and took most of their leadership into exile. This biblical narrative is confirmed by both archaeology and Assyrian texts. As Shiloh and its temple burned, the Levitical priests fled southward to Jerusalem, bringing with them the documents we know as E and D. No doubt, they brought many other works we no longer possess.

Some of the Zadokite priesthood who controlled the Jerusalem Temple, however, felt revulsion at the way the two Shiloh books elevated prophets to a position comparable to that of priests. Furthermore, the insistence of D that all Levites were priests was intolerable for the Jerusalem priesthood jealous for their claim to a monopoly on Israelite sacrifices. E's narrative of Aaron's golden bull in terms reminiscent of the bulls erected at Dan and Beth-el by Jeroboam repulsed them.

Even their own J document was defective as an alternative to those deficient northern traditions. That lengthy Yahwistic document gave no recognition of the importance of the Zadokite priesthood's control of temple sacrifices and ritual or of its God-given laws. Furthermore, that ignorant layman thought their ancestors had known God by the covenant name Yahweh even before Abraham. Had he been a well-educated priest like themselves, he would have known better. Someone had to tell the world the truth.

Shortly after 722 BCE, a Jerusalem priest set out to refute all three versions of the Hebrew ethnic traditions with his own version: the Jerusalem Temple tradition. This tradition would serve as a defense of their position as the pre-eminent spiritual leaders of the nation.

To grasp that story fully, let's pick up the history of the Jerusalem priesthood from several centuries earlier.

Flashback

Zadok, ancestor of the Jerusalem chief priests, had served as one of two chief priests under David. Wisely (or shrewdly), Zadok supported Solomon for the throne when the other chief priest, Abiathar, supported Adonijah. When Solomon won out and succeeded David, Solomon banished Abiathar to his estate at Anathoth. This move left Zadok as the sole royal high priest. From that time forward, only Zadok's descendants officiated at the altar in Jerusalem. Through the centuries the Zadokite priesthood aggressively accumulated prestige, power, and great wealth through control of the temple sacrifices.

The failure of the J and E narratives and the D version of the Mosaic laws to recognize the unique position of the Zadokite priesthood in Jerusalem stimulated an anonymous Jerusalem priest to write a third narrative of the history of Israel from the Creation, through the primordial period, the patriarchs, and the Exodus. Possibly this priest had already been working on this project in reply to J even before the books from Shiloh arrived in Jerusalem. This new history of Israel—the P Document—published during Hezekiah's reign became the basis for a religious reformation under that great king. It also served as the Jerusalem Temple priesthood's semi-official rejoinder to the other two narrative histories and the Deuteronomist's law code.

Timeline of Traditional Historians

1290–1250 BCE	The Exodus
1250–1000 BCE	Israel settles in Canaan
1030–1010 BCE	Saul's reign
1010–970 BCE	David's reign
970–931 BCE	Solomon's reign
931 BCE	Rehoboam's reign over Judah begins, Jeroboam's reign over Israel begins
After 931 BCE	The Yahwist writes J, the Elohist writes E
Between 931 and 722 BCE	The Deuteronomist writes D (chs. 12–26)
722 BCE	Assyrians destroy Israel
After 722 BCE	The Zadokite Priest writes P

Ancient Traditions

Although the Jerusalem Priest's P document was written after 722,[2] the material in it goes back much earlier, even pre-dating the D Document we looked at in chapter 2. To say the P material pre-dates the D material does not mean that the P Document was written before that work. It does mean, though, that the Jerusalem Priest who wrote the P stratum used written documents and oral traditions originating long before his own period of history.

The hand of several different authors can be discerned in the P materials, showing that the final priestly author used materials from numerous men who came before him. Nevertheless, we will refer to P as "the Priest," because clearly some single priest put into its final form material collected and written by many hands before him. This anonymous priest under Hezekiah pulled together the work of his predecessors and merged them into a single document with a unified point of view. He did not merely cut and paste, however. He was a genuine author, even though he used and merged various ancient compositions.

The Priest wrote a continuous narrative of the patriarchal period, the Exodus, and the wilderness wanderings. His material has a distinctive flair, and his hand can be discerned in many parts of the book of Genesis, much of Exodus and Numbers, and essentially all of Leviticus. Much of his material strikes us as exceedingly dull—like reading a telephone book. (On the other hand, how creative could he be with genealogies, legal statutes, architectural plans, and tabernacle furniture?) Some of his narratives, however, exhibit captivating narrative creativity.

The Priest's adaptation of the traditional stories of Israel's origins tracks well with the versions of that history written by the Yahwist and the Elohist. Like them he tells the stories of Abraham, Isaac, Jacob, and Joseph and then moves on to Moses and the Exodus. The Priest gave us the account of God's revelation as El Shaddai to Abraham and later to Jacob, along with a number of beautiful stories of God's interactions with Abraham and Sarah, Jacob and Laban. He concluded the patriarchal narratives with Jacob's arrival in Egypt and meeting the pharaoh, followed by Jacob's death and burial in the family tomb at Hebron.

The Priest valued genealogies connecting the people of Israel with their primordial past and various outside groups.[3] He loved descriptions of the Tabernacle[4] and recounting laws and rituals.[5] Essentially the entire book of Leviticus given over to legal and ritual matters comes from his hand, as does a great deal of the book of Numbers. Many of the narratives of Leviticus and

Numbers have to do with ritual matters and assert the sacral authority of the Aaronic priesthood, of which he was a member.[6]

Always the priest strived to elevate Aaron and the Aaronic priesthood as the ancestors of the Zadokite priesthood, to reduce other Levites to mere assistants of the priests, and to ignore the prophets entirely. In this respect he wrote to refute the D Document directly. Most of the Priest's writing amounts to the ancient equivalent of Ambien, but even that part of his work provides us with essential information concerning laws, rituals, sacrifices, and genealogies of ancient Israel. In addition to his genealogies, lists, censuses, legislations, and rituals, he also preserved a number of sublime narratives, several of which were duplicates of E narratives.

The most distinctive trait of the Priest's narrative of the Exodus resides in his insistence that God (Elohim) was not revealed to the patriarchs as Yahweh, but only as El Shaddai[7] (Genesis 17). In this insistence, interestingly, the southern priest from Jerusalem agreed with the northern priest from Shiloh.[8] Evidently this was a priestly point of view both north and south, suggesting that the Levitical priests of Shiloh and the Zadokite priests of Jerusalem possessed a common Levitical tradition. Only the Yahwist—a layman—of the three authors of patriarchal materials believed the patriarchs knew God by the covenant name Yahweh.[9]

The Priest also presented a theological doctrine of the conquest and destruction of the Canaanites in two passages in Leviticus and two in Numbers.[10] The priestly Leviticus passages describe the land of Canaan as "vomiting out" its inhabitants because of their many idolatrous abominations and warns Israel not to follow their example lest the land "vomit" them out.[11] In Numbers, Moses commands Israel to "drive out" Canaan's inhabitants, destroy their idols, and demolish their high places. If they do not do so, Moses warns, the Canaanites will become "barbs in your eyes and thorns in your flesh."[12]

In Numbers the Priest does describe God commanding total annihilation of the men of Midian (who were not Canaanites), allowing the soldiers to take the women, children, and wealth for themselves.[13] This act of *cherem* was for "revenge," presumably for having corrupted Israel through their women.[14] Still, the Priest did not believe that God commanded the genocide of all Canaanites as the Deuteronomist insisted. This difference of viewpoints, a difference he shared with the priest of Shiloh who wrote E, is striking. Later on, the Deuteronomistic Historian will follow the Shiloh Deuteronomist's view rather than that of other priests of both Shiloh and

Jerusalem. Evidently even many of the ancient Israelites were deeply troubled by the idea that God commanded the genocide of the Canaanites.

Before moving forward with our story, let's address some questions nagging many readers of this discussion.

Reflections on the Story

Were the patriarchs historical?

For people who believe God is revealed in history, the question of what actually happened really does matter. Unfortunately, we have no extra-biblical literature with which to compare the patriarchal narratives to assess their factuality. Furthermore, not even archaeology helps us here, for archaeology knows nothing of Abraham, Isaac, Jacob, or the twelve patriarchs; but then archaeology rarely discovers evidence of individuals this far into the past. Still, historians do use traditional materials to build genuine histories of the Franks of Europe, the Saxons of England, and the Vikings of Scandinavia and develop pictures of their heroes.

Historians frequently rely on multiple attestation—if a tradition is attested by two or more independent witnesses, along with other criteria, it may be judged likely. The patriarchal narratives of J, E, and P provide double and in places even triple attestation that Abraham, Isaac, Jacob, and the patriarchs were father, son, grandson, and great-grandsons. That the Yahwist, the Elohist, and the Priest writing in different locations and in different centuries from competing, contradictory points of view report the same genealogical view of the patriarchs indicates there was a strong tradition of this family linkage. This conclusion stands contrary to some interpreters that unrelated legends were brought together to create a fiction of the patriarchal genealogy. The literary evidence does not validate that skeptical conclusion, and at this point there is no other evidence.

Furthermore, the authors of the three great strands of traditional material presented fairly consistent pictures of the patriarchs and of their experience of God, by whatever name the authors believed the patriarchs knew him. The priests of Shiloh and those of Jerusalem agreed that the divine name Yahweh was revealed first to Moses, indicating a strong priestly tradition that prevailed both north and south. Several times the sources present two or more versions of the same story, further supporting a consistent oral tradition.

The reported covenants with God and various social customs can be shown to parallel practices in the early second millennium Middle East. Such items would not likely have been known to writers operating centuries later after the time of David, unless they were working with traditions going back to that period.

The Genesis narrative represents Abraham as having come from the region of Aram Naharaim. He secured from there Isaac's wife Rebekah, daughter of "Bethuel the Aramean" and sister of "Laban the Aramean." Jacob also went back to this same region for his wives Leah and Rachel, daughters of "Laban the Aramean."[15] The biblical evidence, therefore, clearly claims that Abraham and his clan were Arameans.

William Dever, observing that the Arameans had "a similar origin to that of the early Israelites," points out that the Arameans were pastoral nomads "coming originally from northern Mesopotamia," the region Genesis says was the place Abraham left to enter Canaan.[16] With these convergences between the biblical tradition and history and archaeology, it seems very likely historically that Abraham and the ancestors of the Israelites were originally Aramean pastoral nomads as Genesis describes. That origin would answer the nagging question of how the Israelites living in settled villages, towns, and cities got their social ideal of tent-dwelling pastoral nomadism.

In conclusion, we cannot prove the patriarchal stories as true by purely historical standards. We can, however, show that they generally fit the historical period in which the narratives place them. Furthermore, they have multiple witnesses on their side. Likely is as good as it gets in much ancient history, as in much of more recent history. In other respects, however, careful analysis shows the stories have been colored anachronistically by the authors' own setting several centuries after the events.

Additionally, the religious, revelational aspects of these stories is not strictly speaking "history," as we use the word today. How could historians demonstrate anything about God's nature, actions, words, revelations, or covenants? Still, if the general context has evidence of reflecting history, that context provides a solid background for the religious claims. I accept the patriarchal narratives at face value while allowing for undeniable anachronisms in the telling of their stories.

Did the Exodus actually happen?

What about the Hebrews' slavery in Egypt, their exodus, the Sinai revelation, and their forty-year wilderness wandering? The Copenhagen School of Thomas Thompson denies the Exodus ever happened (or, for that matter, that Israel existed until the Hellenistic period or that the entire Israelite history from David to the Exile ever happened). Israel Finkelstein holds that ancient Israel arose out of a rebellion by Canaanite peasants against their overlords. Conservative scholars insist it all happened exactly as recorded in the Bible. Between the extremes of the Copenhagen School and the conservative view, there are a multitude of opinions. What does the evidence say?

Here, the nonbiblical evidence is almost entirely absent. With all the hieroglyphic material discovered in Egypt, not a word appears about the escape of Hebrew slaves in the delta. Of course, the Egyptians would not want to admit that their slaves escaped; and the elites who write history do not generally care about the peons who do the work. Perhaps, therefore, this lack of evidence does not prove much.

Furthermore, archaeology has found no evidence of millions of Hebrew slaves in the Egyptian delta or of their exodus from Egypt, residence at Sinai, wandering in the wilderness, or almost forty-year campout at Kadesh-Barnea. Single campfires of a few travelers have survived the desert sands for centuries and millennia. Why not hundreds of thousands of campfires, cast-off belongings, massive garbage dumps, and multitudinous privies of two-and-a-half million people camped out for forty years and trampling thousands of acres of wilderness terrain?

For that matter, we do not even know where Mount Sinai/Mount Horeb was located. The traditional location for Mount Sinai in the Sinai Peninsula as depicted in the backs of most of our Bibles has only been so designated since Byzantine times (since 330 CE). Various scholars have proposed at least twenty different sites from the southern Sinai to northwestern Saudi Arabia for the biblical Mountain of God, without persuading a majority on any site.[17] This gap in our knowledge greatly complicates the issue of the facticity of the Exodus, Mount Sinai, and the wilderness wanderings.

Furthermore, the Hebrew language has been shown to be simply southern Canaanite, as Ugaritic is northern Canaanite. Consistently with the linguistic evidence, early Israelite religious festivals correspond largely to Canaanite agricultural festivals.

The evidence (and lack thereof) forces us to adjust our picture of Israel's origins, but we should not move too quickly or too radically. Let's look at some other external evidence from archaeology along with the internal evidence from the Pentateuchal literature itself.

In support of the Exodus tradition, Bernard Baruch has shown that the knowledge of Egypt displayed in Exodus is of Late Bronze Age Egypt (before 1200 BCE), when those events were generally supposed to have happened. They do not reflect Egypt of the Iron Age (after 1200 BCE), the period during which our sources were written.[18] This evidence seems both relevant and significant.

The current trend among archaeologists and historians tends toward recognizing that at least some of ancient Israel entered from outside Canaan rather than arising as a purely Canaanite population (as Israel Finkelstein as well as the Copenhagen School have argued).[19]

Furthermore, we have at least three independent traditions that the Israelites emerged from slavery in Egypt and invaded Canaan from the outside: the Elohistic narrative (E) from Shiloh and the Yahwistic (J) and Priestly (P) narratives from Jerusalem. In addition, numerous psalms and prophetic comments reflect separate traditions from those represented by the Pentateuchal sources. Taken together, this multiplied attestation of the Exodus narrative carries considerable weight. It must be based on something other than imagination. Where did this wide-ranging group of traditions come from if it never actually happened?

As for the Hebrew language merely being southern Canaanite, most immigrants to a new country adopt the language of that country by the second generation at least. For example, the Philistines almost certainly spoke Mycenaean Greek when they arrived in Canaan but quickly adopted a "Semitic language related to Hebrew."[20] If twelfth-century Philistines quickly switched from Greek to Canaanite, why not the Israelites from Aramean to Canaanite? The linguistic argument is useless for determining the original ethnicity of the proto-Israelites, just as my speaking English is for determining my ethnic derivation.

More importantly, Israel clearly introduced a new conception of God—Yahweh worship—along with a new ethical concern and social ideal. Why did the Israelite priests and prophets abandon the worship of the Canaanite goddess Asherah? True, archaeology shows worship of Asherah as the consort of Yahweh continued,[21] but why did the religious leaders who produced our biblical texts universally reject her? And where did their emphasis on the Sabbath and circumcision as ethnic and religious markers originate? Where did the institution of the Levites with Egyptian names[22] come from? And why did they create a new Hebrew alphabet from the old Canaanite alphabet? Why not just keep the Canaanite alphabet they already had?

If the Israelites were merely Canaanites who had never lived in the desert in tents, whence their social ideal of a pastoral life in tents in the desert? Where did the stories about Mount Sinai/Mount Horeb begin? Where did the idea of the wilderness Tabernacle originate? The idea of a pervasive projection of Solomon's temple backwards into a wilderness, nomadic tent-dwelling period that never existed—not even in their deepest memories—simply does not ring true. My incredulity is only increased when I remember that the Tabernacle was so much like the tabernacles the pharaohs used when traveling[23] and also the portable shrines of the desert Bedouin.[24]

Archaeology provides a wealth of detail concerning changes the proto-Israelites brought to the hill country of Canaan—new communities, population growth, a new kind of house, changes in pottery, and dietary changes. Any proposed narrative of the origins of ancient Israel must simultaneously account for these features of the early proto-Israelites in addition to the troublesome lack of evidence from archaeology. Neither the conservative response (ignoring the evidence) nor the entirely too skeptical reaction of the minimalists and revisionists (rejection of the biblical narrative in toto) seems adequate.

The four-room pillared house so distinctive of the new Israelite culture that arose in Canaan in the thirteenth to eleventh centuries finds a parallel in the correct period in Egypt. Similar four-room houses built of reeds have been found near Thebes and dating to the Raameside period (when Israel is believed to have been slaves there). Furthermore, scholars do not consider this kind of house Egyptian but Canaanite, and the occupants of these houses appear to have been slaves.[25]

There remains the problem concerning the two and a half million Israelites supposedly leaving Egypt. Why did such a massive multitude greater than most large cities today leave no trace of themselves in the wilderness? Why did they not swell the population of Canaan by two million instead of by just a few tens of thousands?

The answer may lie in the fact that Hebrew numbers present notorious problems of transmission. Additionally, the Hebrew word *eleph* means variously thousand, a military unit of a thousand, captain of a thousand, and even clan, or just a family.[26] The original numbers may have been corrupted through misunderstanding the meaning of *eleph* ("thousand" having been substituted for "families") and centuries of copyists' errors.

Considering the total lack of any archaeological evidence for the Hebrews in the wilderness of Sinai or at Kadesh-Barnea or for an influx of millions of immigrants into Canaan, I conclude that the slaves who escaped from Egypt were a relatively small company—possibly a few thousand. Still, we must explain that tradition somehow, and fictive imagination hardly does justice to all the evidence—literary, historical, and archaeological.

It is difficult to imagine that a group of disaffected Canaanite peasants alone created out of whole cloth a new kind of house; scores of new communities; a population explosion in the hill country; a new God, religion, and cult; a new ethic and set of ethnic markers; and a new worldview—all in only two centuries. Archaeology and linguistics have exposed significant similarities between ancient Israel and the Canaanites; archaeology and history reveal even more glaring differences between the two groups. Furthermore, as Victor Matthews has observed, "It seems almost inconceivable that a people would choose to create and perpetuate a foundation myth in which they were slaves."[27]

Baruch Halpern has argued that the story of the Exodus reflects a valid folk memory in ancient Israel. Ziony Zevit in his unique, magisterial, multidisciplinary study of ancient Israel observes that the necessary external evidence does not now exist to make conclusive statements concerning the rise of ancient Israel. He further observes that only the biblical narrative provides a basis for accounting for the rise of faith in Yahweh among ancient Israelites.[28]

Finally, the book of Exodus says the Hebrews left Egypt with a "mixed multitude." The historical record shows that at the same time the proto-Israelites were settling into the hill country of Canaan, a large number of other immigrants of varying ethnicities also were arriving. I suspect, as archaeologist William Dever suggests, that the early proto-Israelites consisted of ex-slaves recently escaped from Egypt along with a vast "mixed multitude" of other national and ethnic groups who quickly assimilated with local Canaanites from the then deteriorating Canaanite culture.[29]

The influx of foreign peoples along with the displaced Canaanites led to a population explosion in the hill country numbering in the tens of thousands and the settling of scores of new villages. This mixture of "invaders" of various ethnicities—Amorites, Aramaeans, Hurrians, Midianites, and Hebrews—merging with a larger number of disaffected Canaanites developed into ancient Israel with its distinctive alphabetic script, diet, pottery, homes, God, religion, and cult, along with such practices as circumcision.[30]

I think it likely that the thrilling exodus traditions of a relatively smaller number of former Egyptian slaves among multiple immigrant groups became the founding tradition of the entire Israelite people. The few hundreds or thousands of people who escaped from Egypt became corrupted by the vicissitudes of time, memory, understanding, and copying into millions. Their God, Yahweh, and their religious institutions and cultural practices became those of all Israel; and the rest, as they say, is history.

Considering the biblical source evidence, archaeology, and history simultaneously, the books of Exodus through Numbers seem to record a legitimate, valid folk memory transmitted in the oral traditions of one of Israel's founding peoples—the Hebrews—that became the founding tradition of the entire nation.

How do we as Christian believers handle these historical conundrums? We could say that only the theology matters, but that is incompatible with the biblical picture of historical revelation. The preservers of the ancient founding traditions not only preserved valid traditions of the antecedents of a key people group who became in time the Israelites, but they also saw Yahweh's own self-revelation in those events. The stories and the revelation those spiritual giants saw in them served as the backdrop for God's revelation through the other movements of the Hebrew faith we are about to examine.

What do the traditions narratives reveal about God?
The Elohist, Yahwist, and Priest presented three different versions of their stories—the northern and southern priestly versions and the southern lay version. Their stories of the patriarchs—Abraham, Isaac, and Jacob—described an intensely personal God to whom they related as friend to friend. Their stories of the Exodus and wilderness wanderings described God as elevated and removed from human contact. In other words, the patriarchal stories spoke of an imminent God, while the exodus and wilderness stories spoke of a transcendent God.

Wisely, ancient Israel kept both sets of stories and both visions of God without attempting to harmonize them, evidencing their careful manner of dealing with received traditions. That these authors preserved each set of traditions as transmitted without harmonizing them suggests they were preserving authentic traditions of events and revelation that actually happened.

Furthermore, they conceived of God in purely spiritual terms, not in the crudely physical way of the mythical religions. These early Hebrews had no images to represent Elohim/Yahweh. They communed with him, not by bowing before idols, but by talking to him, by words rather than images or rituals. In this respect, the Hebrew traditions movement marked itself as radically different from surrounding cultures. This early difference from prevailing religious ideas began a process that would ultimately produce a radically different religion that would transform the Western world's conception of deity.

At the same time, Israel's preservers of ancient Hebrew traditions laid the groundwork for a third aspect of the biblical conception of God—historical revelation—God personally working in history. To be sure, the preservers of the traditions had no concept of scientific historiography such as we practice today. Still they worked with the best historical sources they had—oral traditions and written versions of oral tradition. In that folk history they saw God uniquely at work, in grace electing their people to a special personal relationship and redemptively setting them free from bondage.

Fourthly, in recording the divinely given laws of Israel, the Elohist, the Priest, and the Deuteronomist laid the groundwork for the monumental ethical concern of the Hebrew prophets who were just beginning to preach their messages to the two nations.

Finally, their demand that Israel worship no other god than Yahweh laid the groundwork for true monotheism. Granted, the earliest records only assert that Israel should worship no other god than Yahweh—that is, they asserted henotheism rather than monotheism. Still, their absolute demand would eventually culminate in prophetic ethical monotheism. Thus, Israel's earliest efforts at writing the history of its people, though not yet mature in either its historiography or its theology, laid the groundwork for all the theological developments that would follow in subsequent centuries.

Notes

[1] I refer to the P Document as "the Jerusalem Temple tradition," because it represented the viewpoint of the Jerusalem Temple priesthood and became the official doctrine expounded in the Pentateuch as eventually published around the time of Ezra.

[2] Because our early (pre-exilic) dating of P here runs counter to Wellhausen's late dating (exilic or even post-exilic) long favored by many scholars, it seems wise to describe briefly the progress of the voluminous research supporting it. Avi Hurvitz of Hebrew University in Jerusalem ("The Evidence of Language in Dating the Priestly Code," *Revue Biblique* 81 [1974]: 24-56) argued linguistically that P was classical Early Biblical Hebrew (EBH) as exemplified by the J and E materials and not Late Biblical Hebrew (LBH) as exemplified by Ezekiel, Chronicles, and Ezra-Nehemiah. Further, Hurvitz systematically eliminated differences in subject matter, genres of literature, or authors, along with any archaizing attempt by P, as explanatory of the differences between P and LBH.

Two years later Robert Polzin (*Late Biblical Hebrew: Toward An Historical Typology of Biblical Hebrew Prose* [Missoula, MT: Scholars Press for The Harvard Semitic Museum, 1976], esp. 99-102) concluded that the JE material, the Court History, and D were all classical Hebrew (EBH). He saw two corpora of the Priestly material, Pg (the original P material, the "groundwork") and Ps (the later "secondary" material), both somewhat later than classical Hebrew and representing a transitional stage on the way to LBH. Gary Rendsburg ("Late Biblical Hebrew and the Date of P," *Journal of the Ancient Near Eastern Society* 12 [1980]:

65-80) reviewed Polzin's book, critiqued him at length, and concluded that Pg and Ps were both classical EBH and not LBH.

Ziony Zevit ("Converging Lines of Evidence Bearing on the Date of P," *Zeitschrift fur die Alttestamentliche Wissenschaft* 94 [1982]: 65-80) argued that P must be older than D and the Deuteronomistic History, since both cite P and even quote P verbatim from Leviticus and Numbers.

Avi Hurvitz followed his earlier article with another ("Dating the Priestly Source in the Light of Historical Study of Biblical Hebrew a Century after Wellhausen," *Zeitschrift fur die Alttestamentliche Wissenschaft* 100 [1988]: Supplement, 88-100) citing other research supporting the relative antiquity of P, including the unpublished Ph.D. thesis of M. Paran submitted to the Hebrew University of Jerusalem ("Literary Features of the Priestly Code—Stylistic Patterns, Idioms and Structures," 1983).

Mark F. Rooker (*Biblical Hebrew in Transition: The Language of the Book of Ezekiel* [Sheffield, England: Sheffield Academic Press, 1990]) basically agreed with Polzin's analysis but critiqued him considerably. Rooker, like Rendsburg, agreed with Polzin that the JE material, the Court History material, and D are all EBH, virtually indistinguishable linguistically. In contrast to Polzin, however, Rooker argued that Pg and Ps show signs of a beginning shift toward Late Biblical Hebrew, as does Jeremiah, but are not yet even a true transitional state between EBH and LBH. He concluded that Ezekiel exemplifies the true transitional state between EBH and LBH; and Chronicles, Ezra, Nehemiah, and Esther represent full-blown LBH. (See particularly pp. 36-37, 52-53, 177-178, 185-186.)

Avi Hurvitz defended his thesis of P as EBH in various articles that take on his critics. In a 1997 article ("The Historical Quest for 'Ancient Israel' and the Linguistic Evidence of the Hebrew Bible: Some Methodological Observations," *Vetus Testamentum* 47 3 [J/1997]: 301-315) he challenged P.R. Davies' claim that no chronological development can be discovered in ancient BH and that the entire biblical corpus was created and written during Israel's Persian Period (sixth–third centuries BC).

Three years later Hurvitz ("Once Again: The Linguistic Profile of the Priestly Material in the Pentateuch and its Historical Age," *Zeitschrift fur de Alttestamentliche Wissenschaft* 112 [2000]: 180-191) refuted J. Blenkinsopp's challenge to his views (argued in "An Assessment of the Alleged Pre-Exilic Date of the Priestly Material in the Pentateuch," *Zeitschrift fur de Alttestamentliche Wissenschaft* 108 [1996]: 495-518). More recently still, Hurvitz argued (in "The Recent Debate on Late Biblical Hebrew: solid data, expert opinions, and inconclusive arguments," *Hebrew Studies Journal* 47 [Annual 2006]: 191ff) for a chronological interpretation of variations in linguistic usage from EBH to LBH rather than varieties of contemporaneous usage.

Researches such as that of Hurvitz, Rendsburg, Rooker, and Zevit along with his own studies have convinced R.E. Friedman of the antiquity of P as classical pre-exilic EBH (*The Hidden Book in the Bible* [HarperOne, 1998], 358-359, 362). For the contrary opinion and a good summary of the evidence and arguments against the early dating of P and for an exilic or post-exilic date for this material, see Philip J. Budd, *Word Biblical Commentary: Numbers* (Waco, TX: Word, 1984), xviii-xxi.

One final note: this same line of evidence is persuasive against the idea that J and E were not written until the late seventh century BCE, the time of Ezekiel, for by that time Hebrew was transitioning into Late Biblical Hebrew (LBH). Certainly, this information rules out Israel Finkelstein's insistence that J and E were not written until the Persian period and even more so Thomas Thompson and the Copenhagen school of archaeology's contention that these works were written in the Hellenistic period.

³Gen. 11:27-31, 25:12-20, 36:1-30, 46:6-27; Numbers 1, 26.

[4]Exodus 25–31, 35–40—a tremendous amount of the book of Exodus.

[5]Exod. 12:1-20, 40-50; almost the entire book of Leviticus is taken up with legislation and ritual; Numbers 1–9 is given over to ritual matters, as well as Num. 16:1-11, 15-23, 27a, 35, 17–19, 30:2-17.

[6]Num. 33:50-56, 34–36.

[7]Exod. 6:2-3 is from the Priest.

[8]Exod. 3:15 is from the Elohist.

[9]Ziony Zevit, *Religions of Ancient Israel*, (New York: Continuum, 2001), 687, describes Syrians of the 18th–16th centuries BCE, to the north of Canaan, using the name Yahweh in names of both people and places, especially among Amorites (closely related to the Aramaeans from whom the Hebrews came). Zevit also points to a gap of 600-800 years until the name Yahweh becomes pervasive again in tenth-century Judah-Israel. Possibly the Yahwist was not entirely wrong in thinking the patriarchs had known God as Yahweh. R.E. Friedman, for instance, thinks the Yahwist is correct. Nevertheless, we are still left with the quandary concerning the contradictions between the Yahwist on the one hand and the priests of Shiloh and Jerusalem on the other hand. Both views cannot be correct.

[10]We will examine later the historical issues surrounding the conquest and slaughter of the Canaanites.

[11]Lev. 18:24-30, 20:22.

[12]Num. 33:50-56.

[13]Numbers 31.

[14]Num. 25:6-18.

[15]Gen. 12:4; 24:1-4, 10; 25:20; 28:1-2, 5; 29:1, 4. See also F.T. Schumacher, "Aram," A. Jeffery, "Aramaic," and R.A. Bowman, "Arameans," in vol. 1, *Interpreter's Dictionary of the Bible*, ed. George Buttrick (New York: Abingdon,1962): 185-193.

[16]William G. Dever, *The Lives of Ordinary People in Ancient Israel: When Archaeology and the Bible Intersect* (Grand Rapids: Eerdmans, 2012), 307.

[17]Hershel Shanks, "Where is Mount Sinai?" *Biblical Archaeology Review* (March/April 2014): 30-41, 66; David Ussishkin, Lily Singer-Avitz, and Hershel Shanks, "Kadesh-Barnea in the Bible and on the Ground," *Biblical Archaeology Review* (September/October 2015): 36-44.

[18]Ziony Zevit displays reluctance to make much of this evidence, but we cannot ignore it. Zevit, *Religions of Ancient Israel*, 118.

[19]Ibid.,121.

[20]Dever, *Ordinary People*, 302-303.

[21]Ibid., 264-265.

[22]Scott Noegel, "The Egyptian Origin of the Ark of the Covenant," in *Israel's Exodus in Transdisciplinary Perspective* (Switzerland: Springer Publishing, 2015), 238 fn 76.

[23]D.W. Gooding, "Tabernacle," in *New Bible Commentary*, ed. F. Davidson (Grand Rapids: Eerdmans, 1962), 1231. See also Noegel, "The Egyptian Origin."

[24]G. Hinton Davies, "Tabernacle," in vol. 4, *Interpreter's Dictionary of the Bible* (New York: Abingdon, 1962), 499.

[25]Zevit, *Religions of Ancient Israel*, 101 fn 32. Manfred Bietak, "On the Historicity of the Exodus: What Egyptology Today Can Contribute to Assessing the Biblical Account of the Sojourn in Egypt," in *Israel's Exodus*, 18ff.

[26]See Francis Brown, S.R. Driver, and C.A. Briggs, *Hebrew and English Lexicon of the Old Testament* (Oxford: Clarendon, 1962), 48-49. Jack B. Scott, "'elep," in vol. 1, *Theological Wordbook of the Old Testament*, ed. R. Laird Harris et al. (Chicago: Moody, 1980): 109, objects to the definition of the word *eleph* as clan or family on a theological and inerrantist, not a lexicographical, basis. Contrary to the argument of Scott, though, those who differ from

them do so not out of a naturalistic bias but because of the lexicographical uses of the word. For uses of the word to designate clans rather than thousand, see Num. 1:16; 10:4, 36; 31:5; Jos. 22:14, 21, 30; Judg. 6:15; 1 Sam. 10:19, 23:23; Mic. 5:2.

[27] Victor Matthews, "Remembering Egypt," in *Israel's Exodus*, 687.

[28] Zevit, *Religions of Ancient Israel*, 687 with fn 134.

[29] William Dever, *Who Were the Early Israelites and Where Did They Come From?* (Grand Rapids: Eerdmans, 2003), 182; see also Amihai Mazar, *Archaeology of the Land of the Bible* (Anchor Bible, 1992), 334, for a similar suggestion.

[30] Brendon C. Benz, "In Search of Israel's Insider Status: A Reevaluation of Israel's Origins," and Avraham Foust, "The Emergence of Iron Age Israel: On Origins and Habitus," in *Israel's Exodus*, 464, 469-470.

CHAPTER 7

The Man Who Saw the Beginning

The Temple Theology of Creation and History

Before the Jerusalem Temple priest sat down to write his version of the founding Hebrew traditions, he conceived of a theology of creation with which to introduce his monumental work. Like the Yahwist two hundred years earlier, he would not have called this narrative "theology." He was simply thinking about God by means of a story. Still, we think of what he did as a narrative theology of creation.[1]

In the ancient Near East the Babylonian creation myth reigned supreme among all the creation myths.[2] Totally rejecting that crude narrative that so many of his contemporaries accepted as a matter of faith, he conceived a creation narrative to refute the myth point by point. He would do so in far fewer words than the Babylonian priests had used, however. The Babylonian myth occupied some one thousand lines of text. The Zadokite Priest, on the other hand, would tell his story in approximately one hundred lines of the most sublime poetic prose ever conceived by a human mind.

The Babylonian Myth

The Babylonians wrote the *Enuma Elish* on seven tablets in almost a thousand lines.[3] In the beginning existed time and light plus the chaos of fresh water (the monster Apsu) and salt water (the monster Tiamat). Apsu impregnated Tiamat, and she delivered the gods Lahmu and Lahamu. She then conceived other gods, who begat still other gods, who multiplied and made so much noise inside Tiamat that she could not sleep.

Eventually the god Ea killed his ancestor Apsu, but Tiamat did nothing to help her lover. Inside Apsu's corpse Ea impregnated Damkina, and she bore Marduk. Marduk nursed at the breasts of the gods and grew so mighty that his godhead doubled. Then Marduk waged war on Tiamat to avenge her failure to help her lover Apsu when Ea murdered him. Marduk created many destructive winds to torture and disturb Tiamat—the four winds, the tornado, the evil wind, the tempest, the whirlwind, "the unfaceable facing wind," and the storm tempest.

Marduk climaxed his war on Tiamat by slicing her in half as a fisherman fillets a fish to fry on the fire. With half of her he made the dome of heaven, a hard-curved pan overhead. With the other half of Tiamat he made the earth. He used her thighs to support the roof of heaven. He also created the sun, moon, and stars as gods.

Then Marduk commissioned Ea to create slaves to provide food for the gods so they would not have to work and could be at leisure. Ea executed the god Qingu for crimes against the gods and created man out of his blood. Ea placed on man all the work of the gods and set the gods free to enjoy leisure and banqueting while humans slaved to feed them. Such was the Near Eastern conception of creation and the place of humanity in it.

The Priest Refutes the Myths

Worshipfully, reverently, communing with the Spirit of God, the Hebrew Priest wrote a Hebrew theology of creation—picturesque narrative God-talk—to contend with the childish myths of his pagan neighbors. He probably built on the work of generations of priests before him, for scholars have discerned several layers from different hands in the creation narrative of Genesis 1:1–2:3.

The idea of the cosmos coming out of chaos did not seem impossible to the Hebrew Priest, for he often felt the entire world stood in danger of sliding back into the chaos of pagan mythology. The idea that chaos created the gods, however, struck him as nonsense. "In the beginning God created the heavens and the earth." God was there before light, time, fresh water, salt water, or even chaos. Furthermore, God created absolutely everything. The heavens and the earth represented a Hebraic way of saying "everything." That meant God created out of nothing, for there was nothing else from which to make the creation. This creation, however, was merely the raw stuff out of which God would bring the world in which we live. It was still chaos—all formlessness and emptiness—without form, and void.

The myths said light pre-existed even the gods. The Hebrew theologian knew that until God created the light, darkness reigned over creation; no light shone in the beginning to dispel the darkness. "And darkness was over the surface of the deep."

The Spirit of God was there, though. The Hebrew word for spirit—*ruach*—meant "wind," then "breath," and by extension "spirit." The wind of

God, the breath of God, the Spirit of God brooded over the chaos of creation like a hen on her eggs. The winds of Babylonian myths were destructive, evil, malevolent, tormenting Tiamat (Tablet 1), stirring up her belly, constipating her, and keeping her from sleeping (Tablet 4). The Wind of God the Hebrew Priest had experienced, however, was creative, loving, nurturing, bringing as-yet nonexistent realities into being.

The myths of Babylon indicated light and daytime existed even before the gods were born; that the gods were born into the light and lived through time that already existed. The Priest wrote, however, "And God said, 'Let there be light,' and there was light." God created with his word alone and nothing else. Nothing in the myths approached the majesty of creation as taking place entirely by the word of God. The Babylonian creation was always by means of pre-existing realities, never by the word of God alone out of nothing.

The assertion that the first three days preceded the creation of sun and moon shows the Priest wrote of theological, spiritual realities and not of mere literal physical entities. Conversely to frequent assertions to the contrary, even the ancients knew daylight comes from the sun. They were neither blind nor stupid. The Priest asserted that all light—physical, mental, or spiritual—comes from God. Forever afterwards light would symbolize for Hebrews knowledge, revelation, the word of God, the presence of God, the glory of God.

The ancients considered the cosmos as being exactly as it looks. They looked at the earth and saw a flat disk. They saw the sky curved overhead like a blue clay pot sitting on the edges of the earth. Since the sky looks hard and firm, they called it the "firmament." They saw the stars as pin holes in the hard firmament, and they observed the sun and moon moving across the face of the firmament. That was the way things looked, and that is how they conceived of them. That is also how our Zadokite Priest saw the cosmos. His "science" was the science of his day, the science he inherited from his culture.

A more accurate cosmology would be constructed almost three millennia later and would come to relative maturity only recently. We cannot fault the ancients if they had no vision of the universe greater than what their naked eyes could observe. The objectionable aspect of the Babylonian myths lay not in their cosmological picture of the universe but in their crude account of its origins from the corpse of Tiamat. The Priest insisted God created the sky, not out of the corpse of a monster, but by his all-powerful creative word.

According to Babylonian myths, Marduk, the greatest of the gods, created all vegetation and land for agriculture. According to the Priest's theology, God spoke and divided the waters under the firmament into seas, allowing the earth to rise out of the waters as dry land. God then demonstrated his sovereignty over the earth and seas by naming them.

Then the one and only God spoke again and the earth brought forth grass, fruit trees, and herbs, each self-propagating by its seed. For the first time, the author wrote, "God saw that it was good," marking the end of the first half-week of his narrative. Heaven and earth now stood complete at the end of the third day, filled with lush plants and trees.

The Priest divided his creation story into two perfectly balanced and parallel three-day segments. With the conclusion of the first three days, four acts of creation have taken place—light, the firmament, dry ground, and vegetation. The next three days will parallel the first three days in beautiful aesthetic symmetry. Earth is ready for God to introduce breathing life.

Whereas Babylonian mythology conceived of the sun, moon, and stars as gods, the Priest insisted they were only natural phenomena created by the one true and living God who also created Israel out of nothing. As the first three-day sequence began with God creating light, the second three-day sequence begins with God creating the sun, moon, and stars as the light sources for earth. "And God saw that it was good."

Then the Priest described the creation of the birds of the air, the whales, and the fish of the sea. For the Babylonians, the primal monsters of the deep were Apsu and Tiamat, monsters who had created the gods. The Jerusalem Temple Priest, however, refused to believe that any monster had created his God. Instead, his God had created all the sea creatures—even the very seas themselves. Again, the creative acts of the second half-week parallel those of the first half-week. The second day of the first half week saw the creation of the firmament; the second day of the second half-week sees the creation of birds to fly across the firmament and fish and whales to swim in the waters below it.

For the first time the Priest mentions God's blessing a portion of his creation—the breathing life portion. God blessed the creatures of both fresh water and salt water. God's blessing commanded and authorized them to be fruitful and increase in number and fill the water. Similarly, God instructed the birds of the air to increase on the earth. Again he wrote, "And God saw that it was good."

In contrast with the prevailing mythology, the priestly creation account knows nothing of monsters and demons but only the creation of animals such as we know—cattle, creeping things, and beasts of the field. The Yahwist experienced the world as ordered, rational, and blessed of God. When he looked at the world with its domestic animals and wild creatures, even the creeping insects and reptiles, he saw evidence of the creative power of God.

Again, we observe a parallel between the two half-weeks of the creation narrative. The third day of the first half-week contains two creative acts: dry land and the plants that grow on the dry land. The third day of the second half-week contains two creative acts: the animals that walk on the dry land and the human beings who rule the dry land and the animals on it.

The half-weeks, though, like the creation week itself, are in the story. The seven days of creation are in the artistry of the narrator, not in the history of this earth. "And God saw that it was good."

In the Babylonian myth, humanity was created from the blood of a god to be slaves of the gods. The Priest insisted that humans were not made out of a god but were created in the image of God. In his sublime vision the Priest saw that the image of God is not in the male alone, but in male and female together.

According to the Atrahasis myth, the gods objected to the multiplication of people on the earth. To stop human proliferation the gods sent famine, drought, and finally a flood to wipe out humankind entirely from the earth. The Genesis account by contrast depicts God as commanding human multiplication. Here we glimpse the Hebrew experience of the grace of God in the Exodus extrapolated backward into creation.

God created humankind to rule over God's creation—not as slaves to give the gods leisure but in freedom to share God's dominion and power. Then he concluded the sixth day of his story: "God saw all that he had made, and it was very good."

Upon the creation of humanity, Marduk commissioned the creation of Babylon and its step-pyramid ziggurat Esagila. Then Marduk invited the gods to a banquet graced with mugs of beer where humans served the gods in cultic worship for the benefit of the lazy and gluttonous deities. How different the Hebrew version of the climactic moment of creation!

We have missed the point of the seventh day of creation, the Sabbath, by focusing solely on God's resting on the seventh day. The Priest gave us several signals that he intended more than the mythical idea that God needed to rest his tired, aching muscles with a day off and an afternoon nap after a hard week's labor:

- The description of the seventh day does not include these words, "And the evening and the morning were the seventh day." The Priest's story concludes with equivalent words for each of the first six days. Why not for the seventh? Answer: God's sabbath has never ended. God still enjoys his sabbath rest. This fact alone shows we are not dealing with a literal "24/7" creation week.

- Whereas the Babylonians saw the gods as set free with the creation of human beings, the Priest saw humanity as given liberty in creation. The Babylonians saw humans as created to serve as slaves of the gods; this new theology saw humanity as created to reign alongside God as his viceroys. The Babylonians saw the image of God as residing in images; the Zadokite saw humanity itself as the image of God.

- In the Babylonian myths every seventh day of the month is accursed. In the temple account the seventh day of each week is blessed and given to man as a day of rest. God created humanity by his free and gracious act and invited all of humanity to share his Sabbath rest. Here we see God's intention for the human race as eternal fellowship with our creator.

The implication of the priestly creation story is that God created humanity to reign over creation and to enjoy eternal Sabbath rest.[4] The remainder of his vision will declare that humanity has refused both gracious offers. Instead of reigning over a glorious creation, humanity has exploited creation and, therefore, constantly risks sliding back into chaos. Instead of enjoying God's Sabbath banquet, humanity must labor like slaves to survive in an alien and hostile world.

In his creation narrative, the Priest stated the problem and the crisis for his coming story. The plot of his later history of the patriarchs and the Exodus will revolve around the quest for a solution to this crisis—entering into that fellowship with God for which we were created.

The Priest's Theology of History

The Zadokite Priest, like the Yahwist two hundred years earlier, followed his theology of creation with a theology of history in the same story-telling medium. Borrowing available traditional material, he laid out an approach to history that would set the stage for the remainder of his narrative.

In Genesis 5 he includes a genealogy that shows Noah was descended from the first man Adam.[5] Even here, though, we are still in the realm of theology; but pre-history is now morphing into proto-history. Since this is the only passage the Priest calls a "book," it seems likely that he relies here on some written document.

In the ancient Near East everyone believed the ancients long before them had lived abnormally long lives. The Sumerian king lists claimed the early kings of Babylon ruled for 20,000–64,000 years, but those kings were seen as demi-gods. The Priest insisted the ancients were not demi-gods, nor even kings, but mere men. Even though the Priest assigned unusually long lives to the ancients in his genealogy, he was careful not to attribute a lifespan of a thousand years or more to any of them. By assigning the ancients lives of less than a thousand years, the Priest insisted on the full humanity of all the characters in the story.[6] Lives of hundreds of years seem impossibly long to us, but for his generation surrounded by myths of kings living thousands of years, those lifespans spoke of perfectly ordinary human beings.

Unlike the Yahwist, the Priest did not provide us with a lengthy account of the pre-patriarchal period. Only two significant stories in the priestly work come from the period prior to Abraham.

Like the Yahwist, the Priest had also received an ancient tradition of a Great Flood that wiped out all humanity. His story differed from that of the Yahwist at several points. The Yahwist had written that Noah took a pair of unclean animals and seven pairs of clean animals into the ark.[7] The priestly account said by contrast that God commanded Noah to take "two of every sort" of animals into the ark.[8] Unlike the Yahwist, the Priest described the dimensions of the ark and specified the time sequences for every step in the Flood's progression until Noah and his family exited the ark.[9]

All in all, however, the two accounts are complementary, exhibiting throughout distinctively Hebrew God-talk. Significantly the Priest, like the Yahwist, assigned a different motive for the Flood from that cited by the Babylonian myths. The myths said the gods destroyed the humans because they had proliferated too much and made so much noise the gods could not rest. Both the Yahwist and the Priest assigned moral reasons for the Flood. Whereas the Yahwist attributed the flood to humanity's evil,[10] the Priest attributed it to humanity's violence.[11] Continuing his moral interpretation of the Flood, Elohim afterward made a covenant with Noah promising not to destroy the earth by water again, giving the rainbow as a sign of that covenant.[12]

The Priest concluded this portion of his work with a genealogy, a key mark of his work, called by scholars the Table of Nations and a genealogy connecting Noah to Terah and Abraham.[13] His Table of Nations has been interspersed by a later editor with comments and stories from the Yahwist.[14] This Table of Nations descending from the new progenitor, Noah, shows the traditional relationships of nations known to him. These were all the nations of the world he knew and do not include nations outside the Near East and North Africa. We find no mention of China or Greece or Rome, and certainly not of the British Isles, the Americas, or the Pacific islands. His concern was to show how the old traditional history connected to Abraham, progenitor of the Israelites.

From this fact we gain a significant insight into the nature of the Bible and its inspiration. These writers were not miraculously endowed with knowledge of facts outside their experience. The Table of Nations reports only Near Eastern and North African nations. The Priest said nothing about any other civilizations or peoples, demonstrating that he worked with the material he had at hand, interpreting it in terms of his experience with God. Divine revelation and inspiration did not reside in provision of the facts of history but in the interpretation of the history the writers already had from previous sources; but that contribution alone demonstrates the inspiration.

With the Priest's production of the P Document, the recording of the earliest foundational traditions documents of Israel came to a close—two hundred years after the process began. These four works—the J, E, D, and P documents—were not yet our Scriptures. Scripture consists of the books we know—Genesis, Exodus, Leviticus, Numbers, and Deuteronomy. These four documents are merely the four books a much later author drew together artistically and theologically to produce our scriptural books.

By the time the Priest wrote his P Document, the Assyrians had bludgeoned the nation of Israel into oblivion, and the nation of Judah struggled to survive. Judah had endured the marauding Assyrian invasion but still contended with Egypt, Babylon, and Canaanite Baalism. Now we turn to the continuing story of the Hebrew prophets' struggle against Canaanite idolatry during Judah's decline and last days.

Notes

[1] For our early dating of the priestly creation narrative, see the documentation in note 2 of chapter 6.

[2] For Canaanite knowledge of the Babylonian myth, see the documentation in note 4 of chapter 3. The dominant myth of the ancient Near East comes down to us in the *Enuma Elish*, the *Gilgamesh Epic*, and the Atrahasis myths, among others. Although the Priest probably did not possess a copy of the *Enuma Elish* or any similar book, he knew the myths at least in an oral form current in Canaanite culture.

[3] The *Enuma Elish* will be cited throughout from the translation by Tore Kjeilen, © 1996–2009, LookLex Ltd., http://lexicorient.com/e.o/enuma_elish.htm.

[4] Evidently, ancient Israel also saw the priestly creation narrative of the Sabbath in similar terms. In this regard see Deut. 5:12-15 (Sabbath related to Israel's slavery and rest from labor) and 12:7-12 (Israel promised to feast and rest with God); Num. 14:1-23; Ps. 95:7-11; Heb. 3:11, 18-19; 4:3-11; and Rev. 14:13, 18:1, 19:6-9.

[5] Many critical scholars consider Genesis 5 to belong to P. Richard Friedman assigns chapter 5 to the Redactor who combined J, E, and P into our present book of Genesis. Since this chapter is in any case clearly priestly material, it seems best to look at it at this point in our story.

[6] I have borrowed this idea from Gordon J. Wenham, *Word Biblical Commentary: Genesis 1–15* (Waco, TX: Word, 1987), xlv-xlvi, lii-liii.

[7] Gen. 7:1-5.

[8] Gen. 6:19-20; 7:8-9, 15.

[9] Gen. 6:9-22; 7:11, 13-15, 24; 8:1-2, 3b-5, 7, 13a, 14-19.

[10] Gen. 6:5.

[11] Gen. 6:13.

[12] Gen. 9:1-17.

[13] Gen. 10:1-7, 20, 22-23, 31-32.

[14] Genesis 10.

CHAPTER 8

Religious Warfare Rages On

The Prophets and the Decline of Judah

The Bible's authors were not the protectors of the status quo we have tried to make them. In many ways they were religious radicals pushing back vigorously against their surrounding culture. When the children of the Hebrew slaves escaped from Egypt arrived in Canaan, they quickly amalgamated with the resident Canaanites. They adopted the language, alphabet, and much of the Canaanite culture, including in many cases their gods—the Baals and their female consorts, the Asherahs. In some cases they mixed their Yahwism with the local religion, for instance, giving Yahweh an Asherah as a wife.

To make matters worse, the Hebrews intermarried and merged with other people groups who arrived in Canaan shortly after them. These other recent immigrants included the Greek Sea Peoples (Philistines), the Aramaeans (from whom they had originally come), the Midianites (into whose tribe Moses had married), and the Amorites, Hittites, Hurrians, and Ammonites. As with the Canaanites, the Hebrews frequently adopted the ways, religions, and gods of these various people groups.

Some among this new people calling themselves Israel remained true to Yahweh. They insisted on following the laws given to them by Moses in the wilderness, worshiping Yahweh alone, maintaining the Sabbath, circumcision, and abstention from divine images or eating pork. Theirs was a lonely struggle, however. In the ninth century Elijah bemoaned before Yahweh that only he was left of all the Yahwistic prophets.[1] Yahweh answered the self-pitying prophet that there were still seven thousand men in Israel who had not "bowed the knee to Baal." Still, this vignette from that prophet's life shows how desperate the struggle remained even three hundred years after the Hebrews with their strange and imageless God arrived in Canaan.

Through the tenth century BCE onward, prophecy developed among the Israelites until it attained its pinnacle during the eighth century. Even Hosea and Amos in Israel and Micah and Isaiah in Judah could not win a final victory over the idolatry, orgiastic worship, and child sacrifice of the native Canaanite Baalism. When we arrive in the seventh century BCE the struggle between Yahwism and Baalism continues, led by four notable Hebrew prophets whose sermons made it into the Bible: Jeremiah, Habakkuk, Zephaniah, and Nahum.

Josiah's Enforced Reformation

Two hundred years had passed since the Yahwist and the Elohist completed their ambitious works. For those two centuries royal court scribes in both Israel and Judah had kept careful records of the deeds of the kings of those nations. In 722 BCE the Assyrians destroyed Israel and took thousands of the northern nation's leaders into exile. The priests of Shiloh fled south into Judah, bringing with them the E Document and the D Document plus other records from the Shiloh temple archives. In addition, priests from other shrine cities such as Shechem, Bethel, Gilgal, and Mizpah almost certainly fled Israel, bringing their archives of written records of oral traditions to Jerusalem. They would have deposited these scrolls in the Jerusalem Temple, as much as it grieved them to give up their treasures to their despised Zadokite rivals.

Now the Hebrew people had only one nation again—Judah—the northern tribes called "Israel" having ceased to exist as a nation. Another century passed. During this time the court scribes of Judah continued to keep careful records of events in their royal court. The nation, however, had largely forgotten much of their Yahwistic heritage—the Mosaic laws, the holy days and festivals, the rejection of idols, and the ethical principles.

In 621 BCE King Josiah of Judah ordered the renovation of the Jerusalem Temple. During the renovation the workers discovered the Book of the Law,[2] stimulating Josiah to initiate a national reformation.[3] Josiah ordered the shrines to Baal and his Asherah removed from the Temple. He destroyed the Asherah poles, the country shrines to pagan gods, and the Topheth (fire pit) outside Jerusalem where infants were sacrificed. He also destroyed the sacred horse images in the Jerusalem Temple and at the Bethel temple to the bull of Jeroboam and the accompanying Asherah pole, and removed all the priests of the idolatrous shrines and destroyed the quarters for the male shrine prostitutes.

We have to notice a key difference between Josiah's reformation and the usual practice of the prophets. Whereas the prophets exercised their ministry by preaching messages challenging their people to return to Yahweh voluntarily, Josiah enforced his reformation by violence at the point of a sword. Remaining faithful to Yahweh in ancient Israel assumed different forms according to who was remaining faithful.

Jeremiah

The greatest of the seventh-century prophets, Jeremiah, began preaching about the time of Josiah's reformation of Israel in 621 BCE. He seems to have approved of Josiah's religious reforms at first, but later he grew disillusioned with what turned out to be only official, not real, revival. He confronted his nation and its rulers with their evils of idolatry and paganism and prophesied that God would bring judgment on Judah. Although Jeremiah only suspected it at the time, the nation was already in precipitous and irreversible decline. Less than forty years remained for Judah's survival when Jeremiah attempted to turn the nation to Yahweh alone.

After Judah fell in 586 BCE Jeremiah continued to preach well into the Exile, even sending letters to the exiles encouraging them to remain true to God in Babylon. John Paterson points out that in one of those letters Jeremiah was the first person known to history to instruct believers to pray for their enemies.[4] For his faithfulness to the message God gave him, Jeremiah suffered imprisonment—once in a dry cistern—and eventually was taken involuntarily into exile in Egypt.

The only prophet besides Elijah and Habakkuk to allow us to see his inner struggles, Jeremiah laid bare his doubts about the validity of his messages, his anger at God, and his near suicidal depression because of the price he paid for his calling.[5] Possibly all the prophets experienced similar anguish, but they never let the outside world see it. They suffered in private, but in public they stood unbending as men of iron.

Jeremiah's greatest prophecy, no doubt, was one in which he gave words to his recognition that violent, official, state-enforced reformations such as Josiah's were worthless.

> The time is coming, declares the LORD, when I will make a new covenant with the house of Israel and with the house of Judah. It will not be like the covenant I made with their forefathers when I took them by the hand to lead them out of Egypt, because they broke my covenant, though I was a husband to them, declares the LORD. This is the covenant I will make with the house of Israel after that time, declares the LORD. I will put my law in their minds and write it on their hearts. I will be their God, and they will be my people. No longer will a man teach his neighbor, or a man his brother, saying, "Know the LORD," because they will all know me, from the least of them to the greatest, declares the LORD. For I will forgive their wickedness and will remember their sins no more. (31:31-34 NIV)

It took a long time, but eventually a true prophet of God realized that genuine faith flows from the heart, not from the sword of the state.

Habakkuk

Also during Josiah's reign Habakkuk represented the lone philosopher among the prophets. He had an anguished question: Why did God do nothing about the injustice, violence, and oppression of the helpless he saw all around him? The inquiring prophet received the revelation that the Chaldeans would bring God's judgment on Judah. His problem still unsolved, Habakkuk then asked why God would use a people worse than Judah to discipline them.

He received neither a theological nor a philosophical answer to his second question. The only answer he received was, "The righteous will live by his faith" (2:4) or alternatively, "The just shall live by his faithfulness" (NIV). Both translations are valid, and Habakkuk probably intended both meanings. God's only answer to Habakkuk's anguished question was relational and experiential—the righteous man who has faith in and is faithful to God will live thereby. In other words, God said to Habakkuk, "Trust me and be faithful to me; and let me worry about retribution and justice." Habakkuk penned the greatest answer to the problem of evil ever conceived by the mind of man, but then he received it from the Spirit of God.

Centuries later in Alexandria, Egypt, Jewish translators of the Hebrew Scriptures into Greek rendered this verse in the Septuagint (LXX) as "The just shall live by my faithfulness."[6] The Septuagint translators may have worked with a different Hebrew text, or possibly they interpreted "his faithfulness" to refer to God's faithfulness. At any rate, they made the faithfulness that would give life to the righteous person God's faithfulness.

All three versions of God's message to Habakkuk would later become determinative for Christian theology. Six hundred years later this verse would become the life verse of the apostle Paul. Fifteen hundred years after Paul it became the keynote of the Protestant Reformation. Five hundred years after the Reformation it still encapsulates the Christian faith—almost three thousand years after Habakkuk spoke those awesome words.

Zephaniah and Nahum

Just prior to Josiah's reformation, Zephaniah (ca. 625 BCE) preached God's judgment on Judah for its sins of idolatry, dishonesty, and totally ignoring the will of God. Soon after Josiah's reformation, Nahum (ca. 613 BCE) triumphantly celebrated the fall of Israel's enemy Nineveh, capital of Assyria.

Both prophets had messages of unadulterated judgment and wrath. Neither preached anything of the grace of God, not even upon repentance. These two prophets were consumed with a sense of the holiness of God and the sinfulness of humans. Though not nearly on the exalted plane occupied by Isaiah, Micah, Amos, Hosea, and Jeremiah, their prophecies also made it into the Hebrew canon of Scripture and thus into the Christian canon.

Pre-exilic Hebrew Prophets	
1000s BCE	Deborah, Samuel
900s BCE	Nathan
800s BCE	Elijah, Elisha
700s BCE	Isaiah of Jerusalem, Hosea, Amos, Micah
600s BCE	Jeremiah, Habakkuk, Zephaniah, Nahum

Theology of the Prophets

The Hebrew prophets not only experienced resistance from common people who disliked having their idolatry and injustice ruthlessly exposed, but they also discovered that certain elements of the religious establishment did not think much of them either. We saw earlier how the priest of Bethel warned Amos to leave the king's shrine city, but the Zadokite priests of Jerusalem apparently cared little more for the prophets than did the high priest of the golden bull at Bethel. The Zadokite Priest's P Document never mentions the prophets and makes no place for them in Israel's religious life. We probably guess correctly if we suspect the temple priesthood deemed the prophets their rivals and preferred to ignore them.

Besides, certain men laying claim to the prophetic mantel clearly sold their services to the highest bidders. The biblical record shows the temple priesthood and their relatives at his hometown of Anathoth opposed Jeremiah.[7] Nevertheless, the legitimate Hebrew prophets helped define, develop, defend, and advance ethical monotheism. Their theology can be summarized under the following points.

Radical Monotheism

The prophets called Israel to radical monotheism in the face of the crude polytheism and idolatry of its neighbors. Today we only have to say "God"—for most people in the Western world assume there is only one God who does not need any other name. For that assumption, we can thank the Hebrew prophets and their doctrine of the zealous God.

Demand for Justice

A salient keynote of their message resided in the prophets' call for public ethics in the courts of law, the politics of the state, and the economics of the nation and individuals. These preachers of righteousness were the first men known to history to proclaim that God desires justice above all else. They rejected the idea that faith is a private matter and has no role in the public arena, along with the notion that faith does not get involved with justice in the courts, economics, and warfare. Their call for public righteousness would eventually translate into the just war theory, abolition of slavery, emancipation of women and children, state-sponsored welfare, Social Security, the United Nations, Medicare and Medicaid, the civil rights movement, the minimum wage, and the Affordable Care Act.

Judgment and Salvation

The Hebrew prophets' forecasts for the future always proclaimed both warning and hope. Their warnings trumpeted that God would not overlook polytheism, idolatry, injustice, violence, and oppression, and would bring judgment on evil. At the same time, they held out hope for the temporal restoration of God's blessings to those who repented and returned to faithfulness to God. These prophets did not write world history in advance but proclaimed God's justice to power and his grace to sinners.

Davidic Throne, Promises, and Hope

The prophets sounded a theme later enunciated by the Hebrew Historian who insisted God had given David his throne and established his dynasty in Jerusalem. Isaiah's famous messianic prophecies also proclaimed that theme and promised that God would fulfill the divine promises to David in the coming messiah.

For to us a child is born, to us a son is given, and the government will be on his shoulders. And he will be called Wonderful Counselor, Mighty God, Everlasting Father, Prince of Peace. Of the increase of his government and peace there will be no end. He will reign on David's throne and over his kingdom, establishing and upholding it with justice and righteousness from that time on and forever. (9:6-7)

That same concern and promise of hope inspired Micah's prophecy of the birth of the Messiah in Bethlehem.[8] Here, too, they proclaimed Yahweh as the "I Am"—the God who remains faithful—the one who fulfills promises to Abraham, to David, and to the nation.

Problematic Views

These great spiritual visionaries, nevertheless, had some problematic views of God's nature and relationship to the world. Micaiah ben Imlah claimed that God had sent a lying spirit to one of the professional prophets.[9] Amos claimed that God causes every natural disaster ("evil" was his word).[10] He also believed that God predicts all his actions to the prophets.[11] Their message of divine judgment through military invasion sets our teeth on edge. God causes warfare—the greatest evil of the human race?

Here as elsewhere, the solution to our difficulties comes in recognizing the principle of progressive revelation—and progressive comprehension of divine revelation. This process would come to its climactic fulfillment centuries later in the life of a single man.

Notes

[1] 1 Kgs. 19:14-18.
[2] 2 Kings 22.
[3] 2 Kings. 23.
[4] Jer. 29:7.
[5] Jer. 20:7-18.
[6] Sir Lancelot C.L. Brenton, ed., *The Septuagint with Apocrypha* (Peabody, MA: Hendrickson, 1999), 1107.
[7] Jer. 11:18-23, 20:1-2, 26:11.
[8] Mic. 5:2.
[9] 1 Kgs. 22:18-28.
[10] Amos 3:6.
[11] Amos 3:7.

CHAPTER 9

The World's Second Historian

The Deuteronomist's Theology as History

Around the time of Josiah's reformation in 621 BCE the second great historian of world history wrote a gigantic tome that now occupies six books of our Bibles (four in the Hebrew canon). Biblical interpreters call Israel's second major historian the Deuteronomistic Historian. This name refers to his following the theology of the core of the book of Deuteronomy, which biblical scholars have identified with the book of the Law found in the temple during Josiah's reign. Since that scholarly label strikes most non-scholars as awkward and off-putting, we will simply refer to this author as the Historian (recognizing that the Yahwist was Israel's first historian). This man was obviously a well-educated, highly placed individual with access to temple and royal archives of now defunct Israel and surviving Judah. He also had access to prophetic and shrine archives from various locations and other documentary sources.

According to one major theory, these historians (plural) were a "school" of writers, a group of scholars united in a common point of view, purpose, and writing style. They labored for several decades, writing two editions of the history, the first (designated Dtr¹) completed in Jerusalem before the Exile and the second (Dtr²) completed about 550 BCE in Babylon.[1]

In *Who Wrote the Bible?* Richard Friedman offers an attractive alternative theory in which he hypothesizes that Israel's second major Hebrew Historian was one man. According to Friedman's theory, Jeremiah's scribe Baruch ben Neriyah was the actual author utilizing the works of many previous lesser Hebrew historians who had penned shorter works prior to his time. Baruch built his history on the theology of the Deuteronomist and that of his employer and friend Jeremiah. Baruch wrote a first edition (Dtr¹) of his history shortly after Josiah's reformation. Within three decades after the fall of Jerusalem (by 556 BCE) Baruch added the last two chapters of 2 Kings along with other alterations in the rest of the text as a second edition (Dtr²).[2]

Friedman bases his view on the striking similarities in vocabulary and phrasing between the history of the Former Prophets and the book of

Jeremiah, almost certainly also penned by Baruch.[3] Although the wording of those concluding chapters is similar to the rest of the work, the last two chapters of 2 Kings do not include the key themes of the rest of the history of the two nations. These observations lead Friedman to the conclusion that those two chapters were written later than the rest of the history but by the same author—two editions by one author. (Baruch would have been at least in his late eighties by 556 BCE, exceedingly old for that period of history, but not impossibly aged.)

If Friedman's theory is correct, then we possess what amounts to the "signature" of the author of this Hebrew history. Nachman Avigad discovered and published in 1980 a *bulla* (clay seal) inscribed "[belonging] to Baruch son of Neriyah the scribe."[4] This *bulla* belonged to the man who probably penned the prophecies of Jeremiah and possibly also wrote the final edition of Deuteronomy in addition to Joshua–Kings! Although Friedman's theory cannot be considered "proven" and is disputed by other biblical scholars, I accept it as likely and assume it in the remainder of this work.

Baruch observed that the book of the Law (Deuteronomy 12–26), proclaimed a particular theology of history, namely that if the nation should turn away from Yahweh, God would bring judgment on his people. Then if they repented and returned to Yahweh, God would forgive their sins, heal their land, and restore to them the divine blessings. Jeremiah's scribe set out to write a history of the nation from Moses to his own time showing how that principle and Jeremiah's theology had worked itself out in Israel's national life.

Baruch wrote a new introduction and conclusion to Deuteronomy (chs. 1–11, 27–34), linking it to his history that followed. In time, Deuteronomy came to be considered the fifth book of the Torah (Genesis, Exodus, Leviticus, Numbers, and Deuteronomy). Originally, though, it was the first book of the Hebrew history (Deuteronomy, Joshua, Judges, Samuel, and Kings). Deuteronomy thus became the link between the founding oral traditions and the documented history of the entire Israelite people—both the fifth book of the Torah and the first book of the Deuteronomistic History. The "first Bible," therefore, apparently consisted of these nine books. The rest of the Bible coalesced around this core.[5]

Simon J. DeVries has made a good case for calling this Hebrew history genuine history. This work is admittedly primarily theology, preaching, and teaching. It sets forth a well thought-out theology of history and preaches a sermon to the nation calling them to faithfulness to God. It teaches the lessons of the end result of unfaithfulness to God.[6]

At the same time the Hebrew Historian used the methods necessary for calling any work "history." He used contemporary or nearly contemporary written sources as much as possible, traced an organic line of development through the narrative, showed a realistic cause-and-effect progression of historical events, and described the historical characters in realistic, credible, three-dimensional terms. His work represented popular history rather than academic history, to be sure, but history nonetheless—the most academic of which that age was capable.

Although Baruch explained the outcome of the two nations' history in terms of divine judgment and blessing, we cannot remove his narrative from the category of history simply because it has a religious component. To do so would necessitate dismissing as history Gregory of Tours' *History of the Franks* (ca. AD 591) and Bede's *Ecclesiastical History of the English People* (ca. AD 731) because they appealed to religious themes. Every historical work holding any interest for anyone other than the academic specialist delves beneath the bare events to discover underlying reasons and wider meaning.

Religious meaning no more disqualifies a work from the appellation "history" than do moral, ethical, economic, material, or political meanings. After all, religious faith is an integral human component, certainly as integral as other concerns; and theistic faith entails the conviction that God actually exists. Today's historians work with the principle of methodological naturalism and thus do not explain outcomes in terms of divine action. The Hebrew Historian, though, was not a twenty-first-century historian with our philosophical biases; so, we cannot hold him to today's standards for professional historians.

Jews have historically referred to the four works Joshua, Judges, Samuel, and Kings as the Former Prophets, in distinction from the four books of the Latter Prophets—Isaiah, Jeremiah, Ezekiel, and the Book of the Twelve (the so-called "minor" prophets Hosea–Malachi). Calling these works the Former Prophets does not mean they were written by any of the known prophets but that they embodied a prophetic critique of the nation. These works were history written from a prophetic point of view. If Friedman is correct, however, then they were in fact also written by a prophet's scribe partly on the basis of that prophet's ideas.

The Second Major Hebrew History

The second major Hebrew Historian built the book of Deuteronomy on the core of the book of the Law found in the Jerusalem Temple. He added a new introduction (chs. 1–11) and a new conclusion (chs. 27–32), plus the Song of Moses (ch. 33) and the Blessing of Moses (ch. 34) from other sources. He also interpolated miscellaneous comments from other sources or his own mind along the way.

This new book of Deuteronomy provided the theology for the entire corpus of the Hebrew history. The rest of the history provides illustration and proof of the validity of that theology. In addition, the history presents an explanation of the logic implicit in the course of the history of Israel and Judah as well as Baruch's understanding of the reason for the decline and fall of both nations.

This Hebrew Historian adopted the later part of volume one of the J Document—the first Hebrew history—and much of volume two as the core around which to compose his books of Joshua and Judges. Much of the material of the book of Joshua appears to have been compiled at Bethel, some think as early as the time of David (early tenth century BCE). The historian supplemented these Benjamite traditions with various holy war traditions, other narratives and lists, and the Covenant Ceremony of Shechem. The Hebrew Historian turned these traditions into our book of Joshua, the fully integrated sequel to the book of Deuteronomy.

In the book of Joshua the Historian summarized Joshua's conquest of Canaan broadly, presenting it as a blitzkrieg subjugation of Canaan. He took the story of Israel down to Joshua's death and burial "in the hill country of Ephraim" (24:30), concluding with these words: "Israel served the LORD throughout the lifetime of Joshua and of the elders that outlived him and who had experienced everything the LORD had done for Israel" (v. 31).

Then the book of Judges begins, "After the death of Joshua," showing the Hebrew Historian intended it as the sequel to Joshua. He captured the theme of Judges in these words:

> Then the Israelites did evil in the eyes of the LORD and served the Baals. They forsook the LORD, the God of their fathers. . . . In his anger against Israel the LORD handed them over to raiders who plundered them. . . . Then the LORD raised up judges, who saved them out of the hands of these raiders. Yet they would not listen to their judges. . . . But when the judge died, the people returned to

ways even more corrupt than those of their fathers, following other gods and serving and worshiping them . . . Therefore the LORD was very angry with Israel. (2:11-20)

This passage summarizes the theology of the book of Deuteronomy. The rest of Judges illustrates this theology in the progression of the nation through apostasy to judgment, to redemption by a judge and restoration to blessing, to renewed apostasy, and the resumption of the cycle.

Both Joshua and Judges have primarily a theological purpose. The author, therefore, schematized his materials according to his theological vision rather than according to strict chronology. This method presents notorious difficulties for the historian attempting to correlate these works with archaeological finds and extra-biblical records. Still, these books describe the general tone of the period between Israel's entry into Canaan and the rise of the monarchy.

Archaeology indicates that the book of Joshua dramatically telescopes and overstates the rapidity, extent, and violence of the Israelite conquest of Canaan. The book of Judges more precisely reflects the actual historical reality: Israel's gradual incremental replacement of the Canaanite culture over a couple of centuries.

The book of Judges comes to a climax with the shocking story of the rape and dismemberment of a Levite's concubine.[7] The author intended this story to shock the reader, to show how depraved the people of Israel had become prior to the rise of the monarchy. The book ends with this assessment: "In those days Israel had no king; every man did as he saw fit" (21:25). This comment prepares the reader for the Rise of Kingship narrative preserved in 1 Samuel. The Hebrew Historian will show that, although the nation's insistence on a king amounted to a rejection of Yahweh as king, God nevertheless selected Saul as Israel's first king.

The book of Samuel picks up the story without a break with the last two judges of Israel—Eli and Samuel. (First and Second Samuel in our Bible were one book written on two scrolls because of its length.) From the time of Samuel on, Baruch relied on written documents at least roughly contemporary with the events they described. Even the J Document he used as the backbone of his own history proceeded in this manner by that point in the story. From this point on, his history has morphed from traditions into documented history.

As in Joshua and Judges, the second Hebrew Historian added to the J Document numerous previously existing compositions to produce the books of Samuel and Kings. Some of those earlier narratives included the ones named at the beginning of this chapter plus Absalom's Rebellion,[8] The Gibeonites' Revenge,[9] and Solomon's Succession Narrative. Probably someone in David's court had written The Rise of Kingship and the History of David's Rise to legitimate his reign shortly after David replaced Saul. Similarly, someone in Solomon's court had probably composed Solomon's Succession Narrative to legitimize his reign after he supplanted his oldest living brother Adonijah through a palace counter-coup. The Hebrew Historian brought all these older works together and provided interpretive and transitional passages, thus producing our present 1–2 Samuel.

The book of Kings (1 and 2 Kings are also one book on two scrolls) actually gives us three of its sources: the book of the Acts of Solomon, the Chronicles of the Kings of Israel, and the Chronicles of the Kings of Judah.[10] The book of Kings continues to trace evidence for the Deuteronomic theology of history through the records of Israel and Judah.

The low point of evil in Israel came with Omri and Ahab, who receive the blame for Israel's fall to the Assyrians. According to the Historian, none of the kings of Israel were faithful to Yahweh, all of them worshiping the Baals and the Asherahs. The northern nation went into moral, spiritual, and political free fall after Ahab's ignominious death at the Battle of Qarqar in 853 BCE. The chaotic last century of Israel ended when the nation finally succumbed to Assyria in 722 BCE.

Judah's nadir came with Manasseh, who receives the blame for Judah's destruction by Babylon. The southern nation, however, received a brief reprieve during the reign of the pious but ill-fated Josiah. Following Josiah's untimely death in the Battle of Carchemish in 605 BCE, Judah also imploded, going into the Babylonian Exile under Nebuchadrezzar in 586 BCE.

The second Hebrew history flows naturally from each book into the next. Moses' death at the end of Deuteronomy flows into Joshua's leadership in the book of Joshua into the period of the judges. Samuel's story blends naturally into David's story in 1 Samuel that continues through 2 Samuel and concludes in chapter 2 of 1 Kings. The book of Kings concludes in the Exile with King Jehoichin of Judah, a well-accommodated prisoner of war in the royal court of King Evil-merodach of Babylon on March 12, 560 BCE.[11] The entire Hebrew history would have been completed shortly after this date.

At this point, it seems wise to attempt to reflect on a couple of questions that we of the twenty-first century cannot resist asking.

The World's Second Historian

Late History of Israel and Judah	
Before 722 BCE	The Deuteronomistic Historian writes D (Deuteronomy 12–26)
722 BCE	Assyria destroys Israel Priests of Shiloh flee to Jerusalem with E and D
621 BCE	D found in Jerusalem Temple under King Josiah
After 621 BCE	Deuteronomistic Historian completes Deuteronomy and writes Joshua, Judges, 1–2 Samuel, 1–2 Kings
586 BCE	Babylonians destroy Jerusalem
After 560 BCE	Hebrew Historian completes Kings

Reflections on the History

Is Israel's history factual?

The minimalist school (following Israel Finkelstein) and the radical revisionists (Tommy Thompson and the Copenhagen school) insist the archaeological evidence refutes the historicity of much or even the entirety of the biblical version of Israel's early history. The minimalists doubt David existed, or else was anything more than a rural chieftain. The revisionists go even further and deny the existence of the nation of Israel until the Hellenistic period (the last two centuries before Christ).

By the nature of the case, Joshua through Kings cannot be proven accurate in detail. Assertions of divine action cannot be a matter of strictly objective documented "history" in any case. How could a historian document anything about God? More to the point of history, though, we run into difficulties with some of the factual materials.

No archaeological evidence exists for the blitzkrieg Israelite conquest of Canaan or the slaughter of the Canaanites as Joshua reports.[12] Even archaeologists who set out to prove the accuracy of the biblical record have concluded that Ai already lay in ruins when Israel arrived. After all, the word "Ai" means "the ruin."

Israelite pottery, while distinctive and somewhat modified, is still continuous with Canaanite pottery, not indicating a totally different people. The Hebrew language, furthermore, is simply southern Canaanite, as Ugaritic is northern Canaanite. These facts along with many others lead some archaeologists and historians to conclude that the ancient Israelites of the late thirteenth and twelfth centuries BCE were simply Canaanites.

On the other hand, Bethel in the central part of Canaan and Taanach and Hazor in the north were indeed destroyed during the late thirteenth century as described in Joshua. Furthermore, Bethel and Taanach were resettled as Israelite cities. Archaeology shows that a number of towns in the Shephelah also were destroyed at that time.

Much of the archaeological evidence is not so straightforward as some would represent. Archaeologist Amihai Mazar points out that in spite of the frequent assertion that Jericho did not exist in the thirteenth century BCE, a late Bronze Age settlement did exist at Jericho. For this reason, "archaeological data cannot serve as decisive evidence to deny a historical nucleus in the book of Joshua concerning the conquest of this city."[13]

The evidence on the Israelite destruction of Shechem is complex and equivocal. The book of Joshua reports certain cities as not conquered, corresponding precisely to the archaeological excavations of these sites.[14] Negative evidence critically assessed is evidence, too.

Ziony Zevit concludes from archaeology that the early Israelites were indeed a new ethnic group entering Canaan and that evidence indicates a thirteenth-century invasion of this people group. Zevit also endorses Adam Zertel's interpretation of the large structure on Mount Ebal as an altar and effectively refutes all the alternative theories,[15] consistently with the narrative of Joshua 8:30-31. Archaeology, furthermore, indicates the accuracy of the Judges 18 narrative of the tribe of Dan migrating from central Canaan to the region of Dan in the north.[16] These archaeological findings support the biblical narrative.

In support of the general narratives of Joshua and Judges, archaeology has proven that in the late thirteenth century and following settlers suddenly appeared in the hill country of Canaan living in four-room houses archaeologists call "Israelite houses." Their pottery, while continuous with Canaanite pottery, was still distinctive Israelite pottery that allows archaeologists to identify these people ethnically. Significantly, the archaeological evidence shows they did not eat pork.

The hill country of Canaan experienced a population explosion[17] from the thirteenth century BCE to the twelfth and eleventh centuries,[18] as well as in Lower and Upper Galilee and Trans-Jordan.[19] This population growth produced scores of new towns and villages, a growth not explicable by simple growth through progeny. Significantly, however, the vast majority of these new building sites were new villages not erected on top of razed and burnt Canaanite towns. What does this mixed and confusing evidence mean?

Even though the archaeological evidence does not support a total conquest of Canaan in a single military sweep as seems to be described in Joshua, the "conquest" reported in Joshua does seem to embody a national memory of a number of provable significant battles and victories in the late thirteenth century and on into the twelfth century. Likely the events of the early Israelite occupation of Canaan have been telescoped and even exaggerated in the narratives of Joshua, but they do rest on a solid factual basis preserved in the folk memory of the ancient Israelites.[20] The book of Judges probably presents the more accurate general picture of a gradual domination of Canaan by the new Israelites until they were strong enough to establish a true state.

When we arrive at the material in Samuel and Kings, on the other hand, we find ourselves in history proper based on contemporary or nearly contemporary documents. Archaeologist William Dever, who describes himself as a secular humanist, argues vociferously for the essential historicity of the books of Samuel and Kings.[21] Furthermore, Ziony Zevit, who perhaps more than any other scholar has mastered an interdisciplinary approach to Hebrew history, asserts that Finkelstein's low dating of sites associated with these narratives (and by implication even more so that of the Copenhagen school) stands outside the mainstream of current Near Eastern archaeologists. Moreover, he concludes that the history recorded in Samuel and Kings from David and Solomon onward is basically factual and is based on much earlier documents going back even to near contemporary times.[22]

Canaanites invented the world's first alphabet in the early second millennium BCE, and the Israelites could have adopted this form of writing as soon as they appear in the archaeological record in the Late Bronze Age (thirteenth century BCE). Archaeologists have uncovered two Hebrew inscriptions in the Old Canaanite alphabet from the eleventh century (the period of Judges) and the tenth century (the period of the United Monarchy).[23] These inscriptions were almost certainly schoolboys' practice lessons, showing that the Israelites were writing before the establishment of the monarchy and that schools were already teaching writing to the young. They clearly could have maintained written records of their history from their early days.

The "House of David" inscription discovered in 1993 indicates the dynasty ruling in Jerusalem was known in the ninth century to have descended from him—a century after David.[24] The fortified Israelite city of Qeiyafa excavated in 2008, a city contemporaneous with King David, supports the picture of Israel as a strong state in the tenth century.[25]

The later history of Israel and Judah can be correlated in detail with corresponding records and dates of the Babylonian, Assyrian, and Egyptian dynasties. The Moabite ruler Mesha mentioned Omri of Israel by name and his son Ahab obliquely on the Moabite Stone. He had this monument carved about 847 BCE after the Battle of Qarqar.[26]

The Assyrian ruler Shalmanezer III named Israel's Ahab of "the house of Omri" in an Assyrian monolith. Shalmanezer says Ahab fought against him with ten thousand foot soldiers and two thousand chariots in the Battle of Qarqar (853 BCE).[27] Shalmaneser III's Black Obelisk portrays "Jehu son of Omri" in his submission to the Assyrian king.[28]

The Battle of Carchemish in which Josiah died in 605 BCE is well known to historians of the Middle East. Although Josiah is not named in the Babylonian Chronicles, the account in 2 Kings correlates well with Babylonian records.

Historians no doubt will in time develop a more complex and nuanced picture of the history of the rise of ancient Israel in Canaan. That history, I predict, will include the elements reported by the founding traditions and Israelite history under the headings of Exodus, Wilderness Wanderings, Conquest, and Judges.

Still we must remember that the purpose of the Hebrew Historian was theological and pastoral, not academic history. He wrote with a spiritual purpose, not as a professor of history at a twenty-first-century university. Furthermore, as soon as the seventh-century Historian was able to secure at least nearly contemporary documents for his history, he did so, as had the Yahwist in the tenth century. For this reason the Yahwist and the Historian can legitimately be called the world's first historians, predating Herodotus by centuries.

In addition, as evidence of the reliability of the Hebrew history, the Historian treats his characters with brutal honesty. His clear-eyed descriptions of the violence of Israel's greatest and most beloved king—David—strikes us with devastating force. Whatever the Historian thought of David's protection racket as an outlaw under King Saul or his homicidal deeds then and later, the Historian never claimed they were righteous. He only reported them, leaving the reader to draw his own conclusions. He even reported Josiah's later violent death at Carchemish in contrast with Huldah's prophecy that Josiah would die "in peace." As much respect as the Historian had for prophets, when one of them uttered a prophecy that turned out to be wrong, he reported it.

What is the significance of the Hebrew history?

The most immediate significance of the Hebrew history is the theology derived from the book of the Law discovered in the Temple. The first doctrine of that theology held that God's judgment follows unfaithfulness and forgiveness and restoration follow repentance. The second doctrine demanded exclusive loyalty to Yahweh and avoidance of all idolatry. The Historian offered an explanation of the Exile based on this theology. Canaanite Baalism, according to him, led Israel astray, eventually leading to the defeat of the nation, the burning of its capitol and temple, and the exile of its people.

Second, the Hebrew Historian elevated the prophetic office, showing how God spoke to the nation through Deborah, Nathan, Elijah, Elisha, and Huldah among others. This emphasis paved the way for the transmission of the great works of the Hebrew prophets, which in time became a major part of the Hebrew Scriptures. In the prophetic spirit, the Historian called the nation to faithful ethical monotheism, a characteristic of Judaism ever since.

Third, the Historian rejected economic, political, and military power as the standard for success. Omri, Ahab, and Manasseh, for example, ranked among the more successful monarchs ever to rule Israel and Judah. Even so, the Hebrew Historian condemned them as evil because of their idolatry, tyranny, and oppression. For possibly the first time in history, political, military, and economic success were not considered demonstrations of greatness.

Fourth, one of the Historian's greatest contributions lay in the concept of God's self-revelation in human history—an idea implied in the work of the Yahwist on which he built his history. Because of this conviction, the Historian attempted as no one before him to write his nation's history from the best documents he could find. His historical work represented a monumental accomplishment both in historical and theological terms. While his purpose remained theological and pastoral rather than academic, he set the standard for ancient historians to follow.

Fifth, the Historian's emphasis on the divine establishment of David's throne and the Davidic dynasty[29] set the tone for future Jewish messianism echoed repeatedly in the words of the prophets. The growth of that messianic emphasis led to the concept of the Kingdom of God that would become the keynote of Jesus of Nazareth's preaching.

Sixth, the Hebrew history established a foundation for the Jews' ethnic identity. Forever afterward the Jews saw themselves in a new light. During the Exile the Jews as a people finally came to a commitment to the one God

Yahweh and his demands for justice and equity. Baruch's Hebrew history prepared them for their return to Judea and rebuilding their temple and nation.

Seventh, the Historian presented Israel with a distinct doctrine of grace—God had redeemed Israel from slavery in Egypt to make a great nation solely by undeserved grace. There was nothing in the Hebrew people that had attracted God to them.[30] This doctrine of the divine election by grace alone applied to the nation, however, not to individuals.

Eighth, the evidence indicates the Hebrew history from Deuteronomy through Kings constituted the first block of the Hebrew Scriptures completed essentially as we possess it today. Baruch completed the Former Prophets even before the books of Genesis, Exodus, Leviticus, and Numbers that precede it in our Bible. If this judgment is correct, then all of Scripture stands on the foundation of the Hebrew history—known to Jews as the Former Prophets. Few authors have accomplished so much for a nation, a people, and the world.

Finally, the Hebrew Historian had one idea that presents us with excruciating difficulty concerning the nature of God. The Historian[31] adopted the view of the Deuteronomist[32] that God had commanded Israel to slaughter the Canaanites in *cherem* (holy war). This claim, characteristic only of the Deuteronomist and the Deuteronomistic Historian, has led to the impression that this opinion represents the universal position of the Old Testament. Actually, some authors of Old Testament materials—the Yahwist, the Elohist, and the Zadokite Priest—report that God only ordered that Israel drive out the Canaanites or even that God would personally drive them out. While many strands of materials report Israel's putting individual cities to the sword, they do not all claim that God ordered the annihilation of the entire Canaanite population. Evidently this subject was controversial even in ancient Israel, with various theologians and historians holding conflicting, even contradictory views on the matter.

Notes

[1]Another widely accepted view sees three editions, all completed in Babylon during the Exile, but evidence for that theory is wholly unconvincing to me.

[2]Richard Elliott Friedman, *Who Wrote the Bible?* (SanFrancisco: Harper, 1997), 146-149.

[3]Jer. 36:1-4, 18, 27-28, 33.

[4]Friedman, *Who Wrote the Bible?* 147-148; Amihai Mazar, *Archaeology of the Land of the Bible: 10,000–586 BCE*, The Anchor Bible Reference Library (New York: Doubleday, 1990), 519.

[5]For a detailed exposition of this idea, see Duane L. Christensen's theory of the development of the Hebrew canon of Scripture in *Word Biblical Commentary: Deuteronomy 1–11* (Nashville: Thomas Nelson, 1991), li-lv. See Friedman's *Who Wrote the Bible?*

[6] Simon J. DeVries, *Word Biblical Commentary: 1 Kings* (Nashville: Thomas Nelson, 1985), xxxiii-xxxv.
[7] Judges 19.
[8] 2 Samuel 13–20.
[9] 2 Sam. 9:1-13, 21:1-14.
[10] 1 Kgs. 11:41, 14:19, 15:7, plus many other citations.
[11] T.R. Hobbs, *Word Biblical Commentary: 2 Kings* (Nashville: Thomas Nelson, 1986), 367.
[12] Mazar, *Archaeology of the Land of the Bible*, 329-338.
[13] Ibid., 331.
[14] Ibid., 331-334.
[15] Ziony Zevit, *The Religions of Ancient Israel: A Synthesis of Parallactic Approaches* (London: Continuum, 2001), 121, 107, 111 fn 43 and fn 44, 198 fn 123, 199-201.
[16] Mazar, *Archaeology of the Land of the Bible*, 332-334.
[17] William Dever, *Who Were the Early Israelites and Where Did They Come From?* (Grand Rapids: Eerdmans, 2003), 96-100.
[18] William Dever, *What Did the Biblical Writers Know & When Did They Know It?* (Grand Rapids: Eerdmans, 2001), 110.
[19] Mazar, *Archaeology of the Land of the Bible*, 334-335.
[20] Ibid., 334.
[21] Dever, *What Did the Biblical Writers Know?*
[22] Zevit, *The Religions of Ancient Israel*, 108-109 fn 38; 377-379.
[23] Dever, *What Did the Biblical Writers Know?*, 203; *The Lives of Ordinary People in Ancient Israel: Where Archaeology and the Bible Intersect* (Grand Rapids: Eerdmans, 2012), 228-230; *Biblical Archaeology Review* (January-February 2009): 42-43.
[24] Dever, *What Did the Biblical Writers Know?* 128-129.
[25] Dever, *Biblical Archaeology Review*, 38-43.
[26] Dever, *What Did the Biblical Writers Know?* 163; Dever, *The Lives of Ordinary People*, 320.
[27] Hobbs, *2 Kings*, 39-41.
[28] Mazar, *Archaeology of the Land of the Bible*, 404; Dever, *The Lives of Ordinary People*, 320.
[29] See 2 Sam. 7:4-17.
[30] Deut. 7:6-9.
[31] Deut. 7:1-5.
[32] Deut. 20:16-18.

CHAPTER 10

At Last—the Torah

An Heir to the Temple Apologist Unites the Founding Traditions

Just thirty-five years after Josiah's governmentally enforced religious reformation, the kingdom he attempted to save came to a violent, catastrophic end. The Deuteronomistic Historian insisted Judah's fall came as God's judgment on the nation for its idolatry through the previous six hundred years since entering Canaan. More recent historians give other, more political explanations for the demise of the nation, based largely on the work of the Deuteronomistic Historian.

In 586 BCE Nebuchadrezzar besieged Jerusalem, eventually stormed it, burned its temple and royal palace, and took its leadership to Babylon. On the way out of Jerusalem, the priests managed to grab their precious scrolls from the temple archives. Those scrolls included the documents we now identify as the J, E, D, and P documents, plus the writings of many of the prophets, a number of the psalms in our Bibles, royal court chronicles cited in later books, and other works no longer extant.

A dark curtain descended over the next century and a half. We can only surmise what transpired during those years from hints in Jeremiah and Ezekiel plus extrapolations from Babylonian and Persian history and from later Israelite history. One thing we do know, however: A century and a half after the Exile began, we first see what appears to be the Torah as we know it.

The climactic year was 458 BCE.[1] A man named Ezra was holding the Torah at his commissioning by Artaxerxes of Persia to return to Jerusalem to lead the returned exiles already back in the area around Jerusalem. Artaxerxes is reported to have spoken to Ezra of "the Law of your God, which is in your hand" (Ezra 7:14).

Another ancient historian recorded that after returning to Jerusalem, Ezra stood before the people of Israel for seven days from sunrise until noon reading the book of the Law of Moses.[2] As far as the record shows, that week marked the first time in history anyone heard the Torah as we now possess it read aloud.

Timeline of the Exile and Return

722 BCE	Israel falls to Assyria
586 BCE	Judah falls to Babylon, exile begins
537 BCE	Cyrus' edict allows Jews to return to Jerusalem
535 BCE	Return to Jerusalem begins
By 458 BCE	A priest in Babylon merges J, E, and P into Genesis, Exodus, Leviticus, and Numbers
458 BCE	Ezra reads the Torah to Jews returned from exile to Jerusalem

Who was this Ezra?

He was a Levitical priest descended from the Zadokite priesthood that had presided over the Jerusalem Temple for almost 400 years from the time of Solomon until the Exile.[3]

Who was the historic figure who wrote the Torah Ezra read?

We do not know. Some traditions say it was Moses; others say Ezra. Most biblical scholars today cannot accept the tradition that Moses authored it, based on evidence from the Torah itself.

Richard E. Friedman argues that Ezra was in the right place, at the right time, with the correct skill set and the right point of view to qualify as author of the Pentateuch as we have it. Until someone offers a better candidate, I conclude Ezra was the author of the Torah—although we cannot prove it. Still, that hypothesis is consistent with ancient Jewish tradition and the known facts. If Ezra did not write the Pentateuch, he certainly introduced it to the world. For the rest of this chapter, at any rate, we will refer to the literary genius and spiritual giant who wrote the Torah as Ezra.

Throughout Israel's history an internal struggle had taken place among their religious leaders to define the nature of Yahwism. The Yahwist, Elohist, and Deuteronomist, who respectively wrote J, E, and D, along with the second major Hebrew historian focused on personal relationship with Yahweh. The Elohist and the Deuteronomist insisted that all the Levites were priests on a par with the Zadokite priesthood of the Jerusalem Temple. The Priest who wrote P, by contrast, concentrated on law, sacrifice, and ritual, and portrayed God as transcendent. He insisted that only the Zadokite priesthood of Jerusalem validly claimed the title "priest," and Levites were merely their menial aides.

In the end a priest descended from Zadok wove the J and E documents around the spine of the Zadokite P Document. He began his theological tome with the priestly creation narrative of his spiritual ancestor, but he kept the J Document creation narrative, placing it after the priestly narrative. He displayed integrity in retaining the J and E documents and their points of view as part of his combined work, even though they partially disagreed with the Priest.

Ezra's Spiritual Genius

Ezra began with the documents J, E, and P, plus other documents we no longer possess.[4] Rather than accepting one document, or one vision of God over the others, he merged all the documents together. Amazingly, he retained their conflicting viewpoints and vision of God, priesthood, sacrifice, and law. Rather than taking one creation narrative and casting the other aside, he retained them both. That their internal literal inconsistencies did not bother Ezra tells us he held an entirely spiritual and theological view of creation. He recognized that each creation narrative supplemented and complemented the other—theologically.

He even retained the conflicting views of when the name of Yahweh began to be known—both the Yahwist's view that men had known of Yahweh since earliest times alongside the idea of the Elohist and the Priest that Israel learned of that covenant name of God at the burning bush incident. In so doing, he presented us with a revelation of God far superior to that of any of these documents taken alone.

Ezra came from the Zadokite priesthood, but his genius and the evidence of his divine inspiration come in his ability to transcend the bias of his own origins and accept both the Yahwistic creation narrative and the priestly narrative. The breadth of his view appears also in his ability to keep the E Document written by the Levitical priest of Shiloh alongside the P Document written by the Zadokite Priest of Jerusalem—two authors at war with one another. In combining these documents, he turned three source documents into Scripture. The source documents interest us for their historical value, but Scripture consists of the Pentateuch we have.

Two Visions of God

Ezra presented two different visions of God given in the various records of tradition. The vision of God received by the patriarchs reveals an anthropomorphic (human-like) God who is a divine person, talking with, reasoning with, and fellowshipping with Abraham, Isaac, and Jacob. We find in the revelation to the patriarchs no hint of legislations, legally required rituals, holy days, regular sacrifices, or priesthood—not even in the P materials.

In stark contrast, those same writers reported that Moses received at the burning bush and Sinai a vision of a totally transcendent, holy, and awesome God. We cannot imagine Moses fellowshipping with God over a meal as Abraham did. Moses reported God as a "consuming fire" thundering from the mountain. Moses' God enters into covenant with Israel, but now also makes demands on them. This divine revelation bristles with laws, rituals, a Tent of Meeting or Tabernacle, priests, and sacrifices, and a binding covenant that requires commitments from Israel as well as from Yahweh.

Still, the two visions of God do not contradict but rather complement one another. Together they give us a picture of God that balances a vision of a personal God with holiness, immanence with transcendence, covenant promises with covenant obligations.

Interestingly, the various authors of the stories of the patriarchs and the Exodus wrote almost exclusively from oral traditions or written accounts of oral traditions many centuries after the facts. Still, they did not write monochromatic accounts of the revelation received by the ancients in which the understanding of God in the earlier revelations was identical to that in the later revelations. Furthermore, multiple attestation of this ancient tradition in the various authors and strata of the Pentateuch along with their intrinsic spirituality make the general reliability of the traditions credible. Still, we cannot prove the factuality of the details, and we do see some anachronisms indicating the period during which they were recorded.

The Resulting Vision of God

So what did Ezra tell us about his vision of God in this combined narrative? He told us only one God rules over history—not a multitude of gods as in the myths. He told us God cannot be represented as an idol—as in the religions around them.

He told us God is personal. God loves, feels, speaks, and relates to us. God is not, though, just a super-human person like the gods of the myths—often as immoral and chaotic as the people themselves. While God sometimes came to the patriarchs in human form, that was not the normal means of divine revelation. Most of the time God spoke to them as a voice—whether in their heads or otherwise they do not usually say. God did not ordinarily

At Last—the Torah

come to the patriarchs in visual form, however, indicating they thought of God as Spirit—invisible and immaterial.

Ezra thought of God as immanent—close at hand. Abraham walked with God. He knew God as a friend. He talked to God, and God talked to him. Ezra also thought of God as transcendent—high and lifted up, holy and different from us. While the patriarchs experienced God as immanent, Moses experienced God as transcendent. Ezra retained both emphases, true to his sources.

Pagans thought of the gods as revealed in images. Ezra presented God as one who speaks rationally—in words. Even the divine names constitute a revelation by God's word. Furthermore, God self-reveals through deeds in human events—historical acts of redemption and sometimes of judgment.

Put all of this together and we see God revealed as personal, yet pure spirit. God is high and lifted up and different from us, yet so near we can converse with our creator and hear God speak a rational word.

These revelations began to come to the patriarchs about 1800 BCE and began to be written down by the 900s BCE. Ezra completed the narrative of Genesis–Numbers somewhere around 450 BCE. To this day—more than 2,400 years later—the Western world still holds this concept of God!

A Monumental Accomplishment

The book of the Law Ezra created—Genesis, Exodus, Leviticus, and Numbers—and presented to his people would ultimately become the central divine revelation for Jews. According to R.E. Friedman's view of biblical origins, Ezra completed this accomplishment by 458 BCE, almost two centuries after Baruch completed his history of the Hebrews. With Ezra's accomplishment, Genesis–Numbers was added to Baruch's history. With that event, Deuteronomy became the fifth book of the Pentateuch and also the first book of the Deuteronomistic History. That nine-book collection—Genesis–Kings—became the first Hebrew Bible.

This collection—the Torah and the Former Prophets—gave the Jewish people the most monumental spiritual, ethical, theological, literary, and historical work ever seen on earth to that date. These books would become the foundation for the eventual collection of the Hebrew Scriptures that Christians know as our Old Testament.

Reflections on the History

What does the Pentateuch reveal?

In his unification of the competing founding traditions, Ezra presented a marvelous vision of divine creation. He insisted, in opposition to the prevailing mythology surrounding him, that a rational, righteous, and holy God created the entire natural order purely by the power of the word. He gave us the vision that this God invites us to enjoy a sabbath, that is, to experience the divine presence in a beautiful garden of spiritual delight. Conceiving of the universe as the rational creation of a rational God, the Hebrew theologians envisioned all of creation as rational to its core—setting the stage for science to arise two millennia later.

Ezra followed the Zadokite Priest in recognizing the image of God in man-and-woman-together. "So God created man in his own image, in the image of God he created him; male and female he created them" (Gen. 1:27 NIV). This concept holds profound implications for life—war and peace, ethics and morality, relationships between and among human beings, the dignity of the individual and the race, the sanctity of each human person before God, and the relationship of each human being with God. Genesis provides a fundamental answer to the question, Who are we? No one has ever conceptualized a more fruitful answer.

This concept also rules out any suggestion that God has gender or sex. Since God is beyond gender and sex, all sexist notions are ruled out of court from the first chapter of the Torah. Shockingly, God as "the Father of Israel," as the Bible sometimes has it, does not mean God is male!

Through ignoring God's will, though, the human race has failed to enter God's sabbath, has turned away from the garden of God's presence. All of humanity's cultural achievements—cities, agriculture, animal husbandry, music, art, and architecture—rather than exhibiting the greatness of the race as the myths held actually represent the accomplishments of humanity apart from God. Consequently, the human race has become divided linguistically, internationally, and culturally, and degraded morally and spiritually. God created the human race for glory as co-rulers with God over creation, but through hubris the race has forfeited much of the glory for which it was created.

Then God began again with one man—Abraham. Since humanity failed in its divine calling, God appointed a representative to fulfill that calling and bring humanity back into the glory for which God created the race. God made a covenant with Abraham to bring from him a great nation and through that nation to bring blessing to the entire world.

Then when the chosen people found themselves enslaved, God began again, with one man—Moses. God shaped the people of Israel by giving them the law as a revelation of God's will for them and for all humanity. In spite of humanity's violence, evil, and rebellion, God offers undeserved grace. The Pentateuch reveals God beginning from nothing—again and again and again.

What about inspiration?
Scripture consists of the final product, not of the individual ancient documents Ezra adapted and merged into our Pentateuch. Ezra transcended the partial insights of the Yahwist, Elohist, Deuteronomist, and Priest in the overarching vision of the Pentateuch as we have it. No longer is God seen as either personal or transcendent, but as both. No longer is God either holy or merciful; for the final revelation shows God as simultaneously holy, merciful, and gracious. On and on we could go in delineating how the final product transcends the limitations of the documents with which Ezra began.

This understanding explains to some extent how inspiration came about, recognizing we do not fully understand the process. God revealed the divine power, faithfulness, and grace to the patriarchs and in the Exodus. This revelation came as historical revelation—God displaying power in and through human events.

God then inspired the Bible's authors to interpret that history as they communed with God inwardly. Inspiration, also, came as historical inspiration—God inspired the biblical authors through normal historical processes working in tandem with their inner communion with God. That means they used the normal means of research and thought any writer uses when composing a literary work.

Furthermore, divine revelation was miraculous in that in communion with God these men grasped a vision of God never before conceived by a human mind. God did not miraculously give these men historical facts not available in their sources; nor did divine revelation preserve them from every factual or even ethical or theological error. The miracle resides in God's enabling them—through normal historical processes—to come to an infinitely higher view of God's nature, will, and ways of working with us than anything their predecessors or contemporaries had ever dreamed.

Revelation and inspiration lay in the understanding of God they received. The biblical authors became intoxicated from drinking deeply of the Spirit of God. They lived, breathed, ate, drank, slept, and acted in God's presence.

As a result, what they wrote emitted an aura of the holy, communicating that holy presence to others. God inspired Ezra to see the glory of the insights his predecessors had received and move beyond them to give to the world a work greater than any of his spiritual forebears had ever conceived.

To be sure, even Ezra did not see all God had to reveal to the world, and even he misunderstood some of what he did see. Ezra miraculously saw truths beyond those grasped even by the authors of his sources. The miracle, however, resides in God's continuing to lead his historians, prophets, and wise men to see ever more profound truths, constantly transcending those who came before them. Yahweh of Israel continued to speak to Israel in word and deed until that divine self-revelation came to a fitting climactic moment in a single human life.

Notes

[1] The traditionally accepted date. See H.G.M. Williamson, *Word Biblical Commentary: Ezra, Nehemiah* (Waco, TX: Word, 1985), xxxix-xl. Other scholars insist 428 BCE or even 398 BCE

[2] Nehemiah 8.

[3] Ezra 7:1-10.

[4] It is not clear to me whether Ezra possessed the book of Deuteronomy from the Deuteronomistic Historian or if that work was added to Ezra's Torah later. Although there are J and E passages in Deuteronomy, there are exceedingly few of them and it is not apparent when they were inserted.

CHAPTER 11

The Hebrew Philosophers
Seeing God's Wisdom in the Commonplace

Simultaneously with the traditionalists, historians, and prophets of Israel and Judah, another group of people thought and wrote: the sages of the wisdom movement. This movement came to maturity only during the Exile (after 586 BCE) and the Return (after 435 BCE). It had begun, however, centuries earlier.

Israel's philosophical movement did not engage in the abstract speculative theorizing for which the Greeks earned fame. Hebrew wise men thought and wrote about practical matters—success in family, farming, business, war, politics, what makes for a happy life, why bad things happen to good people, how to succeed in the royal court, and even romance and sex. Hebrew wisdom literature displayed neither the white-hot passion of the prophets nor the historical concern of the traditions and history movements. As far as we can tell from the books they left behind, they did not engage in controversy with other religions or attempt to defend Yahwism from attack from without.

They quietly occupied themselves with the practical purpose of living as Yahwists in daily affairs. They produced several works that still instruct, fascinate, and sometimes puzzle twenty-first-century readers. Only by understanding something of these men and their writings can we grasp the total range of ancient Hebrew thinking.

Hebrew Wisdom vs. Greek Philosophy

As far as we know, ancient Hebrews never engaged in the form of philosophy so beloved by the Greeks. They did not invent systems of logic, mathematics, metaphysics, or ontology. Ancient Hebrews focused on personal truth and personal knowledge—that is, experienced knowledge and truth. They began with life as they found it—already embedded in a world of things, other people, historical movements, families, communities, and God. They did not attempt to figure it all out theoretically. Like all of Hebrew descent, they related to others and to the material world practically, ethically, and spiritually before Yahweh. The sages of the wisdom movement, though, distinguished themselves by making explicit the tacit Hebrew view of truth.

They approached the world personally—that is, experientially, communally, practically, ethically, religiously, historically, and spiritually. They saw all truth as relational—having to do with our relations to God and to other persons. They thought in life-centered categories rather than theoretical abstractions. Possibly that focus explains why their vision of God has prevailed in Western civilization. They experienced truth rather than rationalized it.

We all know, for example, that for a Hebrew to say a man "knew" his wife meant he had sexual relations with her. The unique Hebrew use of the word "know" did not, though, refer primarily to sex. To the Hebrews, to "know" anyone or anything was personally to experience that person or thing. A craftsman "knew" his tools by using them to make a plow. A farmer "knew" his cattle by using them to plow a field. God "knows" us and we "know" God through mutual personal relationship, not by explaining God theoretically.

Careful examination of the Hebrew words in the Bible for the terms know, knowledge, true, truth, reveal, and revelation shows these words almost always had a relational sense. The Greek words used to translate those words in the Hebrew Scriptures and in writing the Christian Scriptures demonstrate the same use. Hebrews rarely used the words "true" and "truth" in the correspondence sense—corresponding to an empirical state of affairs. When they did, we find that usage almost exclusively when commanding witnesses to speak the truth in courts of law. Even in law courts, though, the witness was to testify to what he had experienced. These words in the Bible always have a personal, experiential, relational, or ethical sense. That usage contrasts with the way Greeks used those words and the way we usually use them today.

How can we explain the psalmist's statement, "Your law is truth" (Ps. 119:142)? We do not usually speak of laws as being "truth." The Hebrews used the concept of truth both differently from and more profoundly than did the Greeks. They learned principles for living, not by abstract Platonism or Aristotelian logic, but by personal experience. They learned wisdom the same way a boy learned to engage in combat, a farmer learned to plow a straight furrow with an ox, or an entrepreneur learned to do business with integrity—by doing it, by personal experience.

Early Hebrew Wisdom

While devout scholars among them labored at recording and interpreting traditions, laws, rituals, history, and prophecy, most Israelites focused their energies on more practical pursuits. Hebrew farmers and homemakers created proverbs on how to succeed at farming and finance. Probably a farmer or a craftsman working in his shop coined this proverb: "Lazy hands make a man poor, but diligent hands bring wealth" (Prov. 10:4). Another proverb probably arose in a small town: "Hatred stirs up dissension, but love covers over all wrongs" (10:12). On and on it went, housewives, government officials, and soldiers creating proverbs to encapsulate wisdom gained painfully by trial and error.

Translated into English, these proverbs sound dull and pedestrian. In their original Hebrew, however, they were short, pithy, energetic, earthy puns and even rhyming plays on words.[1] They scored emotionally. They embedded themselves in the minds of youth and guided their every act for the rest of their lives. At least, they made a person feel guilty if he violated them, for he knew full well that he was acting unwisely. That is, he was acting like a fool—contrary to God's will.

Ancient Hebrews had hundreds, possibly thousands, of proverbial rules for growing a good crop, securing a wife, rearing children, and managing a household. They did not attend schools and universities but went to school in their homes and fields where parents and grandparents taught the young what they needed to know to survive in the graduate school of success and failure. Life rewarded them, not with a degree, but with survival, success, and a happy life. Their penalty for failure lay, not in a failing grade, but in poverty, disgrace, or death.[2] In everything, though, wisdom lay in walking in fellowship with God.

The Hebrew Historian described a woman of Tekoa during the time of David (tenth century BCE) as "a wise woman."[3] Although the historian included this passage in the canonical book of Samuel centuries after David, the original source probably penned the narrative much closer to the time of the event. Obviously, people recognized wisdom in Israel even before Solomon and in women as well as in men. Isaiah 29:14 and Jeremiah 18:18 show that ancient Israel recognized a class of wise men alongside the priest and the prophet.

Solomon and the Hebrew Philosophers

Although not a warrior like his father, Solomon exercised all the political skills David had demonstrated. Not nearly as pious as his father, Solomon's faith took a distinctly practical and self-serving turn. We do not read of Solomon's having a court prophet as David did, nor do we read of Solomon's writing passionate spiritual poetry or loving Yahweh with all his heart.

In fact, Solomon was something of an accommodationist in relation to other religions. He built for his many foreign wives temples to their gods and accompanied them to their idolatrous worship. He contracted with the Phoenician King Hiram, a Baal worshiper, to build nothing less than the Temple to Yahweh in Jerusalem. Furthermore, he allowed Hiram to model the Temple on pagan Baalistic Canaanite temples. We can hardly see him as a fierce opponent of Baalism like Elijah or the preaching prophets.

Solomon's piety turned in a cooler, more practical direction. He did not abandon the worship of Yahweh, but he did adopt something of a "health, wealth, and prosperity" spirituality. In his opinion that religion is best that succeeds most. Religious but not particularly passionate about it, his passion ran more toward wealth, power, and—above all—women.

At that time the Egyptian wisdom movement was in its heyday, and Solomon followed that same path. In his eyes the religious ecstasy of his father belonged to the past. The future belonged to cool dispassionate wisdom that alone could build a nation, a standing army with chariot cavalry, and a string of walled fortresses guarding his kingdom. (These biblical claims have been confirmed by archaeology.) All these institutions required vast amounts of wealth and a bureaucracy to administer it. Solomon saw the wave of the future in a new kind of thinking. Probably without consciously thinking about it, he launched the wisdom movement in Israel.

Biblical analysts have concluded that the evidence indicates Solomon did not write much, if anything, that has survived under his name. Someone else almost certainly penned the books popularly attributed to him later, much later. Let's look at those works now.

Song of Solomon
Song of Songs, also called Song of Solomon, could have been written early in the monarchy, 960–870 BCE, although many scholars date it to the postexilic period. This set of love songs possibly arose as early as Solomon's court.[4] In spite of the widely popular view, though, a careful reading of this collection of love poems makes it difficult to imagine Solomon as its author.

Most current interpreters agree the book addresses erotic, romantic love, probably within marriage. I see the book as a collection of songs on romantic love, possibly intended to be sung in a marriage ceremony. One thing remains certain, however: the Hebrew approach to wisdom included the romantic relationship between a man and a woman—including sex.

The Book of Proverbs

The historian who wrote Kings waxed eloquent over Solomon's wisdom and erudition. He said Solomon uttered three thousand proverbs;[5] composed songs; and spoke of agriculture, forestry, and various sorts of animal life. Possibly Solomon's collecting of proverbs accounted for much of his vaunted wisdom. Long after Solomon's death, an anonymous author incorporated many of the proverbs of his collection into the book of Proverbs. These proverbs epitomized the Hebrew philosophy—practical, ethical, spiritual, and relational.

Although the title attached to the book of Proverbs reads "The proverbs of Solomon the son of David, king of Israel" (1:1), we can be certain Solomon did not write the book as it stands.[6] The book we have consists of two Solomonic collections of proverbs, four other collections of proverbs, and the Noble Wife acrostic poem.[7]

Someone, no doubt the final editor of the work, wrote an introduction to the entire book (chs. 1–9) sometime long after Hezekiah. Whoever that final editor-author was, he can be recognized as one of the finest writers and theologians ever to come out of ancient Israel. We will return to his vision of truth later, for he gave us concepts critically important for our own way of thinking.

Many devout believers have thought that the proverbs of the biblical book are divine promises whose outcome God guarantees. That is a mistake. Proverbs are not promises; they are statements of generally valid practical truth. For instance, one proverb reads "He who works his land will have abundant food, but the one who chases fantasies will have his fill of poverty" (28:19).

We should not see this proverb as a divine promise that no one who works hard will ever have poverty or that all playboys will. Instead, this proverb states a general truth that prevails more often than not. Proverbs amount to general rules about how things normally work, not God's absolute promise of blessing for righteous conduct or punishment for the unrighteous. General rules always have many notable exceptions.

Ecclesiastes

Neither did Solomon write the late composition Ecclesiastes, even though its title reads, "The words of the Preacher, the son of David king in Jerusalem." Although Solomon is the star and putative speaker in this little book, many of its lines are impossible to imagine coming from the pen of Solomon himself. In chapter 4 the author bemoans "oppression" that he sees rampant in the land; but Solomon had the power to stop the oppression. If Solomon wrote this work, why not simply right the injustice rather than wring his hands like a helpless peasant?

In 10:5-7 the author writes of fools and slaves occupying positions princes should hold. If this is Solomon writing, why did he not simply correct the situation by fiat rather than moan like a dove pining over injustice in the world? Solomon did not write this work, but its author placed its words in his mouth for dramatic effect. The author was not perpetrating a fraud but skillfully put his ideas into the voice of the man who most exhibited the vanity of riches, power, and earthly wisdom.

It is no doubt significant that the title is careful not to actually name Solomon as its author. Some anonymous wisdom teacher wrote Ecclesiastes well into the return from exile, probably about 200 BCE. Although neither Solomon nor a noble in his court wrote Ecclesiastes, it does belong to the wisdom movement Solomon helped to set in motion.

We find difficulty in interpreting Ecclesiastes for a number of reasons, not the least of which is that it appears to have originally had a different form from the book we have. The book of Qoheleth (the Preacher, its Hebrew name) teaches that every success in life seems empty. Only worship of and obedience toward God can bring meaning to life, for God will judge every deed.[8] We find the whole meaning of life in a faithful relationship with God; for no amount of material, educational, or political success has any lasting meaning. This assertion may not have concluded the original edition of the work, but that is how it ends now; that is what its final editor-author meant and what the book means for us.

Job

We have no idea who wrote the book of Job or when. Different dates have been suggested, all with essentially no objective justification. Its author and date, though, do not really matter. It is sufficient that we have it as it is, a magnificent poetic dramatic fiction of a man suffering unjustly and struggling with his experience in the light of his faith.

In the end, like Habakkuk, Job does not receive a philosophical answer to his agonizing question, Why? He only learns that he must trust God even when he does not understand. On the way to that realization, he and his friends exquisitely explore the subject of undeserved suffering, instructing generations and inspiring novelists and dramatists ever since. In the final analysis the work offers a relational solution to the problem of suffering:

relationship with God. That solution always constitutes the bottom line for Hebrew philosophy, as for all biblical thinking.

Some take offense at calling Ecclesiastes and Job works of fiction. Why? We have no problem in recognizing the parables of Jesus as works of fiction, and we love them supremely. How are these books any different? If we are ever to understand the biblical message, we will have to abandon childish notions and adopt a sophisticated grasp of literary genre, the methods of the biblical authors, and divine inspiration. "Taking it all literally" simply will not work.

The Hebrew Wisdom Movement	
900s BCE	Solomon collects popular proverbs
900s–400s BCE	Song of Solomon
900s–300s BCE	Wisdom Psalms: 1, 32, 34, and 49, for instance
600s–100s BCE	Job
400s BCE	Proverbs
200s BCE	Ecclesiastes

The Introduction to the Book of Proverbs

The introduction to the book of Proverbs represents the high point of Hebrew philosophy. The most important part of the book as it stands came from the pen of its final author. Biblical analysts estimate that the book in its final form dates to about 400 BCE. The final author penned the first nine chapters of the book as an introduction to the collection.

The book appears to have been written by a father from the Hebrew nobility to prepare his son for success in life. Possibly the son was destined for government service. Certainly, much of the first nine chapters seems to assume that situation. Seen in that way, the book of Proverbs can be understood as the Bible's handbook for success.

Throughout the first nine chapters the author spotlights two women: the Woman Wisdom[9]—the personification of God's wisdom—and her counterpoint, the Adulterous Woman.[10] Balancing his negative emphasis on the Adulterous Woman, this father also warns his son about violent men,[11] showing he was not the misogynist so many have thought.

The Woman Wisdom and the Adulterous Woman become the motifs the father uses in attempting to teach his son how to live righteously and successfully. The father urges his son to avoid associating himself with the Adulterous Woman, the personification of immoral women. Instead, the son should pursue an intimate relationship with the Woman Wisdom, the personification of God's own mind. Note that his personification of the mind of God is female—no misogyny or sexism here! By avoiding immoral attachments and living under the guidance of God's wisdom, the man of God can achieve true success.

For this ancient wise man, God's wisdom was the vital expression of the mind and will of God. This Hebrew philosopher pondered on the Woman Wisdom until he elevated her to a status never before conceived, so far as we know, and made her the star of his introduction to Solomon's proverbs.

The Daughter of God

In Proverbs 8 Woman Wisdom says, "The LORD brought me forth as the first of his works, before his deeds of old" (v. 22 NIV). Many interpreters hold that "brought me forth" should be translated here as "acquired me" or "created me." The context, however, seems to demand "brought me forth"[12]—that is, gave me birth—for Wisdom goes on to say, "I was appointed from eternity, from the beginning, before the world began." Then she says clearly, "When there were no oceans, I was given birth, . . . before the hills, I was given birth, before he made the earth or its fields or any of the dust of the world" (vv. 23-26). Proverbs presents the Woman Wisdom as (1) a woman who was (2) brought forth or given birth (3) by God (4) eternally. Thus, she is the eternal Daughter of God.[13]

Furthermore, verses 27-31 say she witnessed the creation of the heavens, the seas, and mankind, rejoicing and playing in the presence of God. Proverbs 3:19-20 goes even further than 8:27-31: "By wisdom the Lord laid the earth's foundations, by understanding he set the heavens in place; by his knowledge the deeps were divided, and clouds let drop the dew."

With these words, this author provided an interpretation of the priestly account of creation in Genesis 1. He says that when God spoke the word of creation, that word was not simply a sound in the air; it was God's own mind expressing God's will to bring forth the cosmos. This author personifies the mind and will of God in such a way as to make this creative word of God a personal word.

Furthermore, combining these passages with other Woman Wisdom passages in the first nine chapters we see that this sublime theologian was saying that God's mind is revealed in the fabric of the universe. To go even farther, he was telling us that when we act wisely, we are acting in tune with the mind of our creator. These concepts hold tremendous promise for our thinking about the nature of God, creation, ethics, wisdom, and even the laws of science. Rarely in history has a theologian come up with a more fruitful concept of God, creation, and the cosmic reality we all experience.

With these passages, Israel's philosophical movement reached its highest point of theology. The movement that began inconspicuously among the common folk, that gained informal recognition with Solomon's collecting traditional proverbs, had now come to its full flowering at the hand of a profound and passionate theologian—and we have no idea who he was!

The "word" by which God created the heavens and the earth in the priestly account has now become God's wisdom, the Daughter of God, through whom everything that exists came into being. The author of the final edition of the book of Proverbs has fallen completely in love with the Daughter of God and made her the star of his book on how to live as God created us to live.

The parallel between the Hebrew concept of wisdom in these Woman Wisdom passages and the Greek divine *logos* concept is startling. What is most amazing, however, is that this Hebrew wisdom author coined the concept of God's eternal wisdom a century before the Stoic Zeno of Citium developed his idea of the divine *logos* (reason) embodied in the cosmos. A century before Zeno, the final author of Proverbs had already pictured the rational principle behind the cosmos as the personal expression of the mind of God. A word of warning, however: these concepts are all poetic imagery, not metaphysical ontology.

Several centuries later the Woman Wisdom will assume a much more important role in light of the statements in Proverbs 3:19-20 and 8:12-31.[14]

Notes

[1] To gain a sense of how Hebrew proverbs felt in the original language, see Roland E. Murphy, *Word Biblical Commentary: Proverbs* (Nashville: Thomas Nelson, 1998). Even Murphy's translation, however, cannot capture the subtle plays on words, even puns, in the original Hebrew.

[2] Charles Fritsch, "Introduction to the Book of Proverbs," in vol. 4, *Interpreter's Bible* (Nashville: Abingdon, 1955).

[3] 2 Sam. 14:1-20.

[4] Duane A. Garrett and Paul A. House, *Word Biblical Commentary: Song of Songs and Lamentations* (Nashville: Thomas Nelson, 2004), 25.

[5] 1 Kgs. 4:32.

⁶Prov. 25:1 proves that the book was still being worked on 300 years after Solomon. In this regard compare also 22:17, 24:23, 30:1, and 31:1.

⁷Prov. 10:2–22:16, 25:1–29:27, 22:17–24:22, 24:23-34, 30:1-22, 21:1-9, 31:10-31.

⁸Eccl. 12:1, 13-14.

⁹Prov. 1:20-33; 3:13-20; 4:5-9; 7:4-5; 8:1-11, 12-36.

¹⁰Prov. 2:16-19, 5:3-14, 5:20, 6:24-29, 7:6-27, 9:13-18.

¹¹Prov. 1:10-19, 2:12-15, 3:29-35, 4:14-17, 6:12-15.

¹²Leonard J. Coppes, "qanah," in vol. 2, *Theological Wordbook of the Old Testament*, R. Laird Harris et al, eds. (Chicago: Moody Publishers, 2003), 804, agrees with this line of thought.

¹³Murphy, *Proverbs*, 52-53, takes this line of interpretation.

¹⁴John 1:1-14; 1 Cor. 1:24, 30; Col. 2:3.

CHAPTER 12

Into the Wilderness Again

Completing the Hebrew Scriptures— and Then Crisis

In Babylon the Hebrew survivors of the destruction of Jerusalem descended into a morass of depression. Everything familiar had been taken from them: No more green hills of Judea or temple glistening with marble white and golden sheen on the crest of Mt. Zion. Only a painful memory remained of royal pomp and panoply on special occasions celebrating the eternal rule of the Davidic family on behalf of Yahweh. Gone the temple worship to the majestic music of the massive choir and orchestra. No more engaging in God-talk over a cup of wine with friends in a downtown Jerusalem cafe. No more glittering future for their children, old age sitting beneath a fig tree, or plans for a new wing on their home or for a new country villa.

The Hebrew survivors struggled to adapt to their foreign land with its strange pagan customs, manner of dress, blasphemous gods, and obscene royal display. Yet, the exiled Jews discovered that something of their reputation had preceded them: their fame for captivating music. Their Babylonian "hosts" insisted they sing their vaunted Jewish music, perhaps to dance for them a joyful celebration step spontaneously choreographed on the spot. The exiles, however, were mired deep in depression.

One of them wrote a dirge expressing his agony: "By the rivers of Babylon we sat and wept when we remembered Zion. There on the poplars we hung our harps, for there our captors asked us for songs, our tormentors demanded songs of joy; they said, 'Sing us one of the songs of Zion!' How can we sing the songs of the Lord while in a foreign land?" (Ps. 137:1). This anguished psalmist concluded his dirge by intoning a shocking execration: "O Daughter of Babylon, doomed to destruction, happy is he who repays you for what you have done to us—he who seizes your infants and dashes them against the rocks" (v. 8).

These demoralized ex-pats struggled for a while in the quicksand of depression before they began to recapture the songs of David and the raucous hymns of their former temple worship. Still, recovery would come in a remarkably short period of time. The exiles built homes, learned the local languages, opened shops, practiced their crafts, began new businesses, entered government service, and tried to make themselves at home in their new surroundings.

The priests and intellectuals studied, thought, and talked to one another. Mostly, they asked questions about what had happened:

- Had Yahweh abandoned the people brought out of Egypt by God's own hand?
- Had the gods of Babylon conquered Yahweh of Israel?
- How could they remain true to Yahweh when they could no longer offer sacrifices in the Temple?
- Had God repudiated the promise to David and his dynasty?
- How were they to make sense of their horrible catastrophe?

Everything they had held dear in theology, politics, and worldview had been brought into question. Their very reason for existence was threatened. Deep depression proved their constant companion, like a dark enemy threatening to drag them into the depths of the Babylonian swamps.

Unfortunately, we know little of this period for certain. What we think we know scholars have surmised, mainly by meticulous examination of the literary works that survive as Hebrew Scripture. The literate exiles concerned themselves more with preserving the records of God's work among Israel in Egypt and Canaan than in preserving the records of their own struggles. Consequently, we have to read between the lines and guess at what went on during these years across which time has pulled an ornate oriental brocade curtain.

The heirs to the literature of Israel continued to pour over old records and complete the Scriptures of their people. Ezra or some other priest before him finished the Torah. Historians continued to work updating the national history. Loving disciples collected and wrote out the messages of the eighth- and seventh-century prophets. Heirs of the wisdom thinkers edited and completed their best works. Within a few decades the various springs gushed forth once more, producing multiple branches and creeks, filling a river flowing from these tributary streams.

In many ways these were glorious years. Somehow, even without most of the greatest names in Hebrew literature and spirituality still among them, this beaten people pulled off the most stupendous accomplishment any community in exile has ever produced. During the Exile and the post-exilic period, they compiled the world's most famous and influential collection of Scripture, completed the first comprehensive national history known to humanity, established the enduring identity of an entire people, and matured into the mother religion of the world's three great theistic religions. (Ultimately, both Christianity and Islam flowed from Judaism.)

In 538 BCE Cyrus the Persian conquered the Babylonian empire and ordered that all exiles be allowed to return to their homelands, and a company of Jews geared up to return to Jerusalem. A century later Ezra returned to Jerusalem to lead the struggling returned exiles. Sometime later Nehemiah returned, and he and Ezra worked together in the struggling repatriated community.

Israel was no longer in its heyday of spiritual fervor and excitement. Now these people existed in survival mode. Scholarship replaced flights of inspiration. Meticulous attention to law and ritual superseded the deep personal relationship with Yahweh known and proclaimed by the prophets. Jewish intellectuals devoted themselves to historical and literary research and writing, interpretation of the Scriptures, and detailed argumentation over its meaning and implications.

Still, even during this dark period, several of the greatest authors of the Hebrew Scriptures labored at the task of writing the ancient epic.

Ezekiel

Ezekiel began his preaching just seven years before the Exile, proclaiming his first prophecy in 593 BCE. He pronounced God's judgment on Judah for its idolatry and injustice and prophesied the fall of Jerusalem. Upon Jerusalem's fall and the exile of its leadership, Ezekiel tried to strengthen the exiles in Babylon to remain true to their monotheistic faith in Yahweh. He encouraged them by promising that God would restore them to their land. He continued preaching until 571 BCE, fifteen years after the fall of Jerusalem. He gave the Jews a vision of the restored Temple. His people would maintain this hope for six hundred years, a hope that would come to fruition at the climax of the national epic—yet not as they expected.

Isaiah of Babylon

Isaiah of Babylon (Second Isaiah, Deutero-Isaiah) wrote anonymously during the Exile. His messages became attached to the book of Isaiah as chapters 40–55, probably because he belonged to the "school" of prophecy founded by Isaiah of Jerusalem before the Exile.[1] He almost certainly preached and wrote in Babylon.

Two traits leap out from his messages. First, a radical monotheist, he delighted in casting delicious ridicule on pagan gods and those who bowed down to images their own hands had made. Second, he preached the marvelous Suffering Servant songs.

In Second Isaiah's earlier Suffering Servant passages,[2] the Servant of Yahweh is clearly Israel whom God called to be a light to the nations. This theme continues through Isaiah 49:1-4, but then in 49:5 suddenly the Servant of Yahweh is called "to bring Jacob back to him and gather Israel to himself." Obviously, at this point the Servant of Yahweh is someone different from Israel who will call Israel back to God. Then the Suffering Servant songs continue through 50:1-9 and reach their climax with Isaiah 52:13–53:12, in which Isaiah of Babylon wrote, "For the transgression of my people he was stricken" (53:8).

Isaiah of Babylon proclaimed that God had called Israel to be a light to the nations to call the entire world to fellowship with the God of Israel. Since Israel had failed in that calling, Yahweh would call one from within Israel to fulfill its calling—and to call both the world and Israel back to God.

Isaiah of the Return

We all tend to divide the human race into "us" and "them"—Jews and Gentiles, Greeks and Barbarians, Americans and aliens, Christians and unbelievers. Standing tall, bold, and courageous, two anonymous post-exilic Hebrew prophets proclaimed that God desires fellowship with everyone of all nations, races, and religions. The first of the duo, Third Isaiah (Trito-Isaiah, Isaiah 56–66, which may have been written by several different members of the "school" of Isaiah), wrote sometime after the return. He foresaw the day that "all mankind" would bow down before Yahweh.[3] In these chapters we see the promise that Yahweh will in time bring divine love, mercy, grace, and redemption to all mankind. He also proclaimed, "My house shall be called an house of prayer for all people" (Isa. 56:7).

Jonah

The second Hebrew prophet of God's universal grace ranks among the greatest of the prophetic works. The book of Jonah, however, has been dealt the ultimate insult of having its marvelous missionary parable turned into a fish tale of the man that got away. The historical prophet Jonah ben Amittai[4] appears to have been a fiercely nationalistic prophet who preached in Israel during the reign of Jeroboam II (782–753 BCE). The book that bears his name, however, was almost certainly written during the post-exilic period.

The anonymous author used the historical Jonah's name in his short story because Jonah ben Amittai was the kind of person who fit the role needed for his parable. This prophetic author chose the most nationalistic of prophets for his anti-hero to proclaim a message the historical Jonah would never have preached. Similarly, he chose the most blood-curdlingly cruel people on earth—the Assyrians—as the object of God's mercy and grace.

Many believers take offense at calling the book of Jonah a fictional short story, but the book itself along with history provides overwhelming evidence for its parabolic nature. First, no evidence comes out of the ancient world that the cruel Assyrians ever repented of anything or turned to faith in the God of Israel. Surely such a development would have made the news somewhere, if nowhere else at least in Israel's two accepted histories. The point of the parable, though, shines through precisely because of the unimaginable cruelty of the people featured in the story—God extends his mercy, grace, forgiveness, and salvation even to such evil people as these. Secondly, the plot of the book so clearly tracks along a path parallel to the history of the people of Israel as to make its nature as a parable obvious and certain.

The book proclaims that God called Israel to bear witness to the nations. The nation refused to heed that calling, was swallowed up by the Exile, and was spit back out into its land. The author almost whispered his question that is only implied, never explicitly stated: Will Israel now heed its call to be a witness to the nations or not? The world was not yet ready for such a message of grace. That such a shocking message found its way into the canon provides evidence for the inspiration of Scripture.

The Third Great Hebrew Historian

The first section of the Old Testament to be completed more or less as we have it today was the Hebrew history—Deuteronomy, Joshua, Judges, (1–2) Samuel, and (1–2) Kings. This first section of Hebrew Scriptures was completed by 450 BCE at the latest and probably a century earlier by the second great Hebrew Historian. During the exilic or post-exilic period an anonymous third historian wrote (1–2) Chronicles.

Basing his history on the earlier books of Samuel and Kings, the Chronicler reinterpreted that history in the light of Israel's and Judah's disastrous history. In addition to revising Samuel and Kings in accord with his own viewpoint, he added to that history other materials he had at his disposal.

He explicitly cited the Book of the Kings of Israel,[5] the Records of Samuel the Seer, the Records of Nathan the Prophet, the Records of Gad the Seer,[6] the Prophecy of Ahijah the Shilonite, and the Visions of Iddo the Seer.[7] These ancient works dated from deep in Israel's past, possibly as much as six centuries prior to the Chronicler.

On at least one occasion the Chronicler felt it necessary to correct a grievous error of the Deuteronomistic History. In 2 Samuel 24 Israel's second great historian recorded that God became angry with Israel and "incited" David to take a census of the fighting men in a manner that violated the Mosaic law of Exodus 30:12. Unable to accept the idea that God tempted a man to sin in order to gain an excuse to hurt his people, the Chronicler rewrote that passage. He asserted in 1 Chronicles 21 that "Satan" tempted David to commit this sin. Clearly, he did not consider the work of his predecessor to be infallibly free of error. Who tempted David? God? Or Satan? Both concepts cannot be correct. That one biblical author contradicted and corrected another teaches us much about the nature of divine revelation and inspiration.

Disagreements Among Biblical Authors

The Chronicler's disagreeing with and correcting the Deuteronomistic Historian brings up a point that has run through this work: biblical writers did not always agree with one another. The Bible's authors constituted a collegial group of men over dozens of generations. These men of deep faith respected but did not hesitate to disagree with one another. On occasion they even contradicted another of their group. Let's look at some of those instances of conflict and disagreement that create problems for many believers today.

The Torah

We saw in Chapter 10 how a priest, possibly Ezra, combined the old documents J, E, and P into our present books of Genesis, Exodus, Leviticus, and Numbers. The book of Deuteronomy that had been completed a century earlier was soon added to these first four books of our Bible to produce the Torah. With this development the Jews received the first block of their Scriptures as they stand today.

A couple of knotty problems arose. First of all, did the human race know God as Yahweh from the earliest times as the Yahwist insisted?[8] Or, did the Israelites first learn of God's name "Yahweh" at the burning bush experience

Into the Wilderness Again

of Moses, as the Elohist and Zadokite Priest insisted?[9] The Torah as it stands includes both assertions, but both cannot be correct.

Secondly, did God command Israel to annihilate all the Canaanites—commit genocide—as the Deuteronomist (followed by the Deuteronomistic Historian) claimed?[10] Or did God only command them to drive out the Canaanites or promise personally to drive them out, as the Yahwist, Elohist, and Priest asserted?[11] Both claims can hardly be correct. Even driving a people out of their homeland is problematic, but the point is that one priest of Shiloh and both authors from Jerusalem flatly disagreed with the other Shiloh priest.

Ezra and Malachi

In the book of Ezra we read that Ezra became outraged that the Israelites returned from exile had married non-Israelite women. He ordered such men to divorce their wives and put them and their children away.[12] The prophet Malachi, however, also preaching to the repatriate community of Jews proclaimed in God's name, "'I hate divorce,' says the Lord God of Israel" (Mal. 2:16). He expanded on this assertion by castigating the returned exiles for breaking faith with "the wife of your youth . . . your partner, the wife of your marriage covenant" (v. 14).

The Solution to Our Perplexity

In all these cases we find the way to deal with these difficulties by recognizing the principle of progressive revelation and by forsaking the old doctrine of biblical inerrancy. Sometimes a later writer came to a better understanding of God and corrected what an earlier author had written. Unless we treat seriously the historical process by which these God-intoxicated men wrote the Bible, we will draw seriously flawed interpretations of the Scriptures.

The authors of the Hebrew Scriptures, however, did not spend most of their time disagreeing with one another. Rather, they built on one another's work to kindle the flame of faith in and faithfulness to Yahweh among their people.

Daniel

The book of Daniel, possibly the last book of the Hebrew Scriptures, came to light during the Maccabean revolt against the Seleucid overlords of Judea (about 165 BCE). These events followed the death of Alexander the Great. This work challenged the Jews under the grinding heel of Antiochus IV

Epiphanes to remain true to Yahweh, who would bring them through victoriously. The book of Daniel was the first work of apocalyptic literature to survive and come down to us.

To this point the prophetic view had predominated among the Hebrew people. The prophetic view saw God as working entirely within human events. The apocalyptic view, by contrast, birthed in Israel's most agonizing time, saw history as given over entirely to evil. Eventually God would break into our human experience in a dramatic act of deliverance for his people. In the prophetic view, all history lay under the sovereignty of God. In the apocalyptic view, the present era of history is ruled by evil; only in the coming era will God enter history, destroy the forces of evil reigning at present, and inaugurate his own reign—the Kingdom of God.

These two views of history were not as divergent and contradictory as some have represented. Even the prophetic view looked forward to the coming of the Davidic messiah who would reign over the kingdom of God; and even the apocalyptic view saw God as sovereign over this present evil age. The difference between the two views was more one of emphasis and literary style than of an absolute dichotomy of theology.

Apocalyptic, however, did have several traits that set it aside from the prophetic literature. The prophetic and priestly writings had depicted historical events in strictly "normal" terms, describing the present and past consistently with our own experience. Apocalyptic literature, by contrast, was heavy with revelation through dreams, monsters representing nations and spiritual forces, symbolic numbers, and eventually cosmic signs of stars falling from heaven and the darkening of the sun and moon. Apocalyptic described the same world as the prophetic and priestly narratives but gave history its theological significance through those great symbolic numbers, monsters, and astral events for which it is famous.

One vision in the apocalyptic book of Daniel would have repercussions its author could never have imagined. In the seventh chapter we read:

> In my vision at night I looked, and there before me was one like a son of man, coming with the clouds of heaven. He approached the Ancient of Days and was led into his presence. He was given authority, glory and sovereign power; all peoples, nations and men of every language worshiped him. His dominion is an everlasting dominion that will not pass away, and his kingdom is one that will never be destroyed. (vv. 13-14 KJV)

This passage proclaims that the people of God—personified in its representative, the son of man—will eventually be exalted and vindicated by God before the world and given the Kingdom of God that will last forever.[13] Little could the visionary who wrote these words have imagined how they would find their fulfillment.

Israel's Scriptures Completed

The Jews in exile and return had reversed the course of the great river flowing through and out of Eden that became four tributary rivers.[14] The four tributary streams of Jewish spirituality and literature—traditions, history, prophecy, and wisdom—had become the well-springs of the mighty river of the Hebrew Scriptures:

- The Torah (Law):
  Genesis, Exodus, Leviticus, Numbers, Deuteronomy
- The Prophets:
  The Former Prophets—Joshua, Judges, Samuel, Kings
  The Latter Prophets—Isaiah, Jeremiah, Ezekiel, Hosea, Joel, Amos, Obadiah, Jonah, Micah, Nahum, Habakkuk, Zephaniah, Haggai, Zechariah, Malachi

For several centuries the Law and the Prophets constituted the acknowledged Hebrew Scriptures. The Law and the Prophets plus the Psalms (for some) had become the Hebrew Scriptures by the first century CE. By the end of that century, eleven more books (thirteen as Christians count them) would be universally recognized as Scripture:

- The Writings:
  Ruth, Chronicles, Ezra-Nehemiah, Esther, Job, Psalms, Proverbs, Ecclesiastes, Song of Solomon, Lamentations, Daniel

Although not all the Writings were acknowledged by Jews as Scripture when the first century CE began, all the works that would become the Hebrew Scriptures had been written. When the book of Daniel was completed, the pens of the Hebrew writers of Scripture fell silent. And into this silence, depression descended.

Israel's Wilderness Crisis

In the 1200s BCE the ancestors of the Israelites had come out of slavery in Egypt into their first wilderness crisis. After an entire generation had died in the wilderness, the Israelites had invaded Canaan and founded a new nation there.

Now they had returned to something of a mirror image of their beginnings. They had come out of exile in Babylon to return to their land anew, only to find themselves entering a new wilderness experience and crisis. With the death of Second Zechariah (Deutero-Zechariah, the author of Zechariah 9–14) about 300–280 BCE, the Hebrew prophets fell silent for the next three hundred years. For the next three centuries the Jews would experience a period of drought such as they had not known since the wilderness of Sinai.

With the writing of the book of Daniel about 165 BCE, the pens of their authors of Scripture ceased. For the next century and a half it seemed that God had withdrawn from them. Through a millennium of Israelite existence the Jews had survived the worst life could throw at them: military invasion and defeat, destruction of their two nations along with their institutions and symbols by the Assyrians and Babylonians, humiliation, and exile. They had returned to their homeland only to find themselves foreigners in their own country. Following the exile in Babylon, they knew themselves as aliens before Persian, then Greek, and later Latin-speaking occupying armies who despised their faith and culture. They no longer had a king. The temple leadership, therefore, moved in to fill the vacuum:

- The *Sadducees*, spiritual and possibly genealogical heirs of the house of Zadok, arose as the priests who ran the Second Temple, its sacrifices, and its rituals.
- The *Pharisees* emerged as a group of lay sages and biblical scholars to offer a counter-weight and a competing ideology and theology to that of the Sadducees. Like the Sadducees, however, they committed themselves to sterile legal niceties, technical arguments, and mind-numbing laws.
- The *scribes* became prominent as copiers of the sacred texts, whose occupation daily turned them into experts in the details of the law.
- The *Essenes*, seeing society as hopelessly evil, withdrew into a semi-monastic order in the desert as they attempted to become the purified people of God.

Into the Wilderness Again

The Jews labored under the heat of the blazing sun of foreign rulers—Persians, Greeks, and Romans. Under the Greek Hasmoneans they resisted and survived the depredations of the successors of Alexander the Great. Eventually they learned to keep their heads down and just try to survive the oppressive atmosphere of their high priestly family. The heavy weight of their own laws restricted every detail of daily life. Bitter struggle for survival characterized their lives. Their golden age under David and Solomon lay in the distant past, only a dim memory preserved in the records of their scriptures.

The defeated, however, frequently find something liberating about being beaten down so low that they can only look upward. Before they could ascend higher, though, something monumental would have to happen. Someday the Messiah would come, and all would be well once more. This Son of David would put down the hated Romans and restore Israel to its rightful dominant place in the world it had known under the Davidic dynasty. The Jews could feel it in their bones. They attended temple and synagogue services. They paid their burdensome taxes to Rome. They prayed and hoped; and well they might, for the stage was now set for something really big!

Somehow, during the Exile and Return, even through their unimaginably deep grief and depression, the Jews kept singing their song composed by the pastoral nomad Abraham. They managed to combine the simple pastoral flute melodies of Creation and the patriarchs with the full orchestrations and choral arrangements of the Deuteronomistic History. Sometimes their song came out as the drum-and-bugle corps signals of the great writing prophets or the gentle strings of the wisdom literature. The resulting epic Concerto of Zion captivated many who heard it.

Yet, it remained incomplete—its climax and resolution still uncomposed. Spiritually sensitive souls among them recognized that terrible truth, for example:

- Jeremiah and Ezekiel prophesying from Jerusalem and Second Isaiah prophesying from Babylon had promised Israel's forgiveness by God and return from exile.[15]
- Jeremiah had promised a new covenant between Yahweh and Israel in which God's law would be written on the hearts of God's people.[16]
- Ezekiel during the Exile and Zechariah among the returned Jews in Jerusalem had promised that along with Israel's return from exile would come the Messiah,[17] the Kingdom of God, and the Messiah's rebuilding of the Temple.[18]

- The successors to Isaiah of Jerusalem along with Ezekiel, Zechariah, and Malachi had promised that one day Yahweh would return to Zion.[19]
- Third Isaiah and Zechariah had foreseen the day when all the nations of the world would turn in faith to the God of Israel.[20]
- The book of Daniel, written during the dark days of Antiochus IV, had foreseen the day when the faith of the people of God would be vindicated when God restored the kingdom to their representative leader, the son of man.[21]

All these promises, however, stuck like sawdust in their mouths—hauntingly seductive yet unfulfilled.

To all appearances, God had withdrawn from his people. Their prophets, historians, wise men, and poets had ceased writing works they recognized as Scripture for the past 150 years. The fulfillment of the divine promises refused to come. Heaven seemed like brass, rejecting their prayers for deliverance. Israel had entered a historic crisis of faith—in God, in the promises to their forefathers, and in the future of their people. Still, most of them persisted in blind faith. Blind faith may have its deficits, but for a people in crisis, it will do.

Notes

[1] A "school" of disciples is mentioned in Isa. 8:16.
[2] Isa. 41:8-10; 42:1-7; 42:18–43:13; 44:1-5, 21-23; 45:4*a*.
[3] Isa. 66:23.
[4] 2 Kgs. 14:25.
[5] 1 Chron. 9:1.
[6] 1 Chron. 29:29.
[7] 2 Chron. 9:29.
[8] Gen. 4:26b (J).
[9] Exod. 3:13-15 (E), 6:2-3 (P).
[10] Deut. 20:10-18 (D); Deut. 2:31-37; 3:1-17; 7:16, 23-26 (Deuteronomistic Historian).
[11] Exod. 23:27-33, 33:2 (E); Exod. 34:11-16 and Josh. 23:1-13 (J); Num. 33:50-56 (P).
[12] Ezra 9–10; especially 10:2-4, 7-8, 44 fn z of NIV.
[13] Dan. 7:18.
[14] Gen. 2:10-14.
[15] Jer. 29:10; Ezek. 36:8-38; Isa. 40:3-11, 45:13, 48:20, 49:22-26, 51:11, 52:11-12, 61:16.
[16] Jer. 31:31-34.
[17] Ezek. 34:23-31, 37:1-28; Zech. 9:9.
[18] Ezekiel 40–47, Zech. 1:16.
[19] Isa. 40:9-11; 52:7-10; 60:13, 19-22; Ezek. 48:35; Zech. 3:11, 8:3; Mal. 3:1.
[20] Isa. 56:6-8, 60:1-12; Zech. 8:22, 14:9.
[21] Dan. 7:13-17.

PART II

Climax and Denouement

A thousand years after Israel's traditionalists, historians, prophets, and sages began their monumental religious and literary labors, the Jewish people were 150 years into the crisis of that epic undertaking. As great as were the Hebrew Scriptures, those divinely inspired works made promises that had never been fulfilled. Since those works were finished a century and a half before, the heavens had remained silent. God had withdrawn his presence from Israel, or so it seemed.

In any great story, though, crisis always promises the climactic conclusion to come. As the first century CE dawned, Israel lay on the eve of the climax of the great epic of the writing of its Scriptures. To tell the truth, however, the climax of three great epics lay just around the corner: the epic of Hebrew history, the epic of divine revelation to Israel, and the epic of the writing of its Scriptures. That last epic, though, is the one that holds our attention in this work. That great climax to three magnificent epics was wrapped up in a single transformative person: Jesus of Nazareth.

Jesus never wrote a word, yet we will not be mistaken if we consider him the true author of the climax to the literary saga of the writing of the Bible. After all, he lived the transformative life that changed history. He was the one from whose birth year (approximately) we now date all history. His life, death, and resurrection inspired the Gospels of the New Testament, the climax of the literary epic that had begun 1,000 years earlier.

We will tell the story of the climax and denouement of our great saga as follows:

- Chapter 13, "The Climax of the Epic," summarizes briefly the story of the writing of the Gospels, the climax of our epic.
- Chapter 14, "The Radical from Galilee," tells the story of the life and death of Jesus, the subject of the Gospels, as he presented himself to Israel.
- In Chapter 15, "Death of a Radical," we will follow the factors from the preaching of Jesus that led to his crucifixion.

- Chapter 16, "Proclaiming the Impossible," examines the claim of the Gospels that God raised Jesus of Nazareth from the dead following his ignominious death.
- In Chapter 17, "Denouement: Unpacking the Story," we will look briefly at the book of Acts, the Epistles, and the book of Revelation that explain the meaning of Jesus, wrap up many of the loose ends, and look expectantly toward the future and eternity.

The entirety of the New Testament outside the Gospels constitutes the denouement of our epic. The death and resurrected life of Jesus drove the early church of the book of Acts. His teachings, death, resurrection, and expected return controlled the Epistles and the book of Revelation. Without writing a word, Jesus inspired the entirety of the New Testament.

CHAPTER 13

The Climax of the Epic
The Good News of Jesus Christ

The first-century Roman province of Palestine housed a maelstrom of religious fervor, expectancy, radicalism, and anti-Roman unrest. The Jews who lived there represented an ancient civilization that could trace its roots back through documented history one thousand years and through tribal traditions another eight hundred years. They possessed two documented histories of their people from their entry into Canaan through the rise and fall of their monarchy and their exile to Babylon. In addition, they possessed several centuries of the writings of their prophets, wise men, novelists, dramatists, and hymnists.

About 150 years before the first century, however, their prophets, wise men, and hymn writers had fallen silent, leaving the Jews with only the unfulfilled promises of their prophets, psalmists, and apocalypticists. The great epic of the Hebrew people had ended without reaching its climax. The Jews had never experienced the fulfillment of all the promises of the prophets. With the apparent withdrawal of the divine presence, Israel knew itself to be in national crisis.

Now the Jews felt they could wait no longer. Rome stomped them under its heavy boot and taxed them until they could hardly pay their bills. The hated prefect who subjugated his people and land on behalf of Caesar had dared to bring idolatrous Roman icons into the sacred city. He had even seized temple funds designated for sacrifices to Yahweh to refurbish his aqueduct.

Centuries before, the prophets had proclaimed how God was working and would yet work through the ordinary processes of history to establish righteousness, equity, and peace. The prophets had died out three centuries ago, however, and now all the people had was an endless stream of apocalyptic preachers. These preachers had given up on God working through the processes of history to put things right. They proclaimed that now only a direct intervention of God in history—smashing the ordinary historical processes—could suffice for such a tormented time as this.

Into this chaotic world strode a refreshing preacher from the small Galilean town of Nazareth, a man named Yeshua, proclaiming a different kind of message. He was an apocalyptic like so many others, but he merged apocalyptic with prophecy. He contended God was indeed breaking into history in a mighty act of deliverance but through historical processes. He did not advocate the overthrow of Rome like the other apocalyptic leaders who led untold thousands to their deaths. Instead, he told the people that unless they ceased resisting Rome, they would all die and their temple would be destroyed. He implied, though, that all the promises of the prophets, psalmists, and sages were being fulfilled at that very moment, in their presence, in his own person.

The preaching of Jesus of Nazareth eventually led the religious leaders of his people to turn on him and hand him over to the Roman prefect to be crucified on the charge of treason against Caesar. As with the apocalyptic preachers before him, that should have brought finality to the proclamation of his message. But three days after his crucifixion, suddenly his followers were preaching in the streets of Jerusalem that he had been resurrected from the dead and the fulfillment of all the prophetic promises was breaking out in their midst.

The Oral Traditions of the Jesus Movement

We would think that a new religious community rising out of the Jewish people would immediately set about to produce its own distinctive Scriptures, but they did not. The nascent church did not have its own Scriptures for more than a century after its birth.

So how did those of the early church function without a Bible? Actually, they had a Bible—the Hebrew Scriptures of Judaism. They also had the Greek translation of those Scriptures, the Septuagint (LXX). Still, they did not have their own Scriptures conveying their unique story and message.

Instead, they possessed an authoritative oral witness to Jesus: the testimony of the apostles and other eye- and ear-witnesses of the life and preaching of Jesus. Almost immediately upon the crucifixion and resurrection of Jesus—possibly even during his lifetime—devoted followers began to write down beloved sayings of their Lord. Other teachers carefully memorized and passed along to others what they knew of the traditional sayings, deeds, death, and resurrection of the one they believed to be the Messiah. Each congregation had its own combination of oral and/or written recollections of the deeds and teachings of Jesus. These writings, though, were not Scriptures. They were just written versions of the oral traditions concerning Jesus.

The Climax of the Epic

James D.G. Dunn believes we can see in the New Testament a particular office of ministers commissioned to carry out this function of memorizing and teaching others the Jesus tradition. The introduction to Luke's gospel says the remembrances of "those who from the first were eyewitnesses and servants of the word were handed down to us" (1:2). The Greek word translated "handed down" is the verb form of the noun translated "tradition" in Jesus' own teaching.[1] The apostle Paul used the verb form of that same word several times to refer to the apostolic traditions handed down to him that he then passed along to the church at Corinth.[2] Ephesians 4:5 mentions an office of pastors and teachers, which may refer to the same office of "teacher of the Jesus traditions."

Clearly the ancient church possessed a well-defined tradition concerning the life, deeds, teachings, and passion of Jesus long before any of the Gospels or the rest of the New Testament were written. Most of these traditions obviously were oral, but some of them were without doubt written documents. We will encounter three of these documents in the narrative to follow—documents biblical scholars call Q, M, and L.

Many of the New Testament epistles were written before any of the Gospels, but the Gospels tell the story of the climax of the thousand-year-long Hebrew epic. Within three decades of the crucifixion of Jesus, several disciples took in hand to record the oral traditions of the life, teachings, death, and resurrection of their Lord.

Creator of a New Genre

About 67 CE an anonymous Christian in Rome made history by composing a literary work in a genre never before seen. The Gospel According to Mark represents more than a biography. A gospel proclaims a message—good news of a spiritual nature. Nothing like Mark's gospel had ever been written.

This artist composed a truly literary work, telling his story in such a way as to accomplish a purpose conceived before he put pen to papyrus. Not being a native speaker of Greek, he wrote in such crude Greek that later gospel writers felt compelled to improve his grammar. At the same time, he used many sophisticated rhetorical devices—foreshadowing, repetition, balanced placement of key events, inductive presentation of his message, phrasing that creates an emotional response, surprise, and even shock, among others.

Who was this theological and artistic genius? The traditional answer for nineteen hundred years has been John Mark, companion of Paul and Barnabas on their first missionary journey. That answer still seems best.

Probably a majority of historical-critical scholars reject Mark's authorship of the oldest Christian gospel, but this tradition has a good pedigree. Eusebius of Caesarea (about 323 CE) quoted a work written by Papias, Bishop of Hierapolis, in about 110–125 CE. Papias quoted an older contemporary he called "John the Elder" who said Mark wrote his gospel based on the preaching of Peter. This report from Papias, though written in the early second century, possibly takes this tradition back to shortly after Mark himself.

Those who would deny that John Mark wrote the gospel have to answer this question: Why would the ancient church have attributed so important a work to a character as obscure as Mark?[3] Were it not for his gospel, we would hardly notice the man in the pages of the New Testament. Many scholars accept Papias' statement that Mark wrote the gospel but think Peter was not the only or even the primary source for his materials.

Still, who wrote the first gospel in history is not nearly as significant as the record he left. Whoever wrote that first gospel set the standard for all future treatments of the life, teaching, and passion of Jesus.

Since "Mark" (whoever he was) was not one of Jesus' original disciples, where did he get his material? Papias said he got his material from Peter. This gospel shows great interest in Peter and was apparently written in Rome around the time of Peter's martyrdom in 64–65 CE. It seems likely, therefore, that the author knew Peter; and the chief apostle was probably one of his sources.

The Epistle of 1 Peter indicates that Mark was with Peter in Rome shortly before the gospel was written.[4] We also know that Mark was associated with both Paul and Barnabas.[5] Furthermore, he was from Jerusalem, where his mother owned a large home.[6] Jerusalem, home of the original church, numbered in its membership all the apostles and earliest disciples of Jesus. Clearly, the John Mark of the New Testament had known many eyewitnesses of the life of Jesus, all of whom could have been among his sources. I suspect Mark wrote his gospel in part from material he received from Peter but also from material he received from many other eyewitnesses to the life of Jesus.

Departing from his practice of not mentioning Paul's aides (except for Barnabas and Silas), Luke mentions John Mark by name six times in Acts.[7] Mark played no great role in the action of Acts or in Paul's recorded ministry, so why keep referring to this otherwise marginal character? Could the evangelist's interest in this obscure associate of Paul's be due to Luke's gratefully highlighting the author of the major source for his own gospel?

Ancient writers always (with one exception) said Mark wrote his gospel in Rome shortly before or after Peter's martyrdom under Nero. This means

Nero's persecution of the church had already begun or was at least impending. Internal evidence indicates Mark wrote his gospel to encourage a people under persecution. He presented the facts of Jesus' life, teachings, and passion from a pastoral concern for a hurting, frightened congregation. He challenged them to endure, knowing that everything they experienced their Lord had already endured.

Mark began his gospel with an implied frontal challenge to the Caesar who at the moment was persecuting God's church: "The beginning of the good news of Jesus Messiah Son of God" (1:1 author's translation).[8] Heralds proclaimed Caesar's coronation or arrival in a town for a visit as "good news." "Messiah" designated the long-awaited Jewish king of God's kingdom. The caesars claimed the title "son of God." Mark presented Jesus' story as the Good News of the arrival of the true King and Son of God, the genuine alternative to the blasphemous false claims of the caesars.

As Papias acknowledged in the early second century, Mark did not present a chronological account of Jesus' life, except for placing his baptism at the beginning and his death and the empty tomb at the end of the story. Otherwise he shaped his sequence of stories and quotations according to theological and pastoral purposes. Still, his narrative shows no evidence of attempting to deceive or sell a fiction. The simplicity of Mark's language and the emotionally reserved way he tells his story argue for honesty, integrity, and seriousness.

Mark displayed his literary skill by ending his gospel with a shocker: the empty tomb. He leaves us hanging—without any resurrection appearances, although Jesus had predicted resurrection appearances, according to Mark's gospel.[9]

Sometime later someone who felt something had been lost from the original gospel added verses 9-20 (KJV)—the "long ending." Most of Mark 16:9-20 is parallel to passages from the other Gospels; but parts are not, leading to the conclusion that these verses draw on other oral traditions current in the second-century church. Someone else also later added a "short ending" that had no resurrection appearances.

Mark's gospel as he wrote it, however, leaves us to draw our own conclusions inductively as to the identity and nature of Jesus based on the evidence he had provided in the previous narrative. The genius of Mark's literary creation is to be seen in the fact that Matthew and Luke both based their gospels on Mark's, even though they clearly had other sources. We owe to this literary and religious genius a great debt for penning the first account of the life of Jesus to survive intact beyond the first century and thereby creating the genre of "gospel."

About fifteen years after "Mark" completed the first gospel in history, a Gentile who read that gospel felt inspired to write a second gospel, presenting Jesus of Nazareth according to his understanding of him.

Evangelist for the Gentile Church

A decade or so after the appearance of the Gospel According to Mark, another believer took it in hand to provide his own written version of the oral and written traditions concerning Jesus current in the church. The early church fathers testified unanimously that Luke, the companion of Paul, authored the gospel that bears his name.

Although most critical scholars reject this identification, many historians accept this report for one simple reason. As in the case of Mark, no one would have created the fiction of the authorship of a major gospel by such an otherwise insignificant character in the early church record. Besides, Luke was a Gentile in a predominantly Jewish church following a Jewish messiah and led by Jewish apostles. The Epistle to the Colossians indicates Luke was a physician who traveled with Paul.[10] Since he used Mark's gospel as his primary source, he wrote at some point subsequent to the publication of that gospel. Most historians date Luke's gospel to the period 70–90 CE, with many insisting on a date around 85 CE.

In addition to Mark's gospel, Luke also had another collection of sayings of Jesus he shared with Matthew. Critical historians call this material "Q" (from the German *Quelle*, meaning "source"). Luke also had access to tradition(s) not used by either Mark or Matthew. We usually call these sources "L." Although both the Q and L materials may have circulated solely as oral traditions, more likely Q was a written document and L possibly represents both oral and written records of traditions.

Luke wrote in much more refined Greek than Mark. Wherever he thought Mark's Greek crude, he corrected it. Wherever he thought Mark's wording less than sufficiently reverent toward Jesus, he improved it. For instance, he removed Jesus' statement that he did not know the time of his return.[11] Wherever he had opportunity to stress Jesus' contact with Gentiles or his acceptance of women and the despised, he did so. His gospel clearly bears his erudite Hellenistic Gentile fingerprints, although researchers have discredited earlier claims that he used distinctively medical terminology.

The Climax of the Epic

Instead of writing his gospel for a community, as the other evangelists did, Luke appears to have written for one particular person—a Gentile Christian named Theophilus (1:3). He probably also envisioned his gospel as eventually having a wider audience of Gentile Christians whom he hoped to encourage and strengthen in their faith in Jesus.

Like Mark, Luke had a particular slant to his gospel. ("Slant" does not mean dishonest, but merely that Luke aimed his story of Jesus at a particular audience.) He wrote in such a way as to highlight his conviction and joy that Jesus had come to save people of all nations, not just Jews. Luke's gospel includes a number of stories not included in any other gospel, stories depicting Jesus' acceptance of Gentiles, women, and otherwise despised people. In many passages, Luke shapes his telling of a story from Mark or a quote from Q to emphasize these same themes. Again, we should not see the stories unique to Luke as created by the evangelist but passed along by him because of his personal situation. (The companion volume to Luke's gospel is the book of Acts, also addressed to Theophilus.)

> **What are we to make of the gospel portraits of Jesus?**
>
> Strict historical studies of the factual accuracy of the gospel portrait of Jesus have produced a generally agreed-upon picture of him. Historical Jesus researchers concur on an understanding of Jesus as a first-century apocalyptic prophet consistent with the portrait painted in the four New Testament gospels.
>
> Even atheists Bart Ehrman (University of North Carolina) and Diarmaid MacCulloch (Oxford University) agree with that general portrait of Jesus. Of course, as atheists they do not affirm Jesus' deity, miracles, or resurrection.[12]
>
> Christian historical Jesus researchers, on the other hand, fill in this broad picture considerably. Three such Christian historical Jesus researchers are Raymond Brown (Union Theological Seminary), James D.G. Dunn (University of Durham, England), and N.T. Wright (St. Mary's College of St. Andrews University, Scotland).
>
> While historical research cannot prove the truth of the Gospels, it does demonstrate that the gospel picture of Jesus is highly likely from a purely historical point of view. This result does not equal proving the truth of the gospel, but it does show that trusting the reliability of the Gospels does not equal credulity.

Re-interpreter of the Hebrew Scriptures

About the same time that Luke's gospel appeared, another written gospel, this time by a distinctly Jewish author, was born. No evidence exists that the apostle Matthew wrote the gospel that bears his name, and few scholars believe he did. "Matthew" (scholars conventionally use the traditional names to refer to each gospel's author) used Mark as the basis for his gospel; and it is inconceivable that an apostle would have used the work of a non-apostle as his model. In addition, an apostle would not have needed to use several different sources as did Matthew. So why did Matthew's name become attached to the first gospel in our New Testament?

Papias wrote that John the Elder from the first century said, "Matthew recorded the oracles in the Hebrew tongue."[13] It appears later generations took Papias to mean Matthew wrote a gospel (as opposed to a collection of sayings), and on that basis they attached his name to our first gospel. Researchers, however, agree the first gospel in our Bibles came to life in Greek, not in an Aramaic original (Papias' Hebrew). Furthermore, the Gospel of Matthew does not consist of merely a collection of sayings (oracles). For these reasons, our first gospel cannot be the oracles collected by Matthew to which Papias referred.

Most critical historians believe Matthew wrote his gospel after 85 CE. Some internal evidence, on the other hand, seems to indicate it was actually written before the destruction of Jerusalem.[14] Any time between 70 CE and 90 CE seems reasonable, but certainly after Mark's gospel achieved some circulation, so most scholars prefer a later date.

Like Luke, Matthew based his gospel on that of Mark. He added to the first gospel material from Q (which he shared with Luke) and M—material used by Matthew but not by the other evangelists. Henry Bettenson ventured the hypothesis that the source Q may be the collection of "oracles" of Jesus written by the apostle Matthew to which Papias referred.[15] In that case, one of Matthew's sources would be none other than an apostle of our Lord; but Bettenson's hypothesis is far from proven.

A plurality of New Testament analysts think Matthew wrote somewhere in Syria. Internal evidence indicates he wrote to a Jewish-Christian congregation near a large Gentile population in a metropolitan city. Antioch fits that bill.

Matthew began with a genealogy of Jesus that differs from Luke's. A popular effort to save the legitimacy of both genealogies holds that Matthew's genealogy is that of Joseph, and Luke's is that of Mary. That could be and fits the natures of the two gospels, but we do not know; and most biblical scholars reject that theory as not fitting the actual words and assertions of the two evangelists.

Matthew also includes some stories surrounding Jesus' infancy and early life not known to either Mark or Luke.[16] In spite of the notorious differences between Matthew's and Luke's birth narratives, Raymond Brown finds several points in common between these independent sets of stories.[17] These points of convergence constitute firm historical justification for certain facts concerning Jesus' origins.

The nine points Luke and Matthew have in common in their otherwise different birth narratives include the following: His mother's name was Mary, and her husband's name was Joseph. Joseph was descended from David; Mary conceived Jesus through the power of the Holy Spirit; and they had not consummated their marriage at the time of Jesus' birth. Jesus was born at Bethlehem during the reign of Herod the Great after Mary and Joseph had come to live together. He was reared at Nazareth. Several of these items we know only from Matthew and Luke. Clearly, the divergent traditions lying behind these two gospels agreed on the most important points of Jesus' origins.

Matthew wrote a highly artistic gospel utilizing many rhetorical devices. Like Luke, Matthew felt free to improve Mark's grammar or to correct wording he felt insufficiently reverent. Still, he kept the statement that even Jesus did not know the time of his return.[18]

Furthermore, Matthew offers a defense of Jesus and his church vis-à-vis the Jewish leadership and establishment. This trait probably reflects the situation of Matthew's church—a body of Jewish-Christians who had been rejected by their people struggling to maintain themselves in a difficult situation. Part of this defense uses an extensive list of Old Testament quotations showing how Jesus fulfilled the Hebrew Scriptures. Matthew does not always appear to cite Old Testament verses as predictions of Jesus, although he sometimes does. He frequently presents Jesus as recapitulating in his own life the history of Israel and fulfilling God's promises to Israel.

Finally, Matthew presents Jesus as radically re-interpreting the Hebrew Scriptures and the rabbinic understandings of them. He describes Jesus as setting aside Old Testament laws (for example, the law of retaliation) for his own commandments (in this case, to forgive) and also forgiving on his own authority without requiring temple sacrifices. Matthew proclaims Jesus as replacing Hebrew scriptural legal demands with God's simple mercy and grace. Matthew thus portrays Jesus as placing himself above Moses and the law and on a par with God. These implied claims shocked and offended the authorities, ultimately leading to Jesus' death.

In his commission to the disciples on the mountain in Galilee, Jesus sent them out to evangelize the nations of the world. Thus, Matthew's gospel ends with the ultimate transcending of the Hebrew Scriptures—God offers grace to the entire world and not just to Israel. Interestingly, the most Gentile of the Gospels (Luke's) and the most Jewish of the Gospels (Matthew's) both agree that Jesus came to save all people of all nations, thus parting with ancient Jewish exclusivity. Evidently this theme derived from the earliest Jesus traditions.

Key Events in First-century Christian History	
27–30 CE	Ministry of Jesus of Nazareth
30 CE	Crucifixion of Jesus
30–33 CE	Oral tradition of passion and resurrection of Jesus formed
30–45 CE	Writing of early narratives and quotations of Jesus
48–60s	Epistles of Paul
64 or 65 CE	Death of Peter
67 CE	Gospel of Mark
75–90 CE	Gospel of Matthew, Gospel of Luke, book of Acts
90–100 CE	Gospel of John; 1, 2, 3 John; Revelation

Theologian of Eternal Life

Shortly after Luke's and Matthew's gospels, another author penned a series of meditations on the life of Jesus of Nazareth. Even an inexperienced reader of the Gospels can quickly recognize the difference of the Gospel According to John from the other three accounts. This gospel has many prickly problems. No one knows for sure who wrote it. Tradition posits the apostle John as its author. Internal evidence indicates it was at least based on the testimony of "the beloved disciple," whoever he may have been.

Some suggest that the testimony of the apostle John stands behind the fourth gospel, but a disciple or disciples of John actually wrote the book itself after his death based on John's testimony. That theory fits the assertion at John 21:24. It would also explain why the gospel presents a picture of Jesus so different from Matthew, Mark, and Luke. On this theory the authoritative testimony belongs to John, but the gospel itself and its wording and theology belong to a highly literate, artistic, philosophically, and theologically minded Hellenistic student of John. Current scholarship leans toward the view that "the beloved disciple" was a disciple of Jesus but not one of the twelve apostles. I personally favor the view that the beloved disciple was John, but I recognize that viewpoint as considerably less than proven.

John's gospel was probably written at Ephesus between 90 and 100 CE, shortly after the death of the person providing the basic testimony to Jesus. Probably the majority opinion among critical interpreters of the New Testament is that the Gospel of John was written by a member of the "Johannine school" at Ephesus, a group of men who were followers of "the beloved disciple." Other members of this school of thought produced the sermon of 1 John, the Epistles of 2 and 3 John, and the book of Revelation—as a block considered "the Johannine corpus."

How do we explain the obvious differences between the fourth gospel and the other three? I share the view of many interpreters in seeing John's gospel as a series of meditations on the life and person of Jesus Christ. While meditating on actual historical events, the author allows his own theology and terminology to intrude heavily into the narrative, even into his reporting of the words of Jesus.

The author of the fourth gospel was a theologian of the first order. Some Greek philosophers envisioned the world as unified by the *Logos*, literally the Word, but meaning "Reason." The Jews had in the book of Proverbs the concept of the mind of God presented as the Woman Wisdom, the Daughter of God. Like the father of a bride, he grasped the world of Greek philosophy with one hand and the world of Jewish piety with the other and united them in a felicitous marriage, opening his gospel with these beautiful poetic words:

> In the beginning was the Word [*Logos*], and the Word was with God, and the Word was God. . . . Through him all things were made. . . . In him was life, and that life was the light of men. . . . The Word [*Logos*] became flesh and made his dwelling among us. We have seen his glory, the glory of the One and Only, who came from the Father, full of grace and truth. (1:1, 3, 4, 14)

The Logos of the Greek philosophers identified with the Daughter of God of the Hebrew Scriptures had been embodied as the Son of God in Jesus of Nazareth!

Many critics dismiss the fourth gospel as a source of historical knowledge of Jesus because of its heavy overlay of theology. It seems to me that this opinion jumps to a conclusion going far beyond the evidence. Oddly, while many historians dismiss the historical value of the Gospel According to John, they generally accept John's view that Jesus' ministry lasted a little over three years rather than the apparently year and a half of the synoptic Gospels. I see John's gospel as a brilliant theological depiction of Jesus based on genuine historical memories belonging to a different tradition than that of the Synoptics. John used his literary genius and spiritual insight to describe the meaning of Jesus in ways a bare bones description of the raw facts of his story do not grasp.

This brilliant theologian portrayed Jesus as Yahweh, the God of Israel, embodied in a human life. In eight "I am" sayings he presented Jesus as the "I AM" (Yahweh) of the Hebrew Scriptures. He also presented Jesus as the fulfillment of the Jewish Holy Days—Unleavened Bread, Tabernacles, and Passover.[19] John gave us the picture of Jesus as the Good Shepherd and the metaphor of the Vine and the Branches.[20] John gave us the stories of Jesus' nighttime interview with Nicodemus, the woman at the well, and the raising of Lazarus.[21]

Most importantly, John presented the gospel not so much in terms of the Kingdom of God but in terms of eternal life. John desired that his readers come to experience eternal life—God's quality of life—both now and in eternity.

John did what all the gospel writers did: He framed the way he told the Jesus story to make his points. The words are his. His personality and style so intruded into his citation of Jesus' words that we frequently cannot tell where he ends a quote of Jesus and where he begins to comment on what Jesus said. This trait indicates his "quotations" of Jesus were heavily overlaid with his own commentary and meditations.

Still, I see no evidence that John created a fictional life of Jesus. John includes stories also included in the Synoptics, for instance the feeding of the five thousand followed by the scene of Jesus' walking on water.[22] Conversely, Luke cites one saying of Jesus that sounds remarkably as if it were written by John.[23] These convergences convince me that John truly dealt with genuine historical events and sermons from Jesus' life. John was certainly a unique, highly creative artist and theologian. Our understanding of Jesus would be much the poorer without his meditations on Jesus' life.

Notes

[1] Mark 7:5, 8, 9 = Matt. 15:2, 3, 6; Col. 2:8; 2 Thess. 2:15, 3:16.

[2] 1 Cor. 11:2, 23; 15:3.

[3] To reply "because of Papias" simply begs the question. Why did Papias and his teachers attribute this gospel to such an otherwise obscure character?

[4] 1 Pet. 5:13.

[5] Acts 13:5, 13, 36-49. Col. 4:10 says he was related to Barnabas.

[6] Acts 12:12.

[7] Acts 12:12, 25; 13:5, 13; 15:37, 39.

[8] One of the oldest Greek manuscripts, Sinaiticus, does not include the words "Son of God," but the equally ancient Vaticanus does, as do a host of ancient translations and church fathers.

[9] Mark 14:28 and implied in 16:7.

[10] Col. 4:14.

[11] Mark 13:32; cf. Luke 21:32 following which Mark places the statement from Jesus but Luke leaves out entirely.

[12] Bart Ehrman, *Jesus: Apocalyptic Prophet of the New Millennium* (Oxford: Oxford University Press, 1999); Diarmaid MacCulloch, *Christianity: The First Three Thousand Years* (New York: Viking, 2009), 65-111.

[13] Henry Bettenson, ed., *Documents of the Christian Church*, 2nd ed. (London: Oxford, 1963), 38-39.

[14] For instance, when Jesus predicted the destruction of Jerusalem in Matt. 24:15-22, he included the instruction that believers pray their flight from Jerusalem not be in winter. Luke omitted that element of Jesus' instructions (21:20-24); because writing after A.D. 70, he knew Jerusalem was not destroyed in winter. This argument, however, does not persuade most historians to move Matthew back to pre-70. Still, his source material is clearly pre-70.

[15] Bettenson, *Documents of the Christian Church*, 39 fn 2.

[16] See Raymond Brown, *The Birth of the Messiah* (New Haven: Yale University Press, 1999), 36-37, for a discussion of Matthew's birth narratives.

[17] Ibid., 34-35.

[18] Matt. 24:36.

[19] John 6, 7, 19-20 respectively.

[20] John 10 and 15 respectively.

[21] John 3, 4, and 11 respectively.

[22] John 6:1-20; compare Mark 6:30-52.

[23] Luke 10:22.

CHAPTER 14

The Radical from Galilee
Jesus of Nazareth as He Presented Himself

The writing of Hebrew Scriptures ceased a century and a half before the birth of Jesus of Nazareth without even approaching a climax. Most of the prophets' promises had not been fulfilled. No one had attempted to answer the self-contradiction of the God of mercy and love revealed in their history and Scriptures commanding genocide, mutilations, and cruelty in those same Scriptures. The Messiah had not come and rebuilt the Temple. Yahweh had not returned to Zion or written his law on the hearts of his people. The nations of the world had not turned to the God of Israel, and Israel had not been vindicated before the world.

The people of Israel had experienced a crisis of 150 years duration, a crisis created by God's apparent withdrawal from their midst. The climax of the great Hebrew religious epic would come long after the last work of the Hebrew Scriptures recorded the divine self-disclosure. Even then, the climax came in a manner no one would have expected or predicted.

Both Apocalyptic and Prophet

About the year 27 CE an itinerant preacher walked the hills of Galilee preaching a message that captured the attention of his contemporaries. Jesus of Nazareth lived in many ways as a typical first-century Jew. He worshiped in the local synagogues and Jerusalem Temple. He generally observed the Jewish Sabbath, ritual laws, and holy days. He read and discussed the Hebrew Scriptures. He preached an apocalyptic message similar to that of many other charismatic preachers of the time.

At the same time, however, he preached and behaved like no other Jewish contemporary. He sometimes ignored the rules surrounding the Sabbath and daily life. He reinterpreted the Scriptures of his people as no one before him had dared. He was a radical in the purest sense of the word—he struck at the very root of the religious and spiritual life of his people.

Like dozens of other first-century apocalyptic preachers, he preached that God was about to break into human history in a mighty act of deliverance. Jesus, however, merged apocalyptic and prophecy into his own brand of apocalyptic-prophecy. Other apocalyptic preachers believed history had become so evil that God had to smash the entire world order to deliver his people. Jesus proclaimed, like the prophets of old, that God was going to work within the ordinary bounds of history to accomplish his world-changing deliverance. Furthermore, God was already disrupting history through Jesus.[1]

For a time, Jesus followed John the Baptist as a disciple. Then he called his first disciples from those of the leather-garbed, locust-eating prophet of the Jordan Valley. After Herod arrested and imprisoned the Baptizer, Jesus launched out into his own ministry preaching the same message as John—but with a critical difference.

Jesus like John preached, "The kingdom of God is near. Repent and believe the good news" (Mark 1:14; cf. Matt. 3:2). For John, however, the kingdom was near, but not yet here. In addition, for John the nearness of the kingdom served as a warning of coming judgment and a call to mourning. For Jesus, on the other hand, the kingdom was coming, yet already here. Furthermore, the good news of the kingdom gave cause for joy and celebration as well as repentance.

Luke reported that Jesus began his public preaching ministry in the synagogue at Nazareth by reading from Isaiah 61:1-2a, which spoke of the spirit of the Lord resting on his messenger "to preach good news to the poor." Jesus read and commented through the words "to proclaim the year of the Lord's favor," but he stopped before the words "and the day of vengeance of our God."[2] John would have relished that latter phrase, but Jesus found it foreign to his calling and message.

Months later John sent from prison asking if Jesus was the one who was coming or should they look for another. Jesus answered by pointing to his works of healing the blind, lame, lepers, and deaf; raising the dead; and preaching good news to the poor,[3] quoting passages from Isaiah.[4] Each of those passages is preceded or followed by words of judgment and vengeance that Jesus did not quote. Those omitted words were precisely the keynotes of John the Baptist's preaching, highlighting the difference between the mission of John and that of Jesus.

Proclaimer of the God of Love and Grace

Jesus never commented, as far as the record shows, on the violent passages of the Hebrew Scriptures. He did, however, teach how his people should relate to their enemies, who would have included Roman soldiers who ground

> ### The Words of Jesus vs. the Voice of Jesus
>
> Debates have raged recently over whether Jesus actually spoke certain words attributed to him in the Gospels. We have to recognize that we probably have the actual words of Jesus in only four places in Mark (5:41, 7:34, 14:36, 15:34). In these four instances Mark quotes Jesus in the Aramaic that he almost certainly used most of the time among an Aramaic-speaking people. (Matthew, Luke, and John always translated his words into Greek.)
>
> Although Jesus probably knew Greek, most of his sermons and conversation would have been in Aramaic. We possess all his other sermons and sayings only in Greek translations of the original Aramaic by the evangelists or their sources.
>
> Still, we can be sure that in these Greek translations we have the genuine voice of Jesus. To be sure, each evangelist translated the Aramaic words of Jesus in such a way as to underscore the points he wanted to make; but we have no evidence that the evangelists created statements to put back into our Lord's mouth.

them beneath their boots. "I tell you who hear me: Love your enemies, do good to those who hate you, bless those who mistreat you. . . . [A]nd lend to them without expecting to get anything back. Then your reward will be great, and you will be sons of the Most High, because he is kind to the ungrateful and wicked. Be merciful, just as your Father is merciful" (Luke 6:27, 35-36).

The life and teachings of Jesus imply that the Deuteronomist and the Deuteronomistic Historian got it wrong when they said God commanded the genocide of the Canaanites. Jesus taught and embodied the very contradiction of such a claim.

We can see the Spirit of Jesus in the non-canonical story of the woman caught in adultery.[5] The law prescribed stoning as the penalty for adultery. Jesus saved that poor woman's life by shaming her accusers until they crept away. We could say Jesus nullified the law—with love and forgiveness. Or we could say Jesus fulfilled the law—filled it full—by reclaiming one who had violated it, reclaiming her with love and forgiveness in the spirit of that same law.

At a dinner in a Pharisee's home, a woman from the lower classes who did not keep the law meticulously fawned over Jesus. She had the temerity to touch his feet, weep tears on them, and pour perfume on them in a vulgar display of adoration. Jesus shamed the incensed Simon with a parable about debtors generously forgiven of back-breaking debts. Then he said to the woman, "Your sins are forgiven." When some took offense at his doing what only God can do—namely, forgive sins—he spoke to her again: "Your faith has saved you; go in peace" (Luke 7:47-48).

On another occasion Samaritan town folk turned Jesus away from their village. James and John wanted to call down fire from heaven on those blasphemous fools. In contrast with the violence of some Old Testament "saints,"[6] though, Jesus rebuked his disciples for their attitude and humbly moved on to the next town.[7]

A New Authority

When Jesus began preaching, "The people were amazed at his teaching, because he taught them as one who had authority, not as the teachers of the law. . . . [T]hey asked each other, 'What is this? A new teaching—and with authority!'" (Mark 1:22, 27). Jesus not only spoke authoritatively in the way he preached his message, but also in the message he preached. He did not hesitate to insult his learned opponents and their scriptural interpretations:

> Woe to you, teachers of the law and Pharisees, you hypocrites! You give a tenth of your spices—mint, dill and cumin. But you have neglected the more important matters of the law—justice, mercy and faithfulness. . . . You blind guides! You strain out a gnat but swallow a camel. . . . You clean the outside of the cup and dish but inside they are full of greed and self-indulgence. Blind Pharisee! (Matt. 23:23-26)

Most shockingly, at times Jesus challenged the Scriptures themselves. In Matthew's Sermon on the Mount, he began by saying he had not come to abolish the Hebrew Scriptures but to fulfill them.[8] The following passage, though, makes it clear that he made this pronouncement precisely because he knew some would think he was abolishing the Hebrew Scriptures. What he said next showed that while he accepted the Hebrew Scriptures, he did not give blind adherence to their every assertion.

Six times in the next few verses Jesus said, "You have heard that it has been said . . . but I say to you . . ." In the first three cases—the laws concerning murder, adultery, and divorce—Jesus re-interpreted and internalized his contemporaries' understanding of those Scriptures. In the next three cases, however, he actually contradicted the Scriptures.

You have heard that it was said, "Eye for eye, and tooth for tooth." But I tell you, "Do not resist an evil person. If someone strikes you on the right cheek, turn to him the other also. And if someone wants to sue you and take your tunic, let him have your cloak as well. If someone forces you to go one mile, go with him two miles. Give to the one who asks you, and do not turn away from the one who wants to borrow from you." (Matt. 5:38-42)

Even allowing for rhetorical hyperbole, Jesus flatly contradicted the eye-for-an-eye command of Deuteronomy 19:21 and other passages. He went on, however, to say: "You have heard that it was said, 'Love your neighbor and hate your enemy.' But I tell you: Love your enemies and pray for those who persecute you, that you may be sons of your Father in heaven. He causes his sun to rise on the evil and the good and sends rain on the righteous and the unrighteous" (Matt.5:43-45).

In the first part of the statement (love your neighbor), he quoted Leviticus 19:18. In the second part of his statement (hate your enemy) he probably had in mind such passages from the Hebrew Scriptures as these: "Do not I hate those who hate you, O Lord, and abhor those who rise up against you? I have nothing but hatred for them; I count them my enemies" (Ps. 139:21-22). "O Daughter of Babylon, doomed to destruction, happy is he who repays you for what you have done to us—he who seizes your infants and dashes them against the rocks" (Ps. 137:8-9).

Jesus did not, however, destroy the prior revelation in the Scriptures. As he insisted before refuting several scriptural passages, he fulfilled it. He filled it full by going to the heart of that revelation and discerning its most profound meaning. He corrected its violent, hate-filled passages by other gracious, redemptive passages from those same Scriptures.

One passage that may have captured his attention lay in the letter Jeremiah wrote to the exiles in Babylon. In that letter to the same exiles who produced the statement glorying in bashing out the brains of Babylonian babies, he gave these instructions: "This is what the Lord Almighty, the God of Israel, says to all those I carried into exile from Jerusalem to Babylon: '. . . seek the peace and prosperity of the city to which I have carried you into exile. Pray to the Lord for it, because if it prospers, you too will prosper'" (Jer. 29:4, 7). Jeremiah flatly contradicted the vengeance-seeking psalmist. Jesus implicitly sided with gracious Jeremiah and rejected the attitude of the bitter psalmist.

On one occasion someone asked Jesus if there was one great commandment to which all the other commands of Scripture could be reduced. He replied, "'Love the Lord your God with all your heart and with all your soul and with all your mind.' This is the first and greatest commandment. And the second is like it: 'Love your neighbor as yourself.' All the Law and the Prophets hang on these two commandments" (Matt. 22:37-40).

Jesus spiritualized the Hebrew Scriptures by rejecting the cruel, hate-filled aspects of some passages and re-interpreting them in terms of their deepest spiritual principles as stated in other passages.

A New Revelation of God

Early in his ministry Jesus healed a lame man at Capernaum and said to him, "Your sins are forgiven." The onlookers were horrified, for only God could forgive sin. Jesus responded to their shocked stares by asking, "Which is easier, to say 'your sins are forgiven' or to say 'arise and walk?'"[9]

Within their cultural context, the crowd knew what he meant: "I can easily say 'your sins are forgiven' and no one can know whether they are or not. If, however, I say 'get up and walk,' everyone will know immediately whether those words are fulfilled. Furthermore, only God can enable a lame man to walk; so if God makes this lame man walk, his walking validates my pronouncement that his sins are forgiven."

Then he said, "Get up and go home"; and the man arose and walked. The onlookers responded, "We have never seen anything like this!" They had just seen a miracle performed by a man who had also claimed God's prerogatives.

Matthew and Luke reported a saying of Jesus that sounds surprisingly like something from John's gospel: "All things have been committed to me by my Father. No one knows the Son except the Father, and no one knows the Father except the Son and those to whom the Son chooses to reveal him" (Matt. 11:27, Luke 10:22). Here Jesus came close to calling himself "Son of God." The temple authorities were correct in one key respect: he had put himself forward as the ultimate revelation of God. Although Jesus never called himself Messiah or Son of God, he regularly spoke and behaved as if he were both.

For the benefit of John the Baptist's disciples, Jesus summarized his ministry by saying: "The blind receive sight, the lame walk, those who have leprosy are cured, the deaf hear, the dead are raised, and the good news is preached to the poor" (Matt. 11:5, Luke 7:21-22).

This response points up a common misconception of the miracles and exorcisms of Jesus. First, in the New Testament, miracle does not mean "an event that violates the laws of nature"—the usual popular definition. Miracle in the New Testament means an event brought about by the power of God that points to God who is working among us. The essence of a miracle resides in its ultimate source and its intended effect on observers. The Gospels never speak of violating a law of nature. That concept belongs to our empirical scientific method, not to the first century and the Bible completed fifteen centuries before the invention of empirical science.

Secondly, exorcism does not necessarily involve disembodied spirits moving malevolently around the earth. First-century people may have conceived of demons and exorcisms that way, but we are not obliged to share that concept. What was the exact nature of Jesus' exorcisms? The New Testament never says, except that they evidenced the power of God to defeat the evil that has invaded human lives. The amazing deeds Jesus performed gave evidence of God's power at work through him, pointing to God's coming into human history to deliver us from moral and ethical evil.

His words did more than point to God, however. They implied so much about himself that in the short space of three years they led inexorably to his death.

Notes

[1] Matt. 11:1-6.

[2] Luke 4:16-19. Whereas Jesus would have been reading from the Hebrew, Luke is clearly quoting from the Septuagint (LXX), and that by memory, for he departs in a couple of minor ways from the LXX. In addition, Luke only quotes the parts of the passage that were relevant for Jesus' points; and either Jesus or Luke inserted a clause from Isa. 58:6 into the middle of the quotation otherwise taken from Isa. 61:1-2. These matters have occasioned great debate as to the factuality of this account, but unnecessarily so, as such variations are fully in keeping with first-century practice, given the difficulty at that time of looking up passages on long scrolls.

[3] Matt. 11:2-6 = Luke 7:18-25.

[4] Isa. 29:18-19, 25:5-6, 61:1.

[5] John 7:53–8:11. This story did not belong to John's original gospel. It occurs in two different locations in manuscripts of John's gospel, in one manuscript of Luke, and with notations in other manuscripts. Still, the early church recognized it as authentic tradition and determined to preserve it. I, therefore, follow their lead in taking it as an authentic story from the life of Jesus.

[6] 1 Sam. 15:33, 18:24-27; 1 Kgs. 18:19, 40.

[7] Luke 9:51-56.

[8] Matt. 5:17.

[9] Mark 2:1-10 = Matt. 9:1-8 = Luke 5:17-26.

CHAPTER 15

Death of a Radical

Jesus' Preaching Leads to His Crucifixion

Jesus struck at the root of everything his contemporaries believed about God, success, and the good life. Most of all, he upended what his people believed about their long-awaited Messiah and the Kingdom of God. As with most radicals, he engendered much opposition and hatred from those who felt threatened by his message and his person. In the end, they killed him.

The Gospels state that Jesus anticipated his execution and deliberately moved toward it. In fact, he contributed to his condemnation by the message he preached. For a time, he only implied his shocking claims and avoided centers of political or religious power. At the end he stopped concealing his claims and avoiding the centers of power. The key to the end of his story lies in his teachings throughout his ministry and his actions at the end.

A New Vision of Messiah

Jesus never claimed for himself the titles Messiah or Son of God, until the night before his death. Throughout his public ministry Jesus regularly spoke of the coming of someone he called "the son of man." The way Jesus used that expression made it difficult to tell whether he spoke of himself or someone else.

As Jesus and his disciples made their way toward Jerusalem for the final climactic events of his life, James and John's mother approached him with a request. She asked Jesus to promise that when he came into his kingdom he would seat her sons in ruling positions on his right and left. The other ten disciples exploded with indignation. Did not all of them deserve to sit at his side in the kingdom? As they argued over which of them was the greater, Jesus made a suggestive comment: "Whoever wants to become great among you must be your servant, and whoever wants to be first must be your slave—just as the son of man did not come to be served, but to serve, and to give his life as a ransom for many" (Mark 10:43-45).

This comment in a highly charged moment tells us precisely what Jesus meant by son of man. First, it tells us he identified the son of man with the Messiah. After all, James and John's mother referred to the messianic "kingdom" in her request. Secondly it tells us the son of man referred to Jesus himself. Thirdly it indicates that Jesus poured all the content of the Suffering Servant of Yahweh into that simple expression "son of man." The words "servant," "give his life," and "many" all come directly from Isaiah 53:10-13.[1] Even the expression "guilt offering" is a rough equivalent of his word ransom.

> Yet, it was the Lord's will to crush him and cause him *to suffer*, and though the Lord makes his life *a guilt offering*, . . . After *the suffering of his soul*, he will see the light of life and be satisfied; by his knowledge my righteous *servant* will justify *many*, and he will bear their iniquities. . . . he *poured out his life* until death and was numbered with the transgressors. For he *bore the sin* of *many* . . . [italics mine]

In this brief comment Jesus merged the scriptural figures of the son of man and Isaiah's Suffering Servant of Yahweh with the Messiah promised by the prophets. Jesus announced that in his vision of Messiah he would not be a conquering general with his garments soaked in the blood of his enemies. He held a vision of Messiah as one who suffers and dies sacrificially for his people.

Where, though, did he get the expression "son of man"? Ezekiel used it to refer to himself, simply meaning "man."[2] Daniel, however, used it to refer to a heavenly "son of man" who would serve as the representative of the people of Israel.[3] Which did Jesus mean? He would make that point explicit only when he faced the Jewish high court the night before his crucifixion.

A New Conception of Atonement

Jesus regularly taught through parables—small fictional vignettes he created to drive home his lessons. In one such story the son of a wealthy farmer leaves home with his portion of the family fortune.[4] (Jesus did not say why the father chose to give the younger son his inheritance before he died.) The wastrel son spends the entire fortune on living the high life. Eventually he finds himself feeding hogs—the ultimate degradation for a Jew. In desperation the son returns to his father, intending to ask for a job as a hired servant. Before the wayward son can complete his appeal for a job, however, his father grabs him in a bear hug, orders a calf killed, and throws a party for him.

Prior to Jesus, like every other people group on earth, Jews dealt with the guilt of sin by offering sacrifices of atonement—a legal concept. Jesus, though, came at the matter of sin and guilt before God in an entirely new way.

In Jesus' conception the father does not wait for the son to pay a price for his rebellion. The father waits only for his son's return, watches for him, runs to greet the returning child, and throws a party to celebrate their reunion. Although only Luke recounted that parable, it states powerfully the epitome of Jesus' theology of the atonement. God forgives, demanding nothing but the return of his wayward child into his arms.

Jesus taught us to approach God as he did. He related to God as his Abba—his own dear Father.[5] (We should not take this emphasis of Jesus as saying God has either gender or sex. We should remember that Gen. 1:27 said that God's image resides in both male and female, thus transcending either gender or sex for God.) Jesus saw salvation and atonement within the concept of family relationships rather than within the framework of law. He saw atonement that way because he related to God that way. Such a radically intimate way of relating to God and speaking about God was bound to stir considerable shock and opposition. And it did.

His Death as Necessity

Apparently, shortly after Peter's statement that Jesus was the Messiah, Jesus gave some of his most misunderstood teaching: "He then began to teach them that the son of man must suffer many things and be rejected by the elders, chief priests and teachers of the law, and that he must be killed and after three days rise again" (Mark 8:31; cf. Matt. 16:21, Luke 9:22). Twice in this one sentence Jesus used the word "must," indicating necessity. What kind of necessity?

Nowhere, however—not in direct statement or parable—did Jesus teach that he or anyone else had to offer God some payment in order to make it possible for God to forgive.

His life and death tell us what he meant by asserting the necessity of his crucifixion. When Jesus combined the Jewish hope for Messiah with Daniel's son of man and Isaiah of Babylon's Suffering Servant, he knew exactly what would happen and repeatedly foretold it. He never once, however, said he must die to "make it possible" for God to forgive.

He "must" die, for two reasons. First, he must die, because he was sent to bear witness to, embody, and bring to humanity the infinite grace of God, even to the point of death. Second, he must die, because that was the nature of his historical situation. In that context, to enter Jerusalem—home base of the temple authorities, where Rome had a palace and temple guard—preaching the message Jesus preached was tantamount to walking into death by crucifixion, the Roman torture reserved for insurrectionists.

As Son of God—the embodiment of God's own character and nature—Jesus' death represented more than the death of a mere martyr for his faith, however. He died as the embodiment of the *Logos* (Mind) of God, giving himself as a sacrificial offering on our behalf to bring us to the Father. Jesus was nothing less than God pursuing us all the way to the Cross. As the fourth evangelist put it the night before the Crucifixion, "[H]e . . . showed them the full extent of his love" (John 13:1).

Mediator Between God and Humanity in Crisis

As Jesus journeyed toward Jerusalem for his last Passover, the evidence indicates he intended a showdown with both the temple authorities and the Roman prefect. As he approached Jerusalem, he sent his disciples to fetch an ass for which he had already arranged and then rode it into Jerusalem in an acted-out allusion to Zechariah 9:9. Without a word, he announced clearly within his Jewish context that he was the long-awaited Messiah.

At the Temple he drove out the money-changers and vendors of sacrificial animals,[6] indignantly proclaiming that the Sadducees had turned the temple God intended to be a "house of prayer for all nations"[7] into a "den of thieves."[8] In so doing, he symbolically asserted his messianic authority to discipline the temple functionaries.

On Thursday night Jesus observed an evening meal with his disciples. Historians disagree as to whether he observed a proper Passover meal. Nevertheless, that meal during the Passover season partook of clear references to Passover; and Jesus intended it as that year's Passover for himself and his disciples. During the meal Jesus presented the bread and wine of the supper as symbols of his body and blood "of the covenant," referring to Jeremiah's promise of a new covenant for Israel written on the heart.[9] His statement that his blood was about to be "poured out for the forgiveness of sins" also referred to Isaiah 53:11-12 and Yahweh's Suffering Servant who would bear the sins of many.

After the meal Jesus and his disciples retired to their camp on the Mount of Olives. There in the Garden of Gethsemane Jesus wrestled with a choice that brought perspiration pouring from his body like water cascading over a fall. He struggled so powerfully that his experience created an expression we still use two thousand years later—"he sweat blood."

His crisis boiled down to one simple question: Would he go through with his calling from his precious Abba? Would he, the embodiment of God's nature and character, pursue his people and the entire human race all the way to a horribly tortured death? His next day and the human race hung in the balance that night as Jesus struggled through his own profound crisis.

Later that same night the temple guard arrested Jesus in his camp in the Garden of Gethsemane. The Sanhedrin sentenced him to death on the charge of blasphemy for claiming to be God. Since they had no authority to pronounce capital punishment, they sent him to Pilate for a legal sentencing on a charge of insurrection for claiming to be Messiah, King of the Jews.

Identity of the Son of Man

On the basis of the varying gospel accounts, researchers debate whether the actual trial of Jesus took place the night before his crucifixion or earlier. Possibly the event on the eve of his crucifixion represented not a formal trial but just a hearing to pronounce a previously decided verdict. Whatever the case—the evangelists have possibly telescoped some of the events for dramatic effect—Mark, Matthew, and Luke agreed on the reasons for Jesus' condemnation.[10]

At his trial or sentencing hearing, when asked if he were the Messiah, Jesus replied: "*I am,* . . . And you will *see the son of man* sitting *at the right hand of the Mighty One* and *coming on the clouds of heaven*" [italics mine]. This passage shows that his term "son of man" derives from Daniel 7:14:

> In my vision at night I looked, and there before me was one like a son of man, coming with the clouds of heaven. He approached the Ancient of Days and was led into his presence. He was given authority, glory and sovereign power; all peoples, nations and men of every language worshiped him. His dominion is an everlasting dominion that will not pass away, and his kingdom is one that will never be destroyed.

The son of man was coming with the clouds of heaven. In Hebrew thought only Yahweh rode on the clouds of heaven. His being worshiped by nations and men of every language again implied deity. His being given authority and an everlasting dominion and a kingdom implied the messianic kingdom. In citing this passage, Jesus made some shockingly bold claims.

His statement to the Sanhedrin also alluded to Psalm 110:1: "The Lord says to my Lord: 'Sit at my right hand until I make your enemies a footstool for your feet.'"

This combination of scriptural allusions shows that his self-designation as son of man constituted a hitherto veiled claim to be both Messiah and Son of God. Not until his trial did he make this implicit claim explicit.

Only a scholar of the Hebrew Scriptures could put together all the pieces of the puzzle Jesus handed the Sanhedrin that night. These scholars instantly connected the dots, convicted him of blasphemy, and had the Romans torture him to death for it.

The Romans used crucifixion almost exclusively for insurrectionists and rebels. If Pilate crucified Jesus, he saw him as a political threat to the Roman government. Why? The Gospels provide a historically credible answer.

Jesus had no army. He mounted no insurrection. He did not preach insurrection. He actually called on his nation to stop resisting Rome.[11] He only threatened Rome, as far as we can see, by implying a claim to be the Davidic messiah—a king. The claim to be the Messiah, however, was not blasphemy for the temple authorities. Jesus' only offense to the Jewish hierarchy lay in his implied claim to deity—to share God's throne. These two implied claims—to deity and to messiahship—gave the temple authorities sufficient reason for his condemnation for blasphemy and then gave the Roman prefect justification to order his crucifixion for treason and insurrection.

The Crucifixion of a Radical Apocalyptic-Prophet

Pilate had Jesus flogged until his back was a mangled mass of bloody tissue. The guards jammed a crown of thorns onto his head and cloaked him in a purple robe, mocking his claim to messiahship. Then they took him out to Golgotha for crucifixion. Ordinarily death by crucifixion took days. Jesus expired in a few hours.[12]

Many messianic pretenders had arisen; but without exception they attempted to establish the kingdom of God in the blood of their enemies. By contrast, Jesus—Son of Man—Messiah—Suffering Servant of Yahweh—Son of God—established his kingdom of God in his own blood.

Now, this most recent claimant to be the Messiah of Israel was dead, and that should have been that. But it was not.

Notes

[1] Jesus quoted Isaiah 53 directly only in Luke 22:37, but here he made an indirect reference to it as he did elsewhere. See also Luke 12:37 and 22:27.

[2] Ezek. 2:1, for example, and many other verses in the book of Ezekiel.

[3] Dan. 7:13-14.

[4] Luke 15:11-32.

[5] Mark 14:36, Rom. 8:15, Gal. 4:6

[6] Mark 11:15-17 = Matt. 21:12-16 = Luke 19:45-47.

[7] Isa. 56:7.

[8] Jer. 7:11.

[9] Jer. 31:31-34. See chapter 8, section on Jeremiah, for a fuller discussion of this passage.

[10] Mark 14:62 = Matt. 26:64. Cf. Luke 22:66-71. John offers a different reason in 11:45-53 following the story of the raising of Lazarus.

[11] Luke 13:1-3 and other passages, such as Matt. 5:9, 39, 41, 44-47.

[12] Mark 15:22-27 = Matt. 27:45-50 = Luke 23:44-46. Cf. John 19:14.

CHAPTER 16

Proclaiming the Impossible
Good News of Jesus' Resurrection

Dozens of apocalyptic prophets and messianic pretenders took to the streets of first-century Galilee and Judea, only to learn what it cost to claim the powers of God without warrant. All of them died, and their movements died along with them. Jesus was the first and only one of many messianic claimants to found a movement that lasted for the next twenty centuries and counting. His was the first messianic movement either to replace or to surpass every other religious or intellectual movement of the era.

Why?

The book of Acts says that fifty days after the crucifixion of Jesus his disciples took to the streets of Jerusalem proclaiming that the crucified Jesus had been resurrected by God from the dead. From that day the ancient church marched through history as a conquering army. For the first three centuries it wielded only the weapon of that incredible proclamation. The good news of the resurrection of Jesus of Nazareth from the dead transformed a failed messiah and his followers into the living Lord of a vibrant church.

For years these stories of the resurrection of Jesus circulated as oral traditions[1] of the apostles and others who were witnesses to those critical events. Shortly, however, disciples of Jesus began to write down those oral traditions. Let's turn now to the oldest written reports of those traditions we possess.

Proclaimers of an Unbelievable Story

The Oldest Tradition of the Resurrection
The oldest record we have of the proclamation of the Resurrection comes in the First Epistle of Paul to the Corinthians written sometime between 54 and 57 CE, twenty-five years or so after the Crucifixion.[2] In that passage Paul specifically asserts that he received this material as tradition, which he had then passed along in his preaching.[3] He gives these key elements of the tradition: Christ died for our sins, he was buried, God raised him from the dead, he was seen by a host of witnesses, and all this occurred in fulfillment

of prophecy. Paul's tradition included appearances of the resurrected Jesus to Peter, the Twelve, five hundred "brethren" at once, James (the brother of Jesus), and belatedly to Paul himself.

This earliest tradition, however, goes back two decades before this letter. In Galatians, Paul reports[4] that he visited Jerusalem about 35–36 CE and talked to Peter and James the brother of Jesus. Certainly, he received their reports of the Resurrection directly from the mouths of these eyewitnesses at that time.

Three years earlier than that, however, Paul would certainly have received instruction in the gospel tradition at Damascus[5] shortly after his conversion. Thus, it seems historically likely that Paul's account of the earliest church tradition of the resurrection of Jesus goes back to within two or three years of the event. Clearly the infant church took off in an amazing growth spurt immediately upon its birth.

The Good News of the Empty Tomb

The earliest gospel account of the Resurrection occurs in Mark 16:1-8. That account famously ends with the empty tomb. (Mark 16:9-20 was added a half century or more later and was not a part of Mark's original book.)

Readers of the Bible have puzzled over why Mark's gospel ended as it did. Internal evidence indicates Mark intended to shock us with his abrupt ending. He did not need to describe the appearances of the resurrected Lord, for his audience already knew those stories. His purpose had been accomplished once he set the passion and resurrection of Jesus in the context of his life.

Much has been made of Mark's statement that the women did not tell anyone of their experience at the empty tomb—as if the women never told it. Yet, Mark knew it! He obviously did not mean that they never reported their experience at the tomb of Jesus. His aesthetic purpose drove the way he told his story. He said the women did not tell anyone, knowing full well that his audience would know the women eventually told someone—or Mark would not know about it, and his readers would not already have heard about it!

Need for proof, though, did not shape the purpose of his gospel narrative. Mark's original readers did not learn the story of Jesus from Mark's gospel. The first generations of Christians did not need the gospels to tell them what had happened in the life of Jesus or to prove he had been resurrected from the dead. Instead they received from the written gospels comfort under persecution, strength to face their opponents, encouragement that the gospel applied to all people—even to outcasts and the downtrodden—and hope for life with their Lord after death.

Still, Mark did hint at one or more resurrection appearances of Jesus. In Mark 14:28 the evangelist reported that Jesus told his disciples at the last supper that after his resurrection he would meet them in Galilee. Then the "young man" at the tomb said, "He is going ahead of you into Galilee. There you will see him, just as he told you" (16:7).

Clearly, by 67 CE or so when Mark wrote the first gospel, early church knowledge concerning the Resurrection had become well established. Mark did not need to rehearse the eye-witness reports again. One issue that will remain in looking at the other resurrection appearance reports has to do with Mark's report that Jesus would appear in Galilee. What about in Jerusalem?

The Good News of a Promise of Jesus Fulfilled

Matthew, writing several years later (ca. 85 CE), based his gospel on Mark's through the empty tomb scene. He picked up on Jesus' prophecy and the promise of the "young man" that Jesus would meet his disciples in Galilee after his resurrection. He interpreted Mark's "young man dressed in a white robe" as an angel. Then his action moved almost directly to Galilee as Jesus prophesied, pausing briefly on the way to mention the appearance to "the women" (earlier identified as Mary Magdalene and "the other Mary") in Jerusalem.[6] The evangelist brings his gospel to its climax with his description of the fulfillment of Jesus' and the angel's promises with an appearance to the disciples on a Galilean mountain top.

Matthew certainly knew of Mark's implication of only Galilean appearances since he based his gospel on Mark's. Equally obviously, Matthew did not consider that his accounts of a Judean appearance to the women contradicted the implication of Mark's account. He certainly made no effort to harmonize the two accounts he used. Matthew's alteration of Mark's original instructs us in Matthew's procedure in handling the traditions that came to his hand. Matthew felt free to alter the wording of his sources while not altering their essential content, but he did not feel it necessary to make every detail in his sources consistent.

This simple observation tells us much about Matthew's method and presumably about that of the other evangelists as well. They all felt free to tell their stories without minute harmonization among the accounts they knew. Further, they wrote with an aesthetic purpose, telling their stories for dramatic and emotional effect.

The Good News of Resurrection and Ascension

About the same time Matthew wrote his gospel, Luke took in hand to pass along the traditions with which he was familiar.[7] He told of Mary Magdalene, Joanna, Mary the mother of James, and "others with them" witnessing the empty tomb.[8] Then he told of the experience of Cleopas and another disciple walking to Emmaus, followed by an appearance to the Eleven in Jerusalem.

Luke's gospel then drove beyond the Resurrection to the climactic moment of the ascension of Jesus from the Mount of Olives near Jerusalem. To focus on the Ascension, Luke placed all his resurrection appearances in Jerusalem on Easter Sunday. Luke's practice underscores the aesthetic nature of the gospel accounts of the resurrection appearances.

In the interests of his purpose—both aesthetics and edification—he omitted Mark's implied Galilean appearances. Clearly, he knew of them since he used Mark's gospel. He also ignored the time gap before the Ascension, which he indicates in his sequel of Acts. The resulting narrative possesses striking aesthetic power, even if we today insist on absolute detailed factual consistency in every assertion in journalism and history. Luke did not let the factual details interfere with his telling of the story, his literary intent, or its emotional impact.

Apparently, he did not consider his narratives inconsistent with Mark's. He had to know that many readers would read both accounts, for he mentions in his introduction that "many" had already written accounts of Jesus' life and ministry. Still, he made no attempt to harmonize his account with others with which he was familiar. This practice shows much about the method and intent of the original gospel authors. In his gospel, Luke telescoped events for impact. In Acts, by contrast, he provided the actual time period, presumably, of six weeks. Thus, he balanced artistry and factuality in the total narrative of his two-volume work.

Good News to a Skeptic

John, parallel to Luke, located all his resurrection appearances in Judea, specifically in Jerusalem.[9] The fourth gospel described the Beloved Disciple's witness to the empty tomb alongside Peter following Mary Magdalene's report. Then he narrated the first appearance of the risen Lord to Mary Magdalene and two appearances to the Eleven. Philip was absent when Jesus first appeared to the Eleven the day of the Resurrection and refused to accept the report of the others. A week later, though, he was present when Jesus appeared again and finally accepted the resurrection of his Lord. John deliberately constructed his resurrection narrative to drive to this climactic conclusion of even the skeptic Thomas' coming to believe.

While we have difficulty correlating the appearances in John with those in the other gospels, this author's story produces a remarkable aesthetic and emotional impact. The Gospels were biographical and historical works only in a fourth order sense. The authors were not conscious of having to live up to twenty-first-century historians' concepts of historical narrative. They were not attempting to provide evidence of the Resurrection, whatever we may choose to do with their accounts. Each gospel writer told the story according to his knowledge and the purposes of his narrative—aesthetic, theological, spiritual, and pastoral.

A Belated Resurrection Story

Sometime after the completion of the fourth gospel, someone added notations describing a Galilean appearance at the Sea of Tiberias.[10] The original author of the gospel or someone closely connected to him added this last chapter of the Gospel of John as we now have it. In this chapter we receive the only report now extant of the experience of Peter, Thomas, Nathanael, James, and John at the Sea of Tiberias (Sea of Galilee). On that occasion Jesus fed these disciples with 153 fish they caught in another last meal with them.

Also on that occasion he led Peter into a confession and granted him forgiveness for his denial of Jesus at his trial. In addition, Jesus commissioned Peter as the primary leader of the apostles. This chapter constitutes a sixth tradition of the resurrection appearances of Jesus, after those accounts by Paul, Mark, Matthew, Luke, and John. But there is at least one more tradition to come.

A Seventh Resurrection Tradition

Biblical scholars recognize universally that the long ending of Mark (16:9-20) does not belong to the original gospel. These verses have usually been attributed to a summary of the resurrection appearances extracted from the other three gospels. Close examination of this passage, however, shows significant difference between this passage and similar resurrection narratives in the other three canonical gospels. Those scholars seem correct who see Mark's long ending as a record of oral tradition independent of the written gospels—a seventh non-canonical source. Significant variations in this narrative at every point indicate it serves as an independent record of oral tradition.[11]

The Long Ending cites appearances to Mary Magdalene, two disciples "walking in the country," and the Eleven. These reports provide multiple attestation to Luke's report of the appearance to the two on the road to Emmaus as well as additional confirmation of the primary appearance to Magdalene and to the Eleven. After an evangelistic missionary commission to his disciples, the Long Ending briefly describes the ascension and enthronement of Jesus "at the right hand of God," providing multiple testimony to Luke's reports of the Ascension in his gospel and in Acts.

Granted, this ending is not evidenced until Tatian's Diatessaron in the late second century. Still, it bears evidence of containing a separate tradition from those in the New Testament.

Examining That Unbelievable Story

Critiquing the Gospel Resurrection Traditions

At this point I step aside from narrative to critique the first-century reports we possess concerning the resurrection of Jesus Christ. In spite of the obvious difficulties of harmonizing the evangelists' resurrection appearances, upon careful examination their points of agreement are even more impressive than their disagreements. Because of the crucial importance of this point we should meticulously count the points of agreement among the evangelists, as we already have of their disagreements.

All four gospel writers—Matthew, Mark, Luke, and John—each of whom had his own sources of tradition, bear independent witness to seven points relating to the Resurrection:

- the lack of expectation of Jesus' resurrection
- the empty tomb
- discovered by Mary Magdalene
- on the first day of the week
- the stone already removed
- the announcement of the Resurrection by someone at the tomb
- appearances of the risen Christ to his disciples (only implied in Mark)

Two gospel writers give us three other points, providing multiple attestation to these items. Both Matthew 28 (presumably the M source) and John 20 (presumably the "beloved disciple") tell of Jesus appearing to Mary Magdalene. Both Luke and John report that Jesus appeared to the Eleven on the Sunday on which Jesus was resurrected. Luke states and John implies that Jesus ascended into heaven.[12]

In sum, the New Testament gospels provide ten points on Jesus' resurrection that are multiply attested by the witnesses to the earliest traditions, in spite of the frequent assertions of how much they disagree. This amount of agreement shows significant consistency among the gospel accounts, rather than the total inconsistency many have alleged.

Furthermore, to use the differences among the Gospels to impugn their plausibility reveals a failure to understand how to evaluate historical evidence. Although scientist Richard Dawkins and others have lampooned this argument, all historians would see agreement within disagreement as an argument in favor of points of agreement in any other historical incident or recent crime. Any historical researcher knows that a difference among documents is not a cause for despair but a call to careful evaluation of the evidence and frequently positive proof of validity. On the other hand, if the evangelists had agreed verbatim, we would be justified in suspecting collusion and therefore harboring doubt precisely because of too much agreement!

The Ancient Church's Confidence in the Resurrection

About 57–58 CE Paul wrote his epistle to the Romans. In Romans 16:7 he probably adds two more witnesses to the risen Lord. Paul names the husband-wife team of Andronicus and Junia as apostles. If this nomenclature carries its usual New Testament meaning, then it implies these individuals were eyewitnesses to resurrection appearances. Furthermore, it provides the astounding instance of a case of a woman apostle!

The whole of the New Testament implies the ascension of Jesus. Within three years of Jesus' crucifixion and more than forty years before Luke wrote, Stephen had a vision of the ascended Lord.[13] Shortly afterward, Paul reported a vision of the ascended Lord.[14] The ascension of Christ was a firm belief of the primitive Christian community as witnessed in several epistles.[15] Within the context of first-century Jewish theology an ascension after death required a prior resurrection.

An evidence of the first-century church's absolute certainty of the factuality of the Resurrection lies in the existence of the New Testament, which is itself a testament to the life of the people who lived out of that certainty.

Christianity's initiatory rite, baptism, celebrates and testifies to the new believer's identification with Jesus in his death and resurrection. The startling transformation of a symbol of death into a symbol of resurrection testifies to the confidence of the early believers.

The Christian rite known variously as Communion, the Lord's Supper, or the Eucharist celebrates Jesus' tortured death by crucifixion. Eucharist, by which many congregations know the rite, comes from the Greek word for thankfulness or gratitude. Early believers gave thanks for Jesus' death, because they knew he had also been resurrected from the dead.

To be sure, following Constantine's "conversion" Christianity spread by the sword as egregiously as did Islam four centuries later. Through the first three centuries, however, the church proliferated through one set of factors alone: the Spirit-filled witness of fervent believers in the resurrected Lord Jesus. Furthermore, if early church traditions are to be believed, every one of the original apostles except for John died a martyr's death, as did many of the early Christians up until Constantine made Christianity a legal religion in 311.

Notes

[1] Witness the testimony of Papias in the early second century: "If ever any man came who had been a follower of the elders, I would enquire about the sayings of the elders; what Andrew said, or Peter, or Philip, or Thomas, or James, or John, or Matthew, or any other of the Lord's disciples; and what Aristion says, and John the Elder, who are disciples of the Lord. For I did not consider that I got so much profit from the contents of books as from the utterances of a living and abiding voice." Henry Bettenson, *Documents of the Christian Church* (Oxford University Press, 1947), 38.

[2] 1 Cor. 15:1-8.

[3] When Paul said in 15:3 "For what I received (*parelabon*) I passed on (*paredoka*)," he was using distinctly traditional language. "Received" in v. 3 is a different form of the same verb as "received" in v. 1 (*parelabete*). Paul used these words in the same way in 1 Cor. 11:23, 25. "Passed on" (*paredoka*) in 15:3 and 11:23 is the verb form of the same word group as the noun translated "tradition" (*paradosis*) when used in a negative sense in Mark 7:3-9 and Col. 2:8. This noun, however, when used in a positive sense is translated "teaching(s)" in 1 Cor. 11:2 and 2 Thess. 2:15 and 3:6 (NIV). Many other passages in the New Testament exhibit this use of these and other word groups to refer to tradition.

[4] Gal. 1:18-19.

[5] Acts 9.

[6] Matthew 28.

[7] Luke 1:1-4. In this passage Luke uses traditional language and specifically states that he is passing along the best traditions of which he is aware. "Handed down" in v. 2 is the same verb (*paredosan*) as Paul used in 1 Cor. 15:3 and from the same word group as the noun translated "tradition" or "teaching" described in Note 3.

[8] Luke 24.

[9] John 20. John's original gospel ended at 20:31, as that verse clearly indicates. Sometime later, either the same author or someone connected to him added chapter 21, not originally a part of the fourth gospel.

[10] John 21.

[11] See, for example, Raymond E. Brown's analysis in *The Gospel According to John XIII-XXI*, The Anchor Reference Bible Library (New York: Doubleday, 1970), 967.

[12] Compare John 20:17 with Luke 24:51. Paul also provides an implied witness to Jesus' ascension in his comments on Jesus' coming *parousia* from heaven in 1 Thess. 1:10 and 4:16. Then the long ending of Mark (16:19) adds a fourth attestation of Jesus' ascension.

[13] Acts 7:56.

[14] Acts 9:3-5.

[15] See 1 Thess. 1:10, 4:16; Eph. 4:8-10; 1 Tim. 3:16, for instance.

CHAPTER 17

Denouement
Unpacking the Story

After a thousand years of divine revelation and literary activity, the story of the writing of the Bible has come to its climax. The story that began with the earliest writing of the traditions of the patriarchs of Israel and the law of Moses finally climaxed more than a thousand years later in the New Testament gospels' report of the life, teachings, crucifixion, and resurrection of Jesus.

The remainder of the New Testament is denouement. Of course, many of the epistles of the New Testament were written before the Gospels. Still, the Gospels present the historical climax of the great Hebrew epic. Without writing a word, we can truly say Jesus wrote the climax of that saga in his preaching, life, death, and resurrection.

The synoptic Gospels (Mark, Matthew, and Luke) describe Jesus as he was experienced and remembered by his contemporaries and their disciples. The Gospel According to John presents a series of meditations on the life of Christ written at the end of the first century after six to seven decades of contemplation on that marvelous life.

Timeline of New Testament Books

Although we do not know the exact dates of the various books of the New Testament, the following approximate dates accepted by many New Testament scholars are accurate enough to guide our understanding.

27 CE	Start of Jesus' preaching ministry
30 CE	Crucifixion of Jesus
32–33 CE	Conversion of Saul of Tarsus (Paul)
47–mid-60s	Epistles of Paul
60–63 CE	Epistles of Peter
Before 62 CE	Epistle of James
67 CE	Gospel of Mark
80s CE	Epistle to the Hebrews
85 CE	Gospel of Matthew, Gospel of Luke, Acts
90s CE	Epistle of Jude
90–100 CE	Gospel of John, Epistles of John
96 CE	Book of Revelation

Even before the authors of the Gospels wrote their narratives, other Christian leaders wrote letters drawing out the implications of Jesus of Nazareth. They developed those implications in terms of church life, ethics, spirituality, and meaning for eternity.

Spiritualizing Atonement

The gospel writers transformed the animal sacrifices of the stalwarts of the Hebrew Scriptures into the personal self-sacrifice of Jesus of Nazareth,[1] the embodiment of the nature and character of God in a human life.[2] They depicted that sacrifice, not as a payment to assuage the anger of God, but rather as the self-giving act of the merciful and gracious God, pursuing his creation all the way to the cross.

Alternatively, these writers depicted Christ as a conquering general defeating the forces of evil and leading his people in triumphal procession over everything that would defeat us.[3] In another metaphor they described believers as having been born anew into the family of God,[4] or alternatively as adopted into God's family.[5] Piling metaphor on top of metaphor, they delighted in painting word pictures to describe God's marvelous work of entering into fellowship with human beings—the objects of radical, inalienable love.

In basing their gospel on eye-witness testimony to the life, teachings, death, and resurrection of their Lord, they demonstrated that biblical faith is not mythological or superstitious but eminently rational, historical, and evidence based. In moving beyond the form of the revelation to its deepest spiritual meaning, the authors of the Gospels implied that there is no conflict between faith and rationality.[6]

Ethical Implications of the Cross

James, the brother of Jesus, known in the Jerusalem Jewish community as James the Just, paid particularly close attention to the ethics of the gospel. He does not appear to have been as concerned for theology as for practicality.[7] He told his flocks to take care of the poor and widows, not to give preference to the rich, to watch their words, and not to slander one another. He warned the wealthy among them to live in consciousness of the coming judgment of God. He concluded his letter by telling believers to bear up steadfastly under persecution and suffering.

Peter, like James, told his congregations in 1 Peter to live as befits disciples of Jesus. Most of his instructions took on a practical slant, for example: submitting to legal authorities, wives and husbands living in faithfulness to one another, and bearing up under suffering for doing good. His one theological concern had to do with the church as the royal priesthood of God. No longer, he taught, did a special priesthood rule ordinary people. From now on the entire church constituted God's royal priesthood, every one of them priests and kings.[8]

Even Paul, particularly given to theology, spent much of his letters instructing the church in ethical matters. In all these cases their instruction flowed not so much from the legal passages of the Hebrew Scriptures (Old Testament for Christians) as from the teachings and example of Jesus. The self-sacrificial cross of Christ served as the template by which they were to mold and measure their lives.[9] Paul's epistles, along with those of James, Peter, and John, taught a radically new ethic of sexual purity, love, forgiveness, and redemptive relationships. In everything, followers of Christ now experienced liberty. "It is for freedom," Paul wrote, "that Christ has set us free" (Gal. 5:1).

The Spiritual Meaning of the Scriptures

We have seen how Jesus spiritualized the Hebrew understandings of messiah, the Kingdom of God, and other ideas of the Hebrew Scriptures. That is, Jesus turned away from the legalisms of rabbinic interpretation of the Scriptures to delve into the deeper spiritual meaning of those texts. The New Testament authors who followed him continued that project, further spiritualizing the teachings of the Hebrew Scriptures. Laying aside their cruder, violent, materialistic, and legalistic aspects, they showed the profound spiritual meaning of those same Scriptures.

The apostle Paul spiritualized the concept of the wrath of God in Romans 1:18-31. There Paul presented God's wrath as the natural outworking of the results of our own rebellion against God rather than foreign invasions and meteorological events.

In the concluding chapters of the Revelation, John spiritualized the last visions of the book of Ezekiel. He transformed them from military and architectural events into spiritual realities. He reached the apex of this spiritualizing process when he said of Ezekiel's rebuilt Jerusalem Temple, "And I saw no temple there; for the Lord God Almighty and the Lamb are the temple thereof" (Rev. 21:22).

Broadening the People of God

Jesus broadened the Jews' sense of calling and expectations based on God's promises. He asserted that his mission was not merely to Israel but ultimately to the whole world. In his letter to the Romans Paul continued to broaden the concept of Israel as the people of God, transforming national Israel into the true Israel of God consisting of all people of faith in God's work in Christ.

The apostle Peter in the opening of 1 Peter broadened the concept of Israel as the chosen people of God in a similar manner. The book of Hebrews continued this tendency, calling Jesus a high priest after the order of Melchizedek—shockingly appropriating to the church a pagan Gentile priest of the Canaanite God Most High. The book of Revelation widened the twelve tribes of Israel until it included believers from every tribe and nation under heaven.[10]

Not being Greek philosophers, neither Jesus nor the authors of the New Testament set out to build a logical propositional system of philosophical theology. They rationalized the divine revelation in the uniquely Hebraic manner of narrative theology.[11]

They portrayed God's call of Israel as not merely a nationalistic prejudice but as truly a call to bless all the nations and peoples on earth. Even more, they preached that this new people of God included the faith-filled and faithful of every nation on earth. They described God's revelation not as a mere myth about actions of the gods in heaven controlling events on earth but as a personal relationship between the Creator and Lord of all who had entered creation to relate to human beings.

Implications of the Gospel for Eternity

The authors of the denouement of this great saga went still further to work out the implications of Jesus' teachings to grasp a vision of eternity. Their spiritual ancestors had developed the creation narratives of the book of Genesis by extrapolating backward from Israel's exodus from Egypt under the guidance of God's Spirit. The New Testament authors proceeded in a mirror image of the process of their forefathers. Reflecting on the history of Jesus, the Spirit enabled them to project those implications forward into eternity.

The New Testament authors did not present these visions of eternity as irrational prognostications like the oracles of Delphi. These prophecies came as rational, spiritual conclusions derived from their own historical context, the ministry of Jesus, and the astounding fact of his resurrection from the dead.

These authors did not provide us with photographic landscapes of hell or a roadmap of heaven any more than their most ancient literary ancestors gave us a video of the moment of creation. They gave us a theology of eternity—a theology of hope—parallel to the Old Testament theologies of creation and history. Using metaphors their contemporaries understood, they provided an eschatology of faith and hope without any pretension to answering all our idle questions.

Jesus' prophecies of the son of man coming on the clouds of heaven reassured them that God would indeed bring the whole of this creation under the lordship of Christ. Using the image and terminology of Caesar's coming to visit a city, they called the Son of God's coming his *parousia* (presence) and its announcement *euangelion* (good news), all three terms borrowed from the emperor cult.[12]

Since Christ had been resurrected from the dead in a glorified body, the New Testament authors were assured that they too would be resurrected in glorified bodies, like his, suitable for eternity in the presence of God. The apostle Paul, however, followed the lead of his Lord by spiritualizing even the resurrection of the body, thus removing it from any crude materialistic conception of mere resuscitation of human corpses.[13]

Their faith in the living God who keeps promises assured them God would not lose the creation whose redemption cost so much in the cross of Jesus. For this reason, they envisioned redeemed humanity spending eternity with God—that is, heaven.

The New Testament writers also recognized that God's self-revelation implied and warned of the possibility of missing that eternal union with the Father. Centuries later the church subsumed all the metaphors of that loss under the rubric of the doctrine of "hell." Neither Jesus nor the New Testament authors, however, explained exactly what form that loss would take. Jesus only said it would be the loss of God's eternal presence—the garbage dump of time and eternity.[14]

The book of Revelation reassured believers suffering persecution under Domitian in the 90s CE that the Roman Empire would not have the last word. The Elder John proclaimed that the true King of Kings and Lord of Lords is not Caesar but Christ. The Revelator ended his book, which fortunately for us became the end of the New Testament, by assuring believers that all Israel's hopes for return to Eden—Paradise—will be fulfilled for all people of faith in God's "new heaven and new earth." The river that originally flowed "out of Eden" to water all the nations of the earth would flow eternally from beneath the throne of God, lined on either side with the Tree of Life. The water of that river and the fruit of that tree would nourish God's people, the New Jerusalem, for eternity. Thus, as in God's providence the books of the Bible came to be assembled as they were by the early church, the last two chapters of that great epic exactly mirrored the first two chapters.

Notes

[1] Rom. 3:25; Heb. 1:3, 2:9; 1 Pet. 1:2; 1 John 2:2; Rev. 5:5-6.

[2] John 1:1, 14, 18; Col. 1:15, 25; 2:9; Heb. 1:1-3.

[3] 2 Cor. 2:14, Eph. 4:8, Col. 2:15.

[4] John 3:3-7; 1 Pet. 1:23; 1 John 4:7, 5:1.

[5] Eph. 1:5, Rom. 8:14-15 (in the Greek).

[6] Luke 1:1-4 specifically states that the fourth evangelist based his gospel on eyewitness testimony to a historical event. First John 1:1-4 also clearly appeals to eyewitness testimony. Again, 2 Pet. 1:16-18 appeals to eyewitness testimony, whether the apostle Peter actually wrote this epistle or not.

[7] The Epistle of James.

[8] 1 Pet. 2:9-10.

[9] Gal. 2:20, Eph. 5:1-2, Phil. 2:5-11.

[10] Revelation 7.

[11] In the second century and following, however, the Christian church committed the near fatal error of doing precisely what the biblical writers never attempted: creating a quasi-philosophical system of propositional theology. We are only now beginning to recover from this devastating error.

[12] Son of God and good news in Mark 1:1 and many other places; *parousia*, usually translated "coming" in 1 Cor. 15:23, 1 Thess. 2:19, Jas. 5:8, 1 John 2:28.

[13] 1 Cor. 15:44.

[14] The word Jesus used most often for the awful estate of those who reject eternal life was Gehenna, referring to the garbage dump right outside Jerusalem.

CONCLUSION

So, What Has Happened to the Bible?

What has happened to the Bible as a result of this journey through history? We have shown that God's self-revelation and inspiration of Scripture are imminently historical, rational, and normal. Inspiration does not entail an abnormal process by which biblical authors received facts out of the air without the normal modes of experience, eyewitnesses, and research. Even so, God still speaks to us through the words of Scripture, although we have now assigned some strange new names to some of its authors.

We can still read the Bible simply, devotionally, for our personal guidance, letting it speak to us just as it is without all the scholarly baggage. Most of us will still choose to read it that way. Most preachers will proclaim its message that way, even if they know its more complicated history. That's the way I read and preach it most of the time.

At the same time, when we come across those notoriously difficult passages, we will know how to deal with them within their context in God's own historical self-disclosure. We know those notorious stories of God's ordering genocide and chopping off of hands are part of the problem—the early human misunderstanding of God. God's grace and redemption in Jesus Christ is the solution, as well as the climax of the narrative.

The Bible remains the beautiful, thrilling, inspired library of books it always has been. We can and should still interpret the Bible as it is, not as its sources used to be. Now, however, we have a more informed, profound understanding of why it is as it is and how it came to be as it is. Now we know how to resolve many of the difficulties that have plagued us all these years.

Jesus—the Interpretive Key

We have learned, furthermore, a fresh understanding of the teachings and person of Jesus of Nazareth. We have learned to see Jesus in terms of mercy, grace, and forgiveness rather than through law, wrath, and hell. We have also learned, I hope, to read the Hebrew Scriptures (our Old Testament) through the lens of Jesus Christ. I hope we will also read Paul, Peter, James, John, and Jude through the lens of the Jesus of the Gospels rather than the other way around.

The only way to read any book is through its climax. We can never understand any novel, for example, through its first few chapters alone. It is not until the end—the climax—that we truly know the meaning of the earlier parts of the story.

The same is true of the Bible. If we try to read Jesus through the slaughter of the Canaanites or the stoning of adulterers, we will never understand either those stories or Jesus. If, on the other hand, we read the whole of the Scriptures through its climax in the gracious, self-sacrificing, God-revealing Jesus, we can truly understand it all.

You see, our ultimate authority is not the Bible. Our ultimate authority is Jesus. Only as we let Jesus teach us how to read the Bible—including the Gospels—will we ever come to know the height, depth, and breadth of the Good News he gave us. Furthermore, we should not even read Jesus through Paul. We should read Paul through the lens of Jesus. Otherwise, we are Paulinians rather than Christians. Paul himself said, "But I am of Christ" (1 Cor. 1:12).[1]

The Bible's Authority

The Bible's authority lies in its nature as the original witness to the vision of God held and taught by one thousand years of God-intoxicated historians, priests, prophets, poets, sages, and ultimately by Jesus of Nazareth, the embodiment of God's own character and nature. That vision grows and matures and even changes somewhat over its millennium of development; but that development has an organic, consistent nature.

Older theologians called that development progressive revelation. We might also call it progressive understanding of the divine revelation. Yahweh, God of Israel, did not change over that millennium, but God's self-revelation did develop over time. Human understanding of that revelation and of the God who gave it also changed. Even the authors of Scripture matured and changed in their understanding of the revelation, just as the church has learned, grown, and changed over the two millennia since its completion.

Most of the problems encountered with the Bible and its message come from misreading it. If we read each sentence and verse as a final revelation of God's nature and will, we inevitably involve ourselves in hopeless contradictions and confusion, necessitating endless specious harmonization and explaining away the very text we claim to revere.

If, however, we read the Bible as we would a rich novel in which the story develops from the initial problem to the climactic conclusion, the divine revelation opens up in all its sublime glory. The problem does not lie in the Bible but in our ignorance of its history and its meaning. Consequently, we read it ignorantly and draw wrong conclusions about it and its message.

We do not find in the Bible a law book in which we look up each legislation under its proper heading. Neither is it a theological dictionary in which we find each theological concept under its alphabetic listing. Nor is it an encyclopedia of speculative propositional philosophical theology that satisfies our bottomless curiosity and answers every question. Nor is it a book of science competing with Darwin in biology and Big Bang cosmology. Finally, it is certainly not a monochromatic repository of theological aphorisms, each a final ultimate revelation of God's nature and will.

The Bible is a record of and witness to divine-human encounter and relationship—period! In that record the understanding of those encounters grows and expands until the God behind the encounters bursts forth in love and redemptive grace in a single human life perfectly reflecting the glory of the Father. As John quoted Jesus, "You diligently study the scriptures, because you think that by them you possess eternal life. These are the scriptures that testify about me, yet you refuse to come to me to have life" (John 5:37).

If we read the Bible as a technical treatise in which every word stands on equal footing, we distort the meaning of Scripture. If, on the other hand, we read every sentence of the Bible through the lens of Jesus Christ, we come to see God in all the glory we earthbound and time-bound creatures can stand. Every facet of the earlier parts of Scripture that is inconsistent with the revelation of God in Jesus Christ is transcended—fulfilled, as Jesus put it—by the glory of the God of radical grace. If every assertion of Scripture does not express the mind of God, how do we know what to believe? Simple: Trust Jesus and let him show you how to read the record of God's self-revelation. Read everything before Jesus and everything after him through the Jesus lens.

We need a Jesus worldview, not a biblical worldview. A biblical worldview just might include slavery, stoning, judicial mutilation, genocide, hatred, and warfare. A Jesus worldview rejects all those for liberty, grace, redemption, and peacemaking.

Deciding the Issue

All of us base our worldviews in part on our personal experience with God or lack thereof. Intelligent, reasonable, good people read the evidence differently. We would all like to have a slam-dunk argument to prove our viewpoint the only valid one, but no such proof exists. In the final analysis, each of us has to take responsibility for our own reading of the evidence and the conclusions we draw from that reading.

No matter how much we want to get off the hook with some absolute proof, some irrefutable argument, we have no escape from personal responsibility. When we read the Bible, and especially the Gospels, we cannot escape our own responsibility for the conclusions we draw concerning the reliability and validity of the gospel record.

Whether an individual accepts the deity of Christ and his resurrection from the dead remains an individual personal response to the evidence and the drawing of the Holy Spirit of God. What we then do with those accounts becomes a matter of personal responsibility—a faith commitment—either way.

The Song of Radical Grace[2]

At great cost to themselves, God-intoxicated men composed an enthrallingly beautiful concerto we might title *The Saga of Radical Grace*. It began with a simple pastoral flute melody played by that ancient Aramean nomad Abraham. Through subsequent centuries his genealogical and spiritual descendants developed and expanded that single motif agonizingly, transposed it into a dozen keys and modes, played it forward and backward, arranged it sometimes for a flute solo, sometimes for drum-and-bugle-corps, and sometimes for a concerto grosso.

Sometimes the simple tune had to struggle to make its tones heard through the jarring cacophonies of alien themes, blaring brasses, and deafening percussives. Through it all, however, that one thrilling song can be heard—if we have ears to hear. In the climax of the divine concerto, that lone plaintive melody resolves out once more into a simple flute solo in the life of Jesus of Nazareth—although even that solo contended with surrounding chaos and cacophony. Suddenly those hints we thought we heard throughout the earlier thunderous orchestrations become plain and simple—for those with ears to hear.

In short, the great epic concerto of the Bible proclaims the glory of relationships—a new relationship to the God who redeems—and a new relationship with other human beings! That one set of concepts—broken and restored relationships—captures the heart of the Hebrew approach to truth. Every doctrine of the biblical revelation can be reduced to relationships—between God and humans and among humans. The Bible revolves around this single leitmotif that resolves out in the person of Jesus of Nazareth—Jesus Christ, Son of Man, Son of God—God's radical grace in all relationships.

Notes

1. I take Paul to be concluding his sentence by saying that whereas others may follow Peter, or Apollos, or Paul, Paul himself follows Christ. At any rate, that is my theology.

2. I learned the expression "radical grace" from Kirby Godsey' book, *When We Talk About God . . . Let's Be Honest* (Macon, GA: Smyth and Helwys, 2006).

Glossary

Old Testament

Baruch ben Neriyah: 7th century BCE. Jerusalem. Scribe who penned Jeremiah's prophecies at his dictation. Possibly also wrote the Deuteronomistic History.

Deuteronomist: Levitical priest of Shiloh. Author of the D document.

D: Before 722 BCE at Shiloh. Probably consisting of Deuteronomy 12–26. Later incorporated into the Torah.

Deuteronomistic Historian: After 621 BCE at Jerusalem. Wrote the first edition of the work now known as the Deuteronomistic History. Possibly Baruch ben Neriyah.

Elohist: Levitical priest of Shiloh. Author of the E document.

E: After 931 BCE at Shiloh. Later incorporated into the Torah.

Ezra: 400s BCE. Zadokite priest. Possibly the author of the Torah while in Babylon.

Former Prophets: The name by which Jews know the Deuteronomistic History—Joshua, Judges, Samuel, and Kings

J: After 931 BCE in Jerusalem. Later incorporated into the Torah and the Deuteronomistic History. (See Yahwist)

Latter Prophets: The name by which Jews know the four books of prophecy—Isaiah, Jeremiah, Ezekiel, and The Twelve (a single volume containing Hosea, Joel, Amos, Obadiah, Jonah, Micah, Nahum, Habakkuk, Zephaniah, Haggai, Zechariah, and Malachi)

Priest, the: Zadokite priest of Jerusalem who wrote the P document

P: After 722 BCE in Jerusalem. Later incorporated into the Torah.

Torah: The Pentateuch—Genesis, Exodus, Leviticus, Numbers, and Deuteronomy

Wisdom Literature: Job, Proverbs, Ecclesiastes, Song of Songs, and a number of the psalms

Writings: The third division of Hebrew Scripture—Ruth, Esther, Chronicles, Ezra-Nehemiah, Job, Psalms, Proverbs, Ecclesiastes, Song of Songs, Lamentations, and Daniel

Yahwist: Layman of Jerusalem who wrote the J document

New Testament

Acts of the Apostles: ca. 85 CE. Anonymous, but possibly by Luke. The second volume of a two-volume work that began with the Gospel According to Luke.

John, Gospel According to: 90–100 CE. Anonymous, but possibly based on the testimony of the apostle John or of another eyewitness to Jesus of Nazareth.

L: By 65 CE. Anonymous. Oral and/or written material contained in the Gospel According to Luke not included in either Mark or Matthew.

Luke, Gospel According to: ca. 85 CE. Anonymous, but possibly by Luke. The first volume of Luke-Acts. Author used the Gospel of Mark as its basis and added material from Q and L.

M: By ca. 65 CE. Anonymous. Oral and/or written material contained in the Gospel According to Matthew not included in either Mark or Luke.

Mark, Gospel According to: ca. 67 CE. Anonymous, but possibly by John Mark. Oldest extant gospel.

Matthew, Gospel According to: ca. 85 CE. Anonymous. Author used the Gospel of Mark as its basis and added material from Q and M.

Oral Traditions: 30–100 CE

Pauline Epistles: 48–59 or early 60s CE. Apostle Paul. Earliest written sources on Jesus. Universally recognized as having been written by Paul: 1 Thessalonians (ca. 49–50), Galatians (ca. 48–55), Philippians (winter of 54–55), 1 Corinthians (early 55), 2 Corinthians (late 55), Philemon (ca. 56), and Romans (ca. 57–58). 40% of critical scholars believe Paul also wrote Colossians (54–63, if by Paul or his disciple; 80s, if pseudonymous). 20% of critical scholars believe Paul also wrote Ephesians (60s–90s, for similar reasons to Colossians). Most critical scholars do not believe Paul wrote 2 Thessalonians, 1–2 Timothy, or Titus, although most conservative scholars do; many critical scholars believe those letters were written by a disciple of Paul after the apostle's death.

Q: By ca. 65 CE. Anonymous. "Q" from the German *Quelle* (source). Possibly entirely oral but probably written. Material common to Matthew and Luke not contained in Mark.

Suggested Reading

Comprehensive Scholarly Studies

Buttrick, George Arthur, ed. *The Interpreter's Dictionary of the Bible*. 5 volumes. New York: Abingdon, 1962.

Freedman, David Noel and John J. Collins, eds. *The Anchor Bible Reference Library*. 115 volumes. New Haven: Yale University Press.

Hubbard, David A. et al., eds. *Word Biblical Commentary*. 52 volumes. Waco, TX: Word.

Sakenfeld, Katherine Doob. *The New Interpreter's Dictionary of the Bible*. 5 volumes. New York: Abingdon, 2006–2009.

Snaith, Norman. *The Distinctive Ideas of the Old Testament*. New York: Shocke, 1964.

Canon of Scripture

Lim, Timothy H. *The Formation of the Jewish Canon*. New Haven: Yale University Press, 2013.

Metzger, Bruce M. *The Canon of the New Testament: Its Origin, Development, and Significance*. Oxford: Clarendon Press, 1987.

The Pentateuch

Baden, Joel S. *The Composition of the Pentateuch: Renewing the Documentary Hypothesis*. The Anchor Bible Reference Library. New Haven: Yale University Press, 2012.

Dever, William G. *Who Were the Early Israelites and Where Did They Come From?* Grand Rapids: Eerdmans, 2003.

Friedman, Richard Elliott. *Who Wrote the Bible?* San Francisco: Harper, 1997.

———. *The Hidden Book in the Bible: The Discovery of the First Prose Masterpiece*. San Francisco: Harper, 1998.

———. *The Bible with Sources Revealed*. New York: HarperOne, 2005.

Levy, Thomas E. et al., eds. *Israel's Exodus in Transdisciplinary Perspective*. Switzerland: Springer, 2015.

Mazar, Amihai. *Archaeology of the Land of the Bible: 10,000–586 BCE*. The Anchor Bible Reference Library. New York: Doubleday, 1990.

Shanks, Hershel, ed. *Ancient Israel: From Abraham to the Roman Destruction of the Temple*. Washington, DC: Biblical Archaeology Society, 2011. (The first three chapters are particularly relevant to this material.)

Wenham, Gordon J. *Word Biblical Commentary: Genesis 1–15*. Waco, TX: Word, 1987.

———. *Word Biblical Commentary: Genesis 16–50*. Waco, TX: Word, 1994.

The Latter Prophets

Paterson, John. *The Goodly Fellowship of the Prophets*. New York: Charles Scribner's Sons, 1948.

Powis-Smith, J.M., *The Prophets and Their Times*. Chicago: University of Chicago Press, 1965.

The Deuteronomistic History
Bright, John. *The Kingdom of God*. Nashville: Abingdon, 1981.
DeVaux, Roland. *The Early History of Israel*. Philadelphia: Westminster, 1978.
Dever, William G. *The Lives of Ordinary People in Ancient Israel: Where Archaeology and the Bible Intersect*. Grand Rapids: Eerdmans, 2012.
———. *What Did the Biblical Writers Know & When Did They Know It?* Grand Rapids: Eerdmans, 2001.
Friedman, Richard Elliott. *Who Wrote the Bible?* San Francisco: Harper, 1997.
Halpern, Baruch. *The First Historians: The Hebrew Bible and History*. San Francisco: Harper & Row, 1988.
Mazar, Amihai. *Archaeology of the Land of the Bible: 10,000–586 BCE*. The Anchor Bible Reference Library. New York: Doubleday, 1990.
Shanks, Hershel, ed. *Ancient Israel: From Abraham to the Roman Destruction of the Temple*. Washington, DC: Biblical Archaeology Society, 2011. (The fourth and fifth chapters are particularly relevant to this material.)
Zevit, Ziony. *The Religions of Ancient Israel: A Synthesis of Parallactic Approaches*. London: Continuum, 2001. (Difficult reading for the non-scholar, but the ultimate in a transdisciplinary study of the religious history of ancient Israel.)

First-Century Preaching of the Gospel
Dodd, C.H. *The Apostolic Preaching and Its Developments*. Grand Rapids: Baker, 1980.
Morris, Leon. *The Apostolic Preaching of the Cross*. Grand Rapids: Eerdmans, 1955.

The Historical Jesus
Brown, Raymond E. *The Birth of the Messiah*. The Anchor Bible Reference Library. New York: Doubleday, 1977, 1993.
Brown, Raymond E. *The Death of the Messiah: From Gethsemane to the Grave*. The Anchor Bible Reference Library. New York: Doubleday, 1994.
Dunn, James D.G. *Christianity in the Making*. Vol. 1: *Jesus Remembered*. Grand Rapids: Eerdmans, 2003.
Wright, N.T. *Christian Origins and the Question of God*. Minneapolis: Fortress, 1992, 1996, 2003.

The Resurrection of Jesus
Brown, Raymond E. *The Gospel According to John XIII–XXI*. The Anchor Reference Bible Library. Garden City, NJ: Doubleday, 1970.
Brown, Raymond E. *The Virginal Conception & Bodily Resurrection of Jesus*. New York: Paulist Press, 1973.
Pannenberg, Wolfhart. *Jesus Christ—God and Man*. Philadelphia: Westminster, 1977.
Wright, N.T. *The Resurrection of the Son of God*. Minneapolis: Fortress, 2003.

www.ingramcontent.com/pod-product-compliance
Lightning Source LLC
Chambersburg PA
CBHW070843160426
43192CB00012B/2291